FROM THE FRONT ROW

REFLECTIONS OF A

MAJOR LEAGUE BASEBALL OWNER

AND MODERN ART DEALER

FROM THE FRONT ROW

JEFFREY H. LORIA

A POST HILL PRESS BOOK
ISBN: 978-1-63758-453-8
ISBN (eBook): 978-1-63758-454-5

From the Front Row:
Reflections of a Major League Baseball Owner and Modern Art Dealer
© 2023 by Jeffrey H. Loria
All Rights Reserved

Cover Design by Justin Striebel and Carly Loman

Interior Design by Yoni Limor and Carly Loman

This is a work of nonfiction. All people, locations, events, and situation are portrayed to the best of the author's memory.

Post Hill Press
New York • Nashville
posthillpress.com

Published in the United States of America
1 2 3 4 5 6 7 8 9 10

For my wonderful parents,
who were a perpetual source of
love, inspiration, and support;

my adored sister Harriet,
whose loving memory endures
forever in my heart;

and my sweet daughter, Nancy,
whose radiant life
was taken too soon.

Table of Contents

INTRODUCTION

THOUGHTS FROM THE FRONT ROW
ON BASEBALL AND ART

Great baseball players have much in common with great artists. Both put their talents on the line, and neither is easily stifled by criticism. And both possess an innate ability to focus on their objectives and block out all distractions; indeed, exceptional talents in all fields share these common threads. This book is the story of my twin passions for art and baseball, two worlds that are not nearly as different and separate as they may seem. To me, a baseball stadium has much in common with an artist's studio. Both are places filled with drama, suspense, and magic, and I have always felt wholly at ease in either a studio or a clubhouse.

For more than five decades, I have been uniquely privileged to witness truly exceptional talent from the front row. The excitement of watching and working with creative people has kept me on the edge of my seat, eager for more. What happens on a baseball field also happens in art, as well as in our lives. What we see turns into what we feel.

I am deeply fortunate to have come of age in an era when art and artists were still very much a face-to-face, and indeed heart-to-heart, enterprise. Authenticity and admiration were not yet pitted against anonymous bidders shrouded behind phone banks at auction houses. I still marvel at how I was able, as a young man in my early twenties, to knock on the artist Edward Hopper's door in New York's Washington Square and have him graciously usher me into his unfurnished living room where he kept his printing press. Art was personal. In much the same way, I later had the good fortune to join professional sports, ultimately being at the helm of Major League Baseball's Miami Marlins, during the twilight of the era of instinct, before athletes were so heavily defined by analytics and when managers could still trust their guts, rather than having to work around algorithms.

OPPOSITE PAGE: *Leonardo's* Mona Lisa, *the iconic image that opened my eyes to both seeing art and the larger world.*

Of course, there have been challenges. The art world is a largely private place that prizes discretion. Art dealers support, encourage, collaborate with, and champion artists, while at the same time, they quietly help collectors and institutions find the perfect work, the object of deep meaning or visual delight. Being with artists inside their private working environments and studios provides an intimate, in-depth look at the creative process, which is powerful to behold. The world of professional sports is, however, the complete opposite. The public spotlight is constant and strong. Owning the Florida (later Miami) Marlins meant experiencing the gamut of emotions from exhilarating—including a 2003 World Series Championship—to challenging, but it was never dull. I learned to live with sensational headlines, and the highs of thrilling celebrations and the lows of withering criticism. Often, the person I read about in the press and the person who I am bore no resemblance to each other, but for many who work in professional sports that is, as the saying goes, the price of admission. I've been very lucky, beyond my wildest imagination, to have achieved success in two very different worlds.

Like most people, my own life has been filled with peaks and valleys. I have known deep tragedy and adversity as well as good fortune, with serendipity, timing, and chance playing their own parts. And I realize now that I was also making memories, which, of course, are the currency of life. I have written this book with the intention of not only sharing stories from my experiences but of making those stories something that the reader can see and feel. In the process of navigating the arenas of the arts and professional baseball, as well as philanthropy, commerce, and education, I have also learned a thing or two along the way, which I hope to convey.

If there is one overarching lesson I would like to share, it is that passion is the key. We may value art, or value athletic talent, in monetary terms, but we cannot put a price tag on passion. There is no substitute for it, in work and in life.

When you are passionate about your work, regardless of whether it involves multiple interests or even seemingly contrasting ones, a drive for excellence becomes the common denominator. If I had pursued only my interests in art, well, I would have done okay and had a great life with extraordinary experiences. Knowing and working with many of the world's most famous artists has indeed yielded a life of curiosity and satisfaction. But like most people, I have had more than one interest. Yet, I didn't stop to worry if these different interests would clash. Instead, I realized that the knowledge I had gained from the art world, including how to navigate myriad rules and guidelines, could help me to achieve even greater success in baseball than I had ever thought possible. Here, I hope that some of my experiences might inspire readers and share with them the varied ways of reasoning and seeing that can help anyone to realize their own victories in their own realms.

Some of the earliest lessons I learned growing up in New York City and later as a student at Yale were to always keep an open mind and continuously look and listen. We are all actors on a stage, but we are also the audience to the greatness that finds its way into our lives. If we take a seat in the front row, we have the opportunity not only to witness the best in life, but also to learn how to call the plays that will ultimately move and shape our world.

J.H.L.
New York, 2022

CHAPTER ONE

DREAMS DO COME TRUE

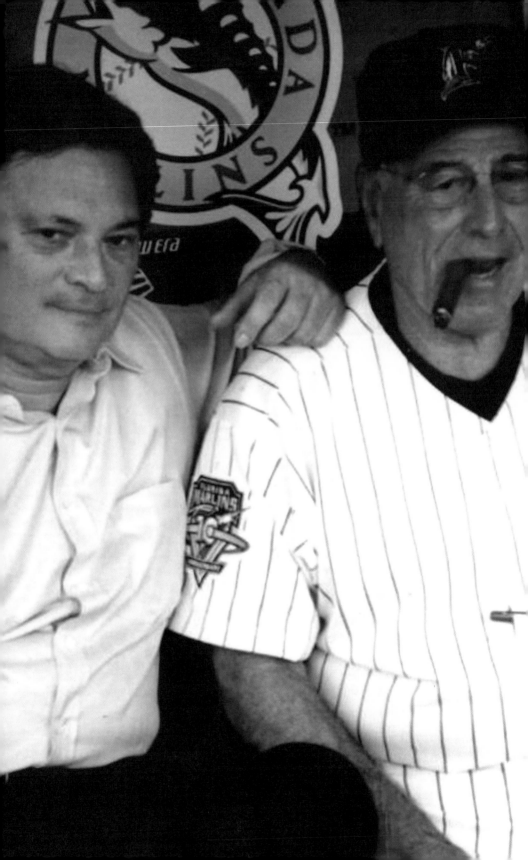

"The greater danger for most of us lies not in

setting our aim too high and falling short; but in

setting our aim too low, and achieving our mark."

– MICHELANGELO

I have experienced other epic moments in stadiums and ballparks across the country. But this day is different. It's a clear, crisp, late Saturday afternoon in October 2003. My mind is racing, and my heart is thumping with excitement. I am sitting in the visitors' dugout at Yankee Stadium, waiting for the first game of the World Series to begin.

Imagine! The little Florida Marlins ball club with a payroll of $54 million going up against the mighty New York Yankees, with their $164 million payroll and storied history, including such legends as Babe Ruth, Lou Gehrig, Joe DiMaggio, and Mickey Mantle. I had chased this dream virtually all my life, first laboring extremely hard to work my way into baseball by purchasing a Minor League franchise and then eventually owning a Major League team.

This was a unique championship series. It was the one hundredth anniversary of the World Series and widely advertised as such. The Yankees were appearing in their sixth World Series in the last eight years. Having amassed twenty-five championships, thirty-nine pennants, and a veritable brand-name status, the Yankees were in a league of their own.

For the Marlins, this was our second trip in six years to the postseason. But our franchise was only ten years old. We were also the first team to be led by a seventy-three-year-old manager, the incomparable "Trader Jack" McKeon, who ultimately became the oldest manager to win the World Series in the history of our national pastime. For some of our players, this was also their first trip to the hallowed Yankee Stadium, and it was evident from the outset that our opponents were masters of intimidation without even trying. The pinstripes alone conjured up apprehension. From the moment we arrived at the stadium and descended the stairs to the visitors' clubhouse, large signs reminded us of who was in charge. Joe DiMaggio's sign declaring, "I want to thank the good Lord for making me a Yankee," stared us in the face before we even took our first steps to the clubhouse level below. That sign, however, made me smile. I had grown up an excited Yankee fan and was now walking those venerable halls with my own Florida team. I still get goose bumps just thinking about it.

It looked, however, like our players did not share my eager emotional state. Sitting in the dugout observing batting practice with Jack and then watching our players return from center field's "Monument Park," where they had glimpsed the bronze faces, plaques, and sheer number of Yankee legends, I realized that the Marlin players seemed intimidated and not their usual confident selves. To further make the point, the public-address system was blasting Frank Sinatra's iconic song, "New York, New York," while the Jumbotron highlighted the Yankees' prior glory in black-and-white film. It was supremely brilliant and not at all subliminal marketing.

As the players descended into the dugout and headed to the visitors' clubhouse to prepare mentally for their first inning, I could see anxiety written all over their faces. Although I too was anxious with anticipation, I felt we had come so far and after so much hard work that fear and failure were not options. I told Jack that I sensed a problem and asked if I could speak with his players. He replied, "Of course. They are not *my* players, they are *your* fucking players. Half of them don't even know if they are in New York or Hoboken."

Jack encouraged me to take a few minutes to address the team, but I only needed sixty seconds. I got their attention by slamming a bat on the table in the middle of the clubhouse. As the players gathered around, I tried to convey to them that we belonged here in the World Series, we had earned it, we had been the hottest team in baseball since the All-Star break. I told them that we also deserved to be here because we were smarter, faster, younger, and better. I reminded them that all those greats in Monument Park had been their age at some point, but they were now retired or dead and could not play tonight. This was *our* time! We were going to beat the Yankees. And we did.

During the New York week of the series, I stayed at my home in Manhattan, and I remember feeling the tremendous energy. Before the first game, on my way to the stadium, I stopped at a bodega on Madison Avenue and bought the *New York Post* and the *New York Times* to see what they were predicting. The headline in the *Post* read FISH FRY. Needless to say, we were the underdogs and not exactly beloved. When our team bus traveled up Madison Avenue, we were booed the entire way. As the series' first game began, emotions were elevated. When our experienced and talented leadoff hitter, Juan Pierre, safely bunted a fastball in the first inning, I had a strong premonition that more success was going to follow. But being super-stitious, like many in baseball, I kept my feelings to myself for fear of jinxing our efforts.

The Marlins won that first game 3–2; our closer, Ugueth Urbina, pitched the ninth inning in his usual heroic fashion. We had handed the Yankees their first home loss during a World Series since 1996.

Back in Yankee Stadium for Game Six, even though the Marlins were leading the series 3–2, the Bronx Bombers were still heavily favored. But as fate would have it, the series didn't make it to seven games. In Game Six, Jack McKeon's tactics were nothing short of brilliant. He decided to start our twenty-three-year-old ace, Josh

Beckett, with only three days of rest—an unheard-of choice in base-ball. Usually, starting pitchers require four to five days between starts.

To get Beckett's mind off baseball for a few hours that afternoon, I had taken him to Barneys New York, the former high-end department store on Madison Avenue in Manhattan, to buy some shirts. I told him his wardrobe needed an upgrade. But Beckett had his own way of releasing the pressure before a World Series start with a unique pregame ritual that I hadn't seen before. When I arrived at the stadium, I found him sprawled comfortably on a clubhouse couch, immersed in watching cartoons and oblivious to his surroundings. I realized then that nothing was going to distract him from winning.

As the game began, I sat, overwhelmed with emotion, next to my security person, John Anderson, who had loyally helped me for years. During one tension-filled moment, John turned and saw the consternation on my face. "Why so serious?" he asked. I explained the weight of this game for me and how a lifetime of memories had come flooding back, a disproportionate number of them involving my late father. The flashback of my dad taking me to my first baseball game in the old Yankee Stadium made me wonder what he would have thought if he could have seen what I was witnessing from my now front-row seat. I'll never forget John's reaction. Without hesitation, he elbowed me hard in the stomach and said, "You're about to win the World Series! Why the hell are you thinking about that right now?"

At the bottom of the ninth, the Marlins were ahead 2–0. A stone-faced Beckett took to the mound and retired the last three batters for the victory. We won the World Series on that Saturday night, October 25, at Yankee Stadium. When we got the third and final out, I could only repeat to myself, "Oh my God. Oh my God. Oh my God." I was told later that the hometown celebration practically stopped traffic on Interstate 95 in Miami. By contrast, on the subway ride back into Manhattan from the Bronx, I was told that it was so quiet you actually could hear the proverbial pin drop.

OPPOSITE PAGE: *With my New York City police escort moments after the Marlins won Game Six to become 2003 World Series Champions. Photo by Dr. Jon LaPook.*

Beckett's pitching made Jack's risky and unconventional choice of starting him with a mere three days' rest seem to be an act of genius. And it was. The complete shutout of the Yankees in the final game made him the first pitcher to accomplish that feat since Jack Morris of the Minnesota Twins did so in 1991. The Marlins also scored the game's only runs on three consecutive two-out singles by Álex González, Juan Pierre, and Luis Castillo in the fifth and Juan Encarnación's sacrifice fly in the sixth.

It's still amazing to recall the opposing lineup. We had beaten future Hall of Fame players Mariano Rivera, Roger Clemens, and Derek Jeter. It was an extremely gratifying experience, but also mind-blowing. We weren't supposed to do this. But isn't that what life is all about? Good things sometimes happen when least expected, and I had learned early on in my life to "expect the unexpected." Jack McKeon is without question an exceptional manager and a very special man. He deserves an abundance of credit for his leadership and for the faith he had in his players. This triumph was a capstone to a truly remarkable career. The Marlins' victory that October was a prime example of expecting the unexpected.

During the celebratory melee on the infield immediately following our victory, everything was a blur. The occasion was obviously highly emotional, not only for our jubilant team but also for the New York fans, who were in a state of utter shock and uncharacteristically silent. They were, however, very classy in defeat. As our players rushed the field, John Anderson and I were escorted by a New York City police officer to the Yankee dugout on the first-base side.

I felt this was my team's time to celebrate, so I did not go onto the field or infringe on their precious moment. Instead, I watched from afar and then entered the Yankee dugout and walked through the underground tunnel behind home plate to the visitors' clubhouse on the third-base side and waited for my team.

As the jubilant players began streaming off the field, I noticed a figure sitting on a bench opposite the clubhouse entrance. When I got closer, I realized it was Don Larsen, a Yankee legend and one of my childhood heroes, who is still the only player in baseball history to

ABOVE: *With David Samson, the Marlins' president, celebrating our championship win inside the visitor's clubhouse at Yankee Stadium.*

pitch a perfect game in the World Series, which he did in 1956. I had witnessed that game with my father. As a player, Larsen was always generous with his time before and after games, always willing to sign autographs and answer questions from young, inquisitive people like me. It had been more than five decades since his historic victory, but he held a special place in my heart for his many kindnesses.

As I neared the clubhouse door, he stood up and said, "I wanted to congratulate you and your team on such a wonderful victory," extending his hand in a gentle manner that I will never forget. Larsen waiting outside our triumphant clubhouse with his message of congratulations from the Yankees was beyond my comprehension. I briefly shared my memories of him and thanked him profusely. It is sometimes said that life often comes full circle. For me, in that brief moment, the clock had turned back to the beginning. We embraced, and, with my emotions almost out of control, I turned and joined the exuberant Marlins celebration.

After a raucous, champagne-drenched celebration, I walked through our dugout to the field to pay my respects to the Yankee lore, to what our beloved team had accomplished, and as an homage to my father's inextricable link to my baseball emotions. I took a quiet walk around the bases, to savor the moment and drink it all in. (*Sports Illustrated* would later erroneously write that I ran around the bases and slid into home plate in a disrespectful way. Nothing could be further from the truth. At my age, I don't slide very well. And more importantly, I had the utmost respect for everyone involved, including Yankees owner George Steinbrenner, a friend whom I also respected greatly. Sadly, sometimes with the media there is no recourse or opportunity to counter inaccurate reporting.)

When I arrived home that night, I vividly remember repeating to myself the words that I had said in the stands as the game ended—"Oh my God. Oh my God. Oh my God."—and those happen to be the exact words that I had inscribed inside my World Series ring. I remained lost in a haze of so many emotions, until I fell asleep.

ABOVE: *The Marlins' win was front page news in New York; the* Daily News' *rival,
the* New York Post, *led with the headline* KING FISH.

My road to winning the World Series began early, as a child in
New York City, avidly watching Yankee games. Five decades later, I
returned to New York with my own Major League team, once again
standing at the starting block of my childhood. If one is fortunate, I
like to think that dreams can and do come true. So, dream big. You
never know.

CHAPTER TWO

THE ART CAME EARLY

> "Art and architecture create a dialogue
>
> between the generations, developing across time."
>
> – VINCENT SCULLY

My father taught me to love baseball, my mother taught me to love art. She and I began that journey when I was five years old. We would spend part of the day in the lush green meadows and tree-lined paths of Central Park, and then, on the way home, my mother would stop at the Metropolitan Museum of Art. What was billed as a quick detour would turn into a slow walk through the collections and exhibitions. My mother particularly liked to linger by the Old Master paintings. She was a highly intelligent and dedicated secondary school teacher who taught history and economics at a time when women were not often hired in those fields. But art was her personal passion. She took me not just to museums but to galleries and auction rooms. The times when my father accompanied us, I remember her doing most of the discussing while my father did all the listening.

One day, she returned home with a small Rembrandt etching. She had carefully saved her teachers' salary to purchase the work from an art gallery, and suddenly the artist whose works she had coveted in the museum now held a place of pride on our living room wall. This moment began my own journey of collecting. I still have the etching as a memory and reminder of the woman who first inspired my eye.

It never occurred to me, or to my parents, that I could not love both baseball and beautiful art—and at least once, my mother's eye for beautiful objects "saved" my sports future. The sidewalks outside our home in the Yorkville section of Manhattan on East Eighty-Sixth Street were not large enough for a baseball diamond, but they were perfect for punchball, a New York street game, which is played exactly like the name suggests: a hard rubber ball punched with one's fist instead of a wooden bat. Once, I executed a perfect punch, sending the ball straight into the third-story window of a neighbor. The police were summoned and went directly to my parents' apartment while I sat in the street, nervously awaiting the outcome. Luckily, the police officer also admired antique furniture, and he started discussing antiques with my parents rather than the broken window. When our neighbors moved no one was happier than my father, who enjoyed watching our punchball games from our third-floor window. But my sister, who was three years younger than me and undoubtedly my biggest fan, always rooted for my team. We were a close, tight-knit family of four.

At Stuyvesant High School, my love of sports had an opportunity to flower. I was both the sports editor for the school newspaper and editor in chief of a sports magazine called *Box Seat*, which I founded. I also played second base for the school baseball team. I was small for my age, so I had no chance to be a power hitter, but I was a solid infielder. On several occasions, I was more than solid. During my junior year, I made an unassisted triple play. With players on first and second base, the opposing team attempted a double steal. As both runners took off, I caught the batter's sinking line drive, stepped on second base, and instead of throwing to first, I chased down the runner and tagged him out. As one of the fastest players on the team, I was well suited for the chase.

At seventeen, I applied to four colleges: Columbia, Union, Trinity, and Yale. Trinity College was by far my first choice. Each summer, my family rented a house in the village of Lake Sheno-rock in upstate New York. My sister and I would remain in the country with my mother while my father, an attorney, returned to Manhattan during the week. The summer of my junior year, I met a Trinity graduate who was a neighbor in Lake Shenorock. He sang the praises of his college experience, so much so that by the time my parents and I traveled to Hartford to visit Trinity, I was primed to be very impressed. On the way home, I told my parents I would only consider attending Trinity. They listened and then suggested we stop briefly in New Haven to see Yale, since it was on our way. I didn't even want to get out of the car, but my mother insisted, and we walked around the Old Campus. I remained adamantly uninterested.

Months later, my college acceptance letters arrived. I was accepted at Columbia, at Union, and at Yale and rejected at Trinity! This was a blessing in disguise—my Yale education would have a defining influence on the rest of my life.

———

While I was at Yale, my parents encouraged me to concentrate on a premedical education so that I could become a physician or even a surgeon. During one of my first days in the zoology laboratory, we were assigned to study the cells of a live palmetto bug. I was instructed to immerse my laboratory specimen in water; instead, I was the only student in the class whose science experiment literally got away from him. Being a true New Yorker, I instinctively swatted the palmetto bug and killed it with my shoe. About two weeks later I received a bill for $25 from the bursar's office for my dead bug. That's when I decided that my nascent medical career was over.

Yale had a required core curriculum, which, as fate would have it, included taking at least one history course. I was not especially interested in general American or European history, but art history sounded more intriguing, and I figured perhaps it would help me understand the works I had seen at the Met with my mother. The general art history course was also well known, even outside Yale, and was taught by leading scholars, including Vincent Scully. I registered, and it is not an exaggeration to say that this course changed my life.

By the end of my freshman year, I had decided to major in art history. The conversation with my parents about my choice was met with silence on the other end of the phone. Was their expensive investment in Yale going toward the pursuit of a questionable future career? Later, my mother and father admitted their profound anxiety. What on earth would their son do with that kind of education? As a parent now, I can understand their concern. But I also know the importance of encouraging one's passion.

I soon realized the value of having a good personal library for my studies and embarked on what became a lifelong interest in collecting art reference books. A fellow student was unwittingly a great help. Yale picked up bulky refuse on Wednesday mornings. Almost every Tuesday night, my upstairs dormitory neighbor discarded a stack of books on the front steps of our dorm. I'm not sure why he didn't keep his books, but it turned out to be the perfect way for me to start my library. That neighbor was Jack Heinz, heir to the famed food-products empire, and we became friends. He was a popular United States senator from Pennsylvania when he was tragically killed in a terrible aviation accident in 1991. Jack was only fifty-two years old.

I had many remarkable teachers, but none more so than the legendary professor Vincent Scully, who made an indelible impression on me, as he did on many others. He was not only a preeminent scholar in art and architectural history, he also possessed a magnetic personality. Being both a brilliant scholar and a showman, when he spoke, you listened. What he taught me I could not have learned anywhere else. He made art and architecture come to life. I have been fortunate to know many of the world's foremost painters and sculptors. Being in Vincent Scully's company was no different. He was just the first.

Vince (as he was universally known) gave me the tools for not only how to see, but also how to analyze and be introspective. How do you measure works against each other and against your own acquired knowledge? Are they good, or are they great? It's all about learning to use your eyes. I wondered then, and probably still wonder now, how he was able to see the things he saw. His eyes missed nothing. He also taught me to see in three dimensions, which was vital for relating to both sculpture and architecture. My deep interest in sculptors and sculptures as an art dealer was clearly attributable to my Yale studies.

Vince had a particularly humanistic approach to architecture. To him, buildings were living entities, not just brick and mortar or slabs of concrete and steel populating the horizon. I came to realize that we live as we do because of the things that surround us. Quality is essential, whether in painting, sculpture, or architecture. When we take too much for granted, when we stop truly seeing our environment, we become comfortable with the status quo. Vince taught me that you don't have to accept being immobilized by visual pollution. I never forgot that.

How I learned to see also mattered no matter what I was looking at. Vince taught me to visualize not only the subject but its underlying elements, which build the composition in two and three dimensions. If we look beyond whatever surface imagery the artist may be trying to use to attract and keep our attention, we begin to find the underlying elements of structure and composition that combine to empower and give depth of meaning to the surface imagery we notice first. The construction and geometry of all the compositional elements then have to move in a manner that supports what we see in front of us—this is what produces great art.

But this process occurs in more than art. In baseball, seeing is crucial to unraveling the subtleties of the game. For both great hitters and pitchers, there exists a formula and a physicality that, when they come together, can yield an extraordinary player. The players who achieve ultimate success usually possess not only athletic talent, but also an ability to see the flow of the game and make necessary adjustments quickly to take advantage of an opponent's flaws.

The most powerful image that I recall Vince teaching me how to "see" was Leonardo da Vinci's *Mona Lisa*, perhaps the world's most famous painting. Known for its subject's iconic smile, the painting actually has a complex pattern of imagery, creating multiple layers and subtleties that produce its overlay of mystery. Da Vinci's composition guides our eyes across the entire painting's surface (not just the figure), and when we pause to concentrate, we see that the enigmatic quality of the Mona Lisa's smile might actually be formed less by the corners of her mouth and more by what's rendered in the background. She is surrounded by a landscape, but on closer inspection, it is a highly mysterious place; the imagery is built on allusions to land and water and winding paths, like an elaborately constructed fantasy. The winding paths beside the figure's shoulders rotate up to the waves in her hair before reaching the foggy edge of a waterscape, which pulls our eyes further into the atmospheric ambiguity of the landscape, where perhaps land, or trees, and/or water meet along an uncertain, broken displacement of fog and sky. It is that enigmatic, mysterious background imagery, which we "see," that fundamentally shapes our experience of the painting. But we must look for it.

Vince taught me that we might think we know what we are "seeing," but if we in fact did, how would Mona Lisa's smile in Da Vinci's masterpiece continue to so thoroughly and brilliantly captivate our collective brains for centuries?

———

Many years after my graduation, Vince called to elicit my help. Yale had decided to demolish the Divinity School's handsome library and alter the complex of Neo-Georgian buildings, which many considered a masterpiece of the architect James Gamble Rogers, who had transformed Yale in the first half of the twentieth century. Vince passionately implored me to call the university's president, Rick Levin, to voice how important these edifices were to Yale and its history. In the end, the Divinity School, although altered, was saved, thanks in part to Vince's herculean effort and President Levin's vital foresight.

When my daughter Samantha arrived at Yale, I suggested that she take Vince's course, as he was nearing the end of his career. Sure enough, the year after she took his class, he retired, although he returned as a visiting professor and gave occasional public lectures. For decades, his trademark opening was to slam his ten-foot pointer on the dais as a signal for the slide projectionist to begin. The deafening noise also captured the students' attention. Suddenly, the lights would dim, and the magical experience of seeing, hearing, and learning from Vince would commence. Years later, when I audited one of Vince's last classes, I noticed that everything was the same, with one exception. Instead of feverishly scribbling notes, students were now typing in rapid-fire keystrokes on their laptops. Without question, Vince had a profound influence on many generations.

The last time I saw Vince was in Miami. I often invited him to come see the Marlins on opening day, and he and his wife, Tappy, would sit with me.

As I began writing this book, I thought repeatedly and warmly about Vince Scully. One of my greatest personal and professional regrets involved the famed twentieth-century master sculptor and painter Alberto Giacometti. Toward the end of his life, Giacometti invited me to visit him in Paris. It was a rare invitation, but I repeatedly postponed my trip, telling myself I would eventually make the visit. I was too late. He died of heart disease before I got to Paris, and I vowed to never let that happen again.

Now, I promised myself that I would call Vince and see him one last time. Exactly twelve hours after I made this promise to myself, Vince died. Glowing obituaries appeared in the *New York Times*, *Washington Post*, Associated Press, and other media, yet they scarcely captured the positive impact he had had on generations of art historians, architects, world leaders, historic preservationists, and most importantly, aspiring young minds.

My mother instilled great curiosity in me and prompted me to always ask questions. Vince taught me how to fundamentally *use my eyes* as the tool to discover the answers.

CHAPTER THREE

THE PATH FORWARD

"Being good in business is the

most fascinating kind of art."

– ANDY WARHOL

I've always been more interested in buying and selling art than in creating it. At Yale, I took one course in drawing and painting at the School of Art. Traditional scholars of art history frown on mixing the two disciplines, believing that the creation of contemporary art does not blend well with the dedicated study of past works. I could appreciate that boundary, but the other truth was, I was not very good at creating original art. I painted four works that I proudly kept in my college room. They were very abstract, probably because I could not draw very well, almost in the style of Jackson Pollock. Shockingly, I managed to trade one with a classmate for a genuine Picasso print. The exchange took several weeks to negotiate. My fellow student was looking for decorative art; I wanted to own the work of an established artist like Picasso. In retrospect, this was hands down the best deal I have ever made, since trading nothing for something is an excellent strategy. The remaining Jeffrey Loria originals were moved from one closet to another, and one of them died a premature death in the trunk of my father's car. Meanwhile Picasso's works have had quite a different trajectory, and so has my life.

OPPOSITE PAGE: *Larry Rivers's portrait of my earliest mentor, Vincent Price, who offered me my first job. Drawn as a study for Rivers's* History of Hollywood *in 2000.*

25

In 1960, I met a Yale classmate whose family had just sold their Texas dairy farm business for $40 million. Even by today's standards that is a big sum but in the early 1960s, it was enormous. The student introduced himself by saying that he didn't know anything about art but had a keen interest to learn. Would I help him? The word on campus was that I knew a bit about art history, and he asked me to accompany him to New York City to buy art. The trip exposed me for the first time to the monetary side of art and to the workings of auction houses, a frenzied landscape even back then. My eyes were opened to a world of financial options that I had never thought possible. Art history degrees generally led to an occupation as an art historian, professor, lecturer, or author. I now saw that perhaps I could turn my education into something financially exciting.

I decided to apply to business school and to explore the possibility of combining art history with finance. In 1962, I was accepted at the Wharton School of Business at the University of Pennsylvania.

I'll never forget my June 1962 Yale graduation weekend. The highlight was a captivating commencement address by President John F. Kennedy. I sat transfixed in the second row while he spoke about the truths and myths of our economy. He called on business and labor to cooperate with the government. It was riveting. No less unforgettable was my conversation with my father following the festivities. Every day, my father read the *New York Times*, which he folded vertically so he could easily carry it on a crowded New York City subway car. Arriving in New Haven with his paper tucked under his arm, he showed me an article about the plans by Sears, Roebuck and Company to expand across the United States, more than doubling its existing footprint of forty stores. Sears had also just hired Vincent Price, a well-known actor both on the stage and in films. He was especially popular for his chilling roles in horror movies. But he had also won *The $64,000 Question* television game show, with art as his area of expertise. As a result, he enjoyed not only fame as a movie star but also widespread esteem for his knowledge of art.

What excited my father was that Sears was planning on selling original art in its stores across the country. Its strategy was to cultivate a new, more affluent clientele and make the Sears brand more upscale by introducing fine art, as opposed to simply selling the tools and home appliances it was known for. My father saw an opportunity and proposed that I write to Mr. Price, to which I replied, "Dad, I'm going to business school at Wharton. You write to him." Well, unbeknownst to me, that is exactly what he did. My father penned a letter to Vincent and mailed it to *Variety* magazine, asking if they would please forward it to Mr. Price. In the letter, he mentioned that we were both Yale graduates, as well as my passion for art, and gave him my home phone number.

Soon after my graduation in the summer of 1962, I was making arrangements to move to Philadelphia. Early one morning, the telephone rang, and the voice on the other end said, "Hello, this is Vincent Price." To which I replied, "Dad, stop fooling around," and hung up. The telephone rang again, and the same voice said, "No, this is really Vincent Price!" He told me he was busy with his Hollywood movie and theater commitments, including performances on the London stage, and he was searching for someone to help him with the Sears project to sell original art. He was glad to see that I lived in New York City, the art capital of the country and probably the world. We spoke for a few minutes and arranged to meet the following week. After I hung up the phone, my mind began to race imagining the possibilities.

A week later I met Vincent for breakfast in the Berkshire Hotel at Madison Avenue and Fifty-Second Street. Afterward, we explored galleries all day, as he sought to assess my eye and taste. We had enjoyed a similar education at Yale and even had some of the same professors, so he viewed me as a somewhat younger version of himself, minus any experience in acting. (He was also more irreverent than me; he was well known for owning an amusing collection of fake drawings, which reflected his oddball approach to the authenticity of art works.) At Madison and Eighty-Second Street, we walked into a gallery called the Drawing Shop. I spied a small ink drawing by Léon Lhermitte, a minor nineteenth-century French Barbizon school artist. The work was a double-sided depiction of a peasant seated in a field. I later told

Vincent that I went back and bought it, to which he replied with great surprise that he had admired the drawing as well and was considering doing the same. I still own that first purchase.

I have never lost my affinity for drawings. They are frequently a unique window into the artist and the artistic process; they are the medium where ideas first enter the world from the mind of the artist. Picasso worked out his ideas on paper. Even for a sculptor, often the initial creation begins in the mind, then finds its way to paper, and only after that to the three-dimensional object. Drawings are also very personal, intimate exercises; they establish a kind of historical record for the artist and their creative process, and many artists are reluctant to part with them.

A few days later, Vincent offered me a job as an assistant buyer at Sears. I was essentially Vincent's ghost, buying art in New York and Europe for a project that none of us knew for sure would work. One of my first important meetings was in Jenkintown, Pennsylvania with Julius Rosenwald, a major Sears shareholder and part owner of the retailer. It was really Vincent's meeting, and I was invited to come along. I didn't want to look like a college student, so I bought a new suit. During our meeting, Rosenwald showed us some of his print collection (much of it was later gifted to the National Gallery of Art in Washington, DC). I was a twenty-one-year-old kid trying to absorb the subtleties of the different prints that he was showing to Vincent.

To fill our inventory, I began searching for works on paper from young new artists as well as older established ones. Our first gallery was scheduled to open in 1963 for a limited time in Phoenix (it was the forerunner of pop-up galleries). It fell under the domain of home furnishings, although art is not a couch, and the home furnishings people could have cared less; in fact, they didn't like giving up floor space in their department. Although "The Vincent Price Collection: Seventeenth Century to the Present" was widely advertised in local newspapers and on radio and television, everyone was nervous, waiting for the response from the public. I still remember when Vincent called to tell me that every picture in the gallery had sold! I was elated. Clearly our concept could work, and people outside New York City were also eager to buy carefully chosen fine art.

After that initial success, the business prospered. I became the youngest full buyer in Sears's history—traveling the country, buying art, and helping set up the galleries. Paintings, drawings, watercolors, mixed-media, and graphics—all had to be purchased, and all the works were expected to be original, many of them unique. The Vincent Price Collection did not deal in reproductions. We established ten to fifteen new galleries a month, each open for about two to three weeks, and moved our inventory around the country, without the help of a computer. Sears arranged for a central warehouse in Chicago to store the art and distribute it from there. There were racks and racks of art, organized and categorized with lists and index cards to tell us where each piece was traveling. I would send a Rembrandt etching and Picasso drawing to places like Las Vegas and Arlington, Virginia, and other works to a new venue in Indianapolis. Transporting sculpture was particularly difficult, but we did occasionally have sculptures in our temporary galleries.

During this time, I even initiated the first mail-order catalog for art; after all, Sears was the largest mail-order company in the country, and it naturally followed that art could be sold that way as well. The catalog achieved enormous success selling graphics by Salvador Dalí, Henry Moore, Pablo Picasso, and others. But I couldn't be an art buyer in New York and attend graduate school at Wharton. I visited the admissions office at Columbia University's School of Business, explained my situation, and asked if they would allow me to transfer from Wharton. Columbia said yes. What should have been a two-year master of business administration degree took me six years to complete because my job involved so much travel and consumed such an enormous amount of time. But I knew that I had made the right decision.

I was also fortunate to make a treasured lifelong friend. Max Davidson was an assistant buyer at Sears for piece goods, while I purchased art for the Vincent Price Collection. Eventually, Max joined the Sears art program.

Today, Max is an important gallery owner and dealer, specializing in kinetic art, with a stable of established and promising American and international painters and sculptors such as George

Rickey, Tom Wesselmann, and Pedro de Movellán. Our friendship has lasted almost sixty years. We still speak several times a week, often reminiscing about our bygone days at Sears.

"Art is meant for everyone, and now can be bought by everyone at Sears. I have personally selected every item offered, and am convinced that the scope of this collection is unparalleled in the world of art. It holds something for every taste as well as something for every budget. I urge you to examine this catalog carefully; its contents will surprise and delight you."

VINCENT PRICE

A work of art is a unique experience, both for the artist who creates it and the observer who lives with it.

The Vincent Price Collection proudly presents an extraordinary opportunity to art collectors everywhere, encompassing Original works of Fine Art from the past Five Centuries...from Dürer to Picasso. These originals include etchings, lithographs, engravings, and woodcuts personally selected by a recognized art collector whose reputation is exceeded only by his impeccable taste and unchallenged ability in the field.

Now, for the first time, Sears offers these original works of art exquisitely framed and ready for hanging in your home and office.

This catalog represents some of the finest works in the Vincent Price Collection. Limited editions are offered as long as they last. Periodically, replacement supplements will be mailed to you to bring your catalog up to date. In the event that your selection is no longer available, we suggest that you indicate an alternate choice.

No reproduction can do justice to these great original works of art. They are unique in every respect; they convey an impression that is intimate and vital, and will lend character and interest to your home.

Begin your own Art collection today. Indeed, with Sears Easy Payment Plan, with which No Down Payment is required for your purchases, there is no need to deny yourself the pleasure and stimulation of owning as many fine works of art as you like.

30

One of the champions of the Sears art program was an executive vice president named George Struthers, who was a visionary corporate leader. He knew that selling fine art at Sears was controversial, but it brought a new clientele of professional people such as doctors, lawyers, and schoolteachers into the stores to see the art. Sears blazed a trail that other department store chains like E. J. Korvette and Alexander's in New York soon copied. Struthers also introduced me to his friend Harry Sundheim, a former toy buyer and a Chicago art collector. Sundheim, in turn, introduced me to the artist René Magritte in 1963. I still remember the first time I visited Magritte in Brussels. His kitchen table had six or seven beautiful gouaches in progress, and his ever-present bowler hat was sitting nearby. (In retrospect, I wish I had purchased some of those gouaches lying on his kitchen table.)

On a typical weekday afternoon, I would purchase prints by Picasso, Matisse, Rembrandt, and other major artists. I would travel to Chadds Ford, Pennsylvania, to acquire watercolors from the esteemed American artist Andrew Wyeth and arrange commissions with other internationally known artists, including Man Ray. On behalf of Sears, I asked him to produce a multicolored lithograph of a still life basket of fruit and often visited with him in Paris, both during the process and afterward. And that is how I came to meet Salvador Dalí.

In many ways, Sears was the perfect venue for Salvador Dalí, who was both a genius and a showman. Having studied Surrealism at Yale, I understood his role as a dominant force in the movement. In the 1920s and 1930s, the Surrealists embraced a philosophy largely influenced by the writings of psychologist Sigmund Freud. Their primary focus was on ideas and imagery born out of the dream state or subconscious mind. As a result, the Surrealists rejected societal rules and institutions, such as the church and government, considering them to be restrictive and burdensome.

OPPOSITE PAGE: *The "inaugural" Vincent Price Collection mail-order catalog for Sears.*

One of Dalí's best-known paintings (and one of Surrealism's most iconic images), *The Persistence of Memory* (1931), epitomizes this notion, with its images of melting clocks in a Spanish village landscape. The painting quite literally bends any traditional understanding of time. Ants appear strangely attracted to the metal casing of a pocket watch, while a distorted, fleshy, semi-self-portrait laid bare in the center of the landscape attracts a melted timepiece. For Dalí, who was raised by a Roman Catholic mother and an atheist father in the Catalan region of Spain, the idea of contradicting traditional imagery may have been implanted early. He tended to side with his father's views and was drawn to science at an early age.

With all of his pronounced eccentricities, one might imagine Dalí as having an affinity for the abstract, but his interests were constructed around allegory and storytelling. Some of his most fantastical paintings from the early 1950s were clearly influenced by great masterpieces in history, particularly the Renaissance, often in combination with science and mathematical reasoning. I was particularly struck by his works like *The Sacrament of the Last Supper* (1955) at the National Gallery of Art and *Crucifixion* (1954) at the Metropolitan Museum of Art.

But while his brilliant compositions and technical mastery were profoundly eye-popping and mind-bending, Dalí was equally at home creating controversy in real life. During the winters, he lived at the Saint Regis Hotel in New York City. He spent the balance of his time in the small fishing village of Port Lligat in Spain, near the Costa Brava town of Cadaqués. Most afternoons when he was in New York, Dalí could be found at the Saint Regis's King Cole Bar, holding court at a conspicuously prominent table. His desire for publicity and controversy were insatiable and a perfect match for my first big proposal: to have Dalí create an original painting and three hundred accompanying numbered and signed colored lithographs for Sears.

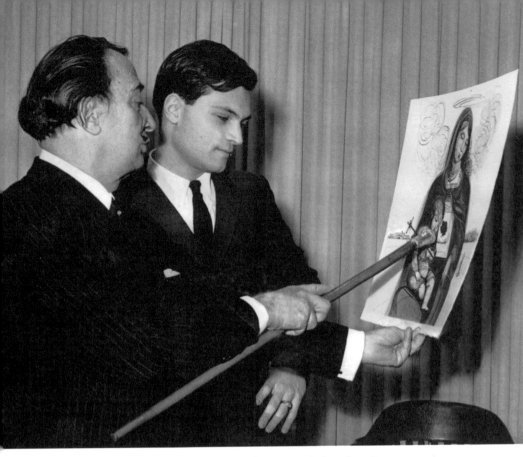

ABOVE: *Dalí sharing the intricacies of his Sears-commissioned work,*
The Mystical Rose Madonna.

When he produced *The Mystical Rose Madonna* painting and the three hundred prints for Sears in 1963, his vision of the impact of science on religion was a wonder to behold. The body of the Madonna was his vehicle for the depiction of the rose in the center of the figure. Painted as a startling focal point, there is a partial image of a doorway that seems to refer to the negative space of a cube. It frames the floating red rose at the heart of the Madonna's life force, as in his *Crucifixion*. Sears, at my urging, spent $25,000 on the project, which was a large sum at the time for a commission, but the project netted the company $120,000 for the prints alone. Sears retained the original painting but later sold it. Today it is part of the María José Jove Foundation art collection in A Coruña, Spain.

Dalí and I became friends, and over the years we saw each other often, both in New York and in Port Lligat. For me, it was a vibrant, life-affirming friendship. Imaginative ideas poured from his fertile mind at such an accelerated rate that the less imaginative among us (and that was just about everyone) really needed to pay careful attention in order to process what he had to say. But it was all worth processing. He had much to share.

One year at the Saint Regis, Dalí decided that it was imperative for him to acquire a pet ocelot. Now, for those of us more accustomed to the company of a domesticated cat, let me put this in perspective: Think of a wild bobcat roaming around an elegant suite at the Saint Regis. Then add a few feline pounds. Dalí named the creature Babou. He was beautiful to look at and, fortunately, not quite big enough to tear off a limb. An ocelot, however, is inherently a carnivorous beast, naturally accustomed to sleeping most of the day and roaming at night in search of prey. Babou's nocturnal travels, other than those on a leash with Dalí, were restricted to the suite's bathroom. He spent a great deal of his time living in the bathtub, where he continually marked his territory, which begs the question, Where did Dalí shower? Dalí's wife, Gala, who genuinely appreciated the virtues of a clean bathtub, kept her own suite across the hall. But no separation was great enough to curb the intense scent of Babou's urine, which permeated the hallway of the Saint Regis and was immediately noticeable the moment one exited the elevator onto Dalí's floor. The odor would hit you like a wild fastball. Dalí's need for this animal in his room was part of his powerful imagination and sometimes absurd obsessions. It wasn't much different from his compulsive need to acquire an elephant skull collection that he warehoused in what he named the "Throne Room" in his Port Lligat home.

Gala often told me that, left to his own devices without her "steadying hand," DALI! as she called him, "would have lived in a house of madness, horrors, and the outrageous." The reality was shocking enough that it can be hard to imagine what those might have been.

Meeting Dalí was one of those milestone moments that, in retrospect, anticipated the very fortunate and unique course my life would take. He was the first painter that I reached out to in my professional career, and perhaps meeting such a liberated mind so early afforded me the opportunity to believe that anything was possible.

———

When I started buying art, I was working for Vincent, but soon I was hired by Sears. One of the company's internal journals placed me on its cover, with the title "Bird Dog on Madison Avenue." But in spite of the art program's success, a new team in the executive offices was not convinced that the public would want Sears-sold art in the future. I saw the handwriting on the wall. In 1965, I established Jeffrey H. Loria & Co., Inc. and became a private art dealer. My father backed my efforts with a $2,000 loan. That seed money was all I needed. I am glad that the eventual result justified my father's early faith in me.

Vincent and I maintained a close friendship until he died in 1993. When I wrote a book titled *Collecting Original Art* in 1965, Vincent was kind enough to write the foreword. At the time, there were no books about collecting fine art. This book answered many of the questions that both new and experienced collectors had asked me during my travels for Sears; now I hoped that it would serve me well as I struck out on my own. My father, who was an inventor as well as an attorney, had convinced me that "an invention is finding a need and then filling it." And that's what I sought to do with my first book and in my approach to business.

In his foreword, Vincent said that I was "not only art excited, but people excited." He was right. That principle would extend to baseball as well, where I often conversed with the players in the clubhouse as well as the fans in the stadium. My passions for art and baseball are really about getting to know the participants and for the engaging conversations that prompt passionate discussions. I've been privileged to experience both of them over a lifetime.

Two years after writing *Collecting Original Art*, I published another book, *What's It All About, Charlie Brown?* The comics of Charles Schulz and his *Peanuts* creations had always fascinated me. He shone a spotlight on a host of fields such as sports, religion, politics, education, and psychology. So after meeting with Schulz several times, I wrote a tongue-in-cheek book about the cartoonist's valuable insights as seen through the prism of the *Peanuts* characters. When Schulz wrote me a personal note, he mentioned that his favorite American artist was Andrew Wyeth, whom I had visited in Chadds Ford and in Maine and knew well. Schulz sent me a drawing to give to Andrew, and they became friends. It was gratifying for me to introduce the iconic American cartoonist to the revered American artist.

From time to time, people ask me, "What does an art dealer do?" Once in a while, I will half jokingly say, I am a "professional hunter." But actually, that is not too far from the truth. Art dealers are often on the hunt for the best works of the highest quality, searching for the finest examples from an artist's total body of work. One needs to develop keen eyes to spot the great work. And one needs to be able to move quickly. Mobility has always been an integral part of my career.

I greatly enjoyed meeting celebrated art dealers and artists. I learned much from, for example, Sam Salz, who dealt in nineteenth- and twentieth-century masterpieces, and from the late Harold Diamond, another private dealer specializing in important twentieth-century art. I admired their flexibility, untethered to any physical location, such as a commercial gallery.

I recall seeing Salz by chance once in the lobby of the Hôtel Plaza Athénée in Paris. He was carrying a parcel as we both entered the elevator. The flat, square-wrapped parcel immediately piqued my interest. By the time we exited on the fifth floor, I had purchased the Picasso drawing that he carried!

It was never my desire to be a merchant with a retail presence. For me, it was critical to spend more time getting to know great artists and collectors. If I had operated a gallery, I could not have been as creative and mobile. It is true that you could miss meeting a great collector or artist by not possessing a public space. But one of the benefits of my life has been that the world became my gallery.

———

There's something about the hunting metaphor that might sound heartless and disconnected from emotional attachments produced by great art. But it isn't uncommon for a dealer to search for something that they either know a client might want or believe a client might be attracted to. So, part of that hunt is for a special work that I, as a dealer, know or suspect a client might eventually connect with emotionally. Of course, emotion is only one of many reasons why a particular work is desirable for a collector. But regardless of a collector's motivation, art always seems to possess an affinity for evolved taste, which exists beyond the immediate needs for sustenance.

Humans, since they began making tools, have valued and collected objects, and since early Neolithic times, some of those objects have been made for the sole purpose of being art. A good art dealer learns how to value both the art and their client with an equal regard, respectfully bringing the two together. A successful merger of this nature can extend the life of the work and enhance the quality of life for those who are fortunate enough to acquire and interact with the art. In this way, a good dealer is indeed a professional hunter of sorts, tracking the finest examples of human creativity and making them available to those who feel nourished by the aesthetic touch of humanity's grand pursuit. Art is not meant to be hidden, and a good dealer understands the value of finding a great work and helping it breathe in new life in a fresh environment, be it a home or a museum.

So, I'll reframe my initial thought and say, I am a professional hunter, tracking my prey with an educated sense of history and understanding, aimed at illuminating the mysteries and meanings of life, as contained in a single, expressive, thoroughly unique work of art.

CHAPTER FOUR

HENRY MOORE

MY FIRST ARTIST FRIENDSHIP

"Great art is the outward expression of the inner life of an artist, and this inner life will result in his personal vision of the world."

– EDWARD HOPPER

Salvador Dalí was the first professional painter I personally commissioned a work from, but the first major artist whom I met was the sculptor Henry Moore. In the winter of 1962, during my senior year at Yale, my parents inquired about my plans for spring vacation. They were expecting me to follow most of my classmates to the beaches of southern Florida, then and now a favorite spring break destination for students. But I surprised them with my response. Inspired by my art history courses, I proposed traveling to London to meet the celebrated sculptor Henry Moore.

World-renowned professors like Vince Scully and George Heard Hamilton had enabled me to see the visual possibilities of shapes and forms. But to me, paintings, sculptures, and drawings were not created to be viewed merely as two-dimensional images projected on a classroom screen. I wanted to translate their slide-

OPPOSITE PAGE: *Henry Moore working in his studio in Much Hadam, England.*

shows into reality, to understand how the artists thought and how they approached their creations in their working environments. I was bold enough to begin that process with Henry Moore, and meeting him began a treasured friendship and conversations that lasted for more than twenty-five years.

In the early 1960s, Moore was represented in New York by the legendary Knoedler Gallery on Fifty-Seventh Street. Harry Brooks ran the gallery and generously welcomed my inquiries, even inviting me to see some bronze maquette studies when they arrived at the gallery. Moore's maquettes were the small-scale first versions of an idea for a large-scale bronze sculpture. Sometimes they were enlarged to a thirty- or forty-inch midsized work, which Moore called "working models." It was from his maquettes and working models that he would choose a subject to consider for a large, full-size outdoor work.

My parents indulged me, and I wrote Henry Moore a letter on Yale University letterhead. He responded with a kind handwritten note, inviting me to visit him at his home and studio, Hoglands, in the village of Much Hadham, Hertfordshire, about an hour outside of London by train. This was one of those moments where timing and approach were everything. In 1962, the world was far less global; communication still relied on tissue-paper letters sealed inside red and white airmail envelopes, and as famous as Henry Moore was, he remained the son of a British coal miner living an English village life. Perhaps he thought I wouldn't come. Perhaps he was intrigued by the idea of an American college student who was interested in his art.

I flew to England and took the train from Liverpool Street in London to the Bishop's Stortford station, and then it was a fifteen-minute taxi ride to the Moore home on Perry Green, where he lived with his wife, Irina. No matter how many times I made the trip in the future, it never changed. I never opted for a driver or drove myself.

He greeted me in the driveway with a beautiful, warm smile I'll never forget, dressed in a light blue cardigan. It was his signature sweater, and I made note of it. For many Christmas holidays after that, I either brought or mailed him a new sweater. Mrs. Betty

Tinsley, his wonderful assistant and long-time secretary, told me that he always looked forward to his Christmas sweater. It was a tradition we both enjoyed.

Henry, as I called him, could easily have been mistaken for a university professor, given his proper, gentlemanly English manner—he usually wore a tie while working in his studio. He was kind and engaging, and on my first visit he immediately took me to his maquette studio, which adjoined his house. He would often spend evenings alone in this space, what he called his "top studio," working on his ideas and experimenting with his plasters. He loved a crowded studio, surrounding himself with finished bronzes back from the foundry and broken plasters, as well as early carvings that he had kept. He would start one sculpture, then leave it, only to later return to and refine it. One plaster could cast multiple sculptures.

Part of the reason why I was so driven to meet artists and see their works and their process was my belief that it is impossible to appreciate a work of art without interacting physically and emotionally with it. From the first time I met him, it was clear that Henry felt that way about his sculptures. "The sculpture wants touching," he would say, and he himself would put his hands all over his sculptures. It was almost an automatic response, like putting your arms around your child. Henry always saw his forms as radiating love and comfort, warm with life, and wanted them to be very inviting. He even regarded the natural oils of the hands as a positive feature when touching a bronze. Caressing one of his sculptures only served to enrich the surface, and he would always encourage this bond between the work and the viewer. Henry once told me about a sculpture of a reclining figure that he had lent to Winchester Cathedral. When the piece was returned, her breasts were highly polished; that's what people had wanted to touch.

I learned so much from Henry and his studios—he later built a studio just for his drawings and prints and a studio for the big plasters needed for his sculpture enlargements (it resembled an airplane hangar) on the grounds of his house. It's difficult if not impossible as an observer to see the techniques in a finished sculpture the way you can in a painting, but sculptures, especially large ones, are often put together in sections, although you may not see where they are welded. Then the surfaces and finishes are carefully and subtly applied by the artist and his assistants. This is why you never want to lift a sculpture by an appendage—it can break at a weak joint.

I went home and saved my pennies, and when I returned a year later, I purchased a small abstract sculpture, *Mother and Child*. Henry told me that at age twenty-three, I was probably the youngest person ever to buy a sculpture from him. In all the years we knew each other, I don't recall that he ever said no to any work I wished to acquire. I probably bought more than eighty works in the more than sixty times I took that taxi ride from Bishop's Stortford to Perry Green. I always felt the same intense excitement to be in his studio and to spend time with him, and he was always warm, friendly, and genuine in return. Henry, who never had a son of his own, became like a second father to me. He made my studies become a reality and made my textbooks come alive.

He was very serious about his work and eloquent when it came to what sculpture was and what it should represent to the viewer. He was also incredibly disciplined, working all day and often late into the night. He was a shrewd collector as well. He would trade his own sculptures with dealers in London for works by other artists. He built his own collection of Impressionist objects and was particularly interested in Cézanne's watercolors of the bathers; he even made a sculpture of the bathers, but the work didn't look like a typical Henry Moore image.

He would also sometimes solicit ideas from me on possible titles for his maquettes. One seated figure, which looked very Rubenesque to me, was given the title *Mother and Child: Rubenesque* after a short discussion. There were also a number of small sculptures that incorporated the seashells I brought him on many of my visits, with titles such as *Seated Woman: Shell Skirt* (1969). He loved adapting nature to create his sculptural imagery. His inveterate interest in natural forms was fascinating to me, and I always felt his use of them was his way of never viewing the past as separate from the present.

ABOVE: *Moore strolling the grounds of his home, Hoglands, in 1967.*

On one occasion, when we were in his maquette studio, I was particularly moved by the way he picked up and gently stroked the back of one of his seated figures. He explained that as a child his mother often suffered from a painful back, and he would caress it to ease her pain. For all his life, he had great reverence for the backs of the figures he created. We don't necessarily know that as the viewer, but we can intuit it from the care that he devoted to the surfaces of his forms. That is part of what gives a work its power.

One aspect of our visits that never changed was our stroll through the rear of his estate, a tradition that we began in the early 1960s. With great pride, he guided me on an expedition along pathways of his natural gardens and manicured lawns, all populated by an incredible array of sculptures and foliage. In the years following, the gardens expanded, and more sculptures were set along the pathways. Figurative and abstract forms were purposely juxtaposed against each other, bringing nature and man's creation together as one. Henry's work was truly magical. The forms and figures were imagined with a pure understanding of space, uncompromised by the love and care he poured into each awe-inspiring creation.

Often, as we drew closer to the studios at the rear of his property, Henry's playful yet competitive nature would emerge. He initiated a game to test the eye's ability to measure an object in space. We would both stop, and he would challenge me to "guess the height" of a base or a pedestal in the landscape. More often than not, I would be close to the right measurement, and it would drive him crazy. I soon learned not to try so hard. He liked winning the measuring game, so I deliberately made poor guesses, which meant he would win.

He was always very pleased to show his newly acquired properties. One piece of land was for grazing sheep. It was his "field of dreams," which prefigured the famous movie line, "If you build it, they will come." In a distant meadow, Henry had sited a large abstract sculpture, which was suggestive of two animals mating. It was under this object that the sheep would gather to seek shelter from the elements. Henry was very proud of seeing the sheep congregate beneath his sculpture, which he eventually named *Sheep Piece*.

Henry began by carving sculptures, but once the scale of his work became larger, he needed the sizable studios at the back of the estate. He made his larger creations by modeling with plaster on armatures, which enabled them to be cast in bronze in foundries in London or Berlin, always in limited editions. The process of creating his large outdoor sculptures piqued my curiosity. His assistants were necessary and present. Chief among them was a talented young sculptor, John Farnham, who worked with him until Henry died in 1986, and then with the Moore Foundation. These assistants helped Henry realize his enlarged monumental sculptures. On almost every visit, Henry would insist on showing me his most recent massive outdoor sculpture, creations like his large *Reclining Figure*, now located at Lincoln Center in New York.

For years, the Moore estate bustled with activity, in what can best be described as a parkland of breathtaking proportions. Trucks arrived and departed, loaded with sculptures for exhibitions and museum loans. Sculptures, both large and small, were prepared for dealers and collectors all over the world. It was said that at one time Henry Moore was the number one cottage industry in England. For several decades even after his death, the invaluable, dedicated, and talented David Mitchinson oversaw the expanding Henry Moore Foundation. In great measure, David made it the celebrated destination that it is today.

In 1977, on one of Henry's and my walks near the large work studios, I noticed a cast of the enlarged 1948–1949 *Family Group* sitting in a corner of one of the storage barns, so majestic and so strong, with the parents sheltering and protecting the child below. I asked Henry who owned it, to which he replied that it was his cast. It was, and still is, an image of astonishing elegance. I offered to buy it. He explained that the billionaire industrialist Norton Simon had an option on it that would expire at noon on the last day of the year. But he said that I could acquire it if the option was not exercised.

I thought about the sculpture all summer and into the fall. Finally, December 31 arrived. I called Henry at 11:30 a.m. London time. He said, with obvious joy, "Jeffrey, it looks as if the sculpture is yours!" I was thrilled. A few minutes later, at 11:55, he called back to apologize and say that Simon had just called and exercised his option. "I'm sorry, Jeffrey, but you certainly know, after all these years, that my word is my word." Today the sculpture still graces the grounds of the Norton Simon Museum in Pasadena, California. Timing is everything.

The good fortune of meeting an artist like Henry Moore was life-affirming for me in many ways. First, it made me believe that it was possible to actually meet very unique and historically signif- icant artists. That knowledge alone was spectacularly exciting. And indeed, the experience of getting to know a living artist, who was completely self-motivated to create a universe of art out of nothing but his own inner vision and drive, was amazing. The serendipi- tous fact that we ultimately developed a friendship gave me an even greater connection to Henry Moore's life, enabling me to examine his insights, purpose, and cultural heritage. This is something I was able to do with other artists as well.

I was also deeply fortunate that Henry himself was a very patient and gentle soul. Both the art and the artist were empa- thetic. Had I initially approached someone else, I might have been too green and immature to see beyond an unconventional façade. That initial foray into the world of Henry Moore was what helped me connect with Salvador Dalí. And Henry introduced me to other excellent sculptors, starting me on my professional journey. So many of the artists that I met in my life were highly dedicated people, driven by an inner desire to create. Each one sought to realize his or her vision. Each one was utterly unique. Most of the very successful ones brought true determination and discipline to their craft.

Moreover, the lessons that they taught me applied to more than the creation of art. They have underlined the importance of face-to-face human connection. If in the twenty-first-century

ABOVE: *In Henry Moore's office in 1966. He was always generous with his time and observations.*

idiom, I had only texted with Henry Moore, I would have been just another guy with a smartphone. There is no substitute for a real relationship. The early lesson that I learned in Henry's studios, that "the sculpture wants touching," carried over to other facets of my life, particularly to my baseball business. You have to be fully engaged and involved to shape, encourage, and praise. Being there, in a hands-on manner, was important to me in guiding team executives and players. It never meant telling players how to play, or managers how to manage, or telling executives which players to scout and sign. Rather it meant being there when needed or when asked to make encouraging suggestions. Caring for the well-being of my employees and players was, for me, a form of "touching," as Henry would say. That yielded only positive results and created many lifelong friendships.

But the baseball phase of my life would come later. For now, I was a young man in a hurry, with many more places to go and artists to meet.

CHAPTER FIVE

MARINO MARINI

ANGUISH AND TENSION

"The aim of art is not to represent the outward

appearance of things, but their inward significance."

– ARISTOTLE

Henry Moore was not only generous with his own time, he was also generous in expanding my circle of knowledge and friendship. During one early foray to Much Hadham, he suggested that I visit two of Italy's leading sculptors, Marino Marini in Milan and Giacomo Manzù near Rome. The mid-twentieth century was another golden age in Italian sculpture, for a culture that had a glorious history of sculptural exploration and appreciation dating back to the ancient Etruscans and, of course, the Italian Renaissance. Henry generously called Marini on my behalf.

The two men were summer friends in Forte dei Marmi, Italy, near Pietrasanta, an artist's haven for carving and casting. Indeed, summer in Forte dei Marmi was a time to carve marble, an old Italian tradition that Henry enjoyed. The pair often met for drinks at the Il Principe, usually in the late afternoon after a day's work in the local marble quarries in nearby Carrara. On more than one occasion, I joined them and witnessed their high regard for each other. In 1962, Marini had modeled and created a bronze bust of Moore, which Henry loved. As a gracious gesture to their long friendship, Marini gave it to Britain's National Portrait Gallery in 1969.

OPPOSITE PAGE: *Marino Marini sculpting a bust of Henry Moore. The bronze cast resides in the National Portrait Gallery in London.*

Meeting new and talented people has always fascinated me. It does not matter who they are or what they have accomplished in life; everyone has a story. Still, I believe that there is a different sense of anticipation on meeting someone who has lived their story and then turned it into something exceptional.

Artists in particular seem to possess the ability to turn their entire lives into vehicles for creation. Those very few and rare artists who perform at the highest levels—those who achieved tremendous critical and financial success and recognition for their ability to bring a unique perspective to visual communication, to create masterpieces that enrich lives or present new imagery ahead of its time—are clearly worthy of admiration. These individuals live a different kind of dedication. There is something exhilarating about a life dedicated to visions that don't conform to expected norms but produce exceptional results, which can make us want to see and learn how that happens.

At the outset of my career, I never would have imagined that I would be fortunate to meet so many important artists who would become lifelong friends. Every artist was remarkably different. Many were household names. Their individual acts of creation varied widely. But a common factor I have repeatedly observed was a self-discipline that kept them dedicated to their work. My closeness to many of these legendary and influential figures changed me profoundly. Much to my initial surprise, most artists also welcomed me freely into their worlds. Marino Marini was no exception.

—————

When I first visited the Marini home at 2 Piazza Mirabello in Milan in 1968, his wife, Marina, greeted me in their living room. The large space was filled with prints and drawings on worktables that she was busy cataloging. Marino soon appeared, looking very dapper and smiling with his trademark mischievous smile. Upon meeting him, I felt as if a new world of artistic discovery had opened seamlessly before my eyes.

OPPOSITE PAGE: *Marino Marini and Henry Moore perched alongside Marini's bronze sculpture,* Miracolo, *in Forte dei Marmi, Italy, summer 1961.*

His studio was downstairs, separate from their family living space, but I already knew I was in the presence of an artist—the scent of plaster and paint was everywhere. Indeed, Marino's whole building smelled like plaster, and I felt the warmth of an artist's studio behind that scent. As soon as we opened the doors to the basement studio, I saw not only his workroom but a range of finished sculptures, in both plaster and bronze, from the 1940s and 1950s. These were artist's proofs, which Marino owned and which he liked to keep close at hand. His overwhelming choice of subjects were horses or horses and riders. The sculptures shone a spotlight on the heart of his vision. He was working persistently to understand the destruction and tragedies he had observed during his lifetime.

During that first visit, I remember hearing a distinct tension in Marino's words, which I never forgot. Even in the 1960s, nearly twenty years after the end of World War II, he was desperately searching for meaning in the world's suffering, past and present. His equestrian subjects displayed those feelings of deep pessimism. His riders never seemed quite able to control their horses. To this day, these mysterious sculptures continue to reveal the human and societal unrest surrounding us. I learned much by merely looking at the objects in his studio, and I always seemed to acquire sculptures from him that expressed the unsettled state of the world. For me, those works revealed human nature at its most vulnerable. There is definitely an endearing quality about the fragile; there's an almost natural instinct to want to protect the weak. That may have been part of those sculptures' allure.

I purchased one sculpture on that first trip, a bronze *Horse and Rider* from 1955, about twenty-four inches high, which sat in a corner of his studio on a pedestal. It was meant to symbolize world events, as Marino saw them, filled with anguish and tension. In a way, he would say he saw his art as representing the end of the world. He increasingly doubted that mankind would survive. He felt that way in 1968 and continued to do so until his death in 1980. He explained to me that the agony of his frightened horses, rearing back and separating themselves from their rider, was a symbol of his fear that the world would come to an end. In the same way that many people saw the annihilation of civilization in Picasso's landmark painting *Guernica*, so too, Marino's *Horse and Rider* series powerfully exhibited his despair. As in *Guernica*, however, in Marino's imagery of death and destruction, there remains an ironic, deep-seated element of hope embedded in the act of creation. After all, if the end is rapidly approaching, why create at all? The very drive to create confounds these depictions of despair. While Marino's message is forceful, his great artistry makes these convictions seem vulnerable and inspires empathy for his work.

Among the sculptures that caught my eye on that first visit was one whose surface had been chiseled with a saw, creating both polished and sharp edges. The work was then finished with hints of applied paint. I had never seen such a combination on the surface of a bronze sculpture before. When I questioned Marino about it, he said with a smile, "I was a painter before I was a sculptor." His early career as a painter also inspired him to use chisels and other tools on the surfaces of his bronzes. He further explained that digging into a bronze with a chisel yielded unusual results, just as a touch of paint also created varied visual effects on the same surface. For him, it was a nod of acknowledgment to ancient Greek and Roman sculpture, a heritage he clearly understood. Marino skillfully embraced the two-dimensional techniques of painting and then applied them to a three-dimensional form. As so often happens, an artist's personality affects the vocabulary of his work. Marino was no exception.

I once asked Marino why he rarely cleaned out the plaster still remaining in the deep chiseled crevices of his bronzes. He was quick to say to me, "Nothing is perfect in the world, so I leave part of the process as evidence of our imperfect world." For him, everything in his artistic language had a meaning, even the casting, finishing, and patination processes.

ABOVE: *A Marini sculpture from 1947, entitled* Horseman, *in the collection of the Tate Modern.*

Whenever I visited with him, Marino enjoyed talking about politics, law, order, and current events. His postwar pessimism can best be seen in his large *Horse and Rider* sculptures of the late 1940s. In one masterpiece from 1947, the horse's head is stretched forward as if in a straight horizontal line, while the rider looks back over his left shoulder in an apparent state of horror about everything around him. For a number of years, the sculpture was part of the Museum of Modern Art, as a gift from the Rockefeller family, until the museum deaccessioned the work in 1982.

During another of my early visits to his studio, Marino encouraged me to visit the Joe Hirshhorn estate in Greenwich, Connecticut, to see one of his masterpieces from 1949–1950. Joe was happy to show it to me, and with great excitement, I navigated my way up the driveway to the Hirshhorn mansion on Round Hill. I still remember how the power and presence of Marini's large outdoor *Horse and Rider* sculpture jolted me. The work dominated the center of the main courtyard. The horse's legs were outstretched to the four corners of the base. It looked as if the rider was about to be thrown off the horse; he seemed powerless to contain the restless animal. Marino later told me that of all his large renditions of this theme, the 1949–1950 Hirshhorn work and the 1947 Museum of Modern Art bronze embodied the essence of his message.

Marino ultimately transformed his *Horse and Rider* sculptures. By the mid-1950s, the *Horse and Rider* subjects became "warriors," as he increasingly viewed the world as lacking civility, peace, and respect. The *Warrior* works were harshly chiseled, and far more abstract depictions of his equestrian subjects emerged from that process. They were executed with pitted and ragged edges, with the legs and arms often indistinguishable from each other. While they were initially less popular among collectors, they have established themselves as equally important images for Marini's overall artistic vision.

Marino Marini was also not an artist to bend his vision to popular taste or the demands of the commercial marketplace. In the summer of 1955, his dealer, Curt Valentin (who also represented Henry Moore), visited him in Pietrasanta to encourage him to return to the style of his more elegant works of the earlier period. Valentin thought they would be more salable. Marino declined. His view of the world was his alone, and commerce was not as important as his principled message. He had no intention of changing his vocabulary. The two men argued, and two days later Valentin died of an apparent heart attack.

In my own visits, I bought several of the later and more abstract *Horse and Rider* sculptures. Every time I examined these mid-1950s works with him, our conversation would gravitate to his sad memories of Curt Valentin, and Marino always mourned and regretted what had happened.

Many years later, in the late 1970s, the collector Walter Chrysler called and asked me to secure one of Marini's *Warrior* sculptures for his museum in Provincetown, Massachusetts. Chrysler was interested in the meaning that the works conveyed, not in their commercial value. I was happy to oblige.

On my next visit, Marino and I had our customary lunch in a small trattoria near his home before he opened his studio. He questioned my interest in this particular work, with its very abstract and nightmarish sculpted contortions. I explained that I sought a piece for a very accomplished collector who was building a museum. The ultimate horrors of war that Marino imagined in sculpture were exactly what the collector wanted. The sculpture arrived in New York a month later, and I delivered it myself to the Chrysler Museum on Cape Cod. Walter Chrysler, who had a brilliantly perceptive eye for art, got what he wanted. Later the work became part of the magnificent Chrysler Museum of Art collection in Norfolk, Virginia.

Clearly, Marino was right to hold fast to his vision and to take the long view. He had told me that eventually the world would understand his message. Indeed, these later 1950s casts, which at first were often relegated to a neglected corner of his studio, have gradually found a more appreciative audience.

But Marino Marini's work and the man were not above some flashes of humor. In the mid-1970s, while on vacation in Curaçao in the Dutch Antilles, I was ambling down a street and saw what I thought to be an original Marini *Horse and Rider* bronze in the front garden of a rather undistinguished house. On my return to New York, I learned that Marino had done three casts of this work, called *Angel of the Citadel*. One bronze had been installed in front of the Peggy Guggenheim Collection in Venice. I was able to purchase the work in Curaçao and had it shipped to New York. But I couldn't afford to keep it, even though I recognized it as a masterpiece. Ray Stark, the movie producer whose credits include *West Side Story*, *Annie*, and *Funny Girl*, was a client, and he bought it from me.

Months later, Ray called me early one morning. I was not prepared for his question: "Where's my penis?" He often spoke in a polite whisper on the phone, so his flagrantly vulgar query was a shock. I was momentarily stunned. Why was he calling me? "Ray," I replied with as much dignity as I could muster, "I don't have your penis."

"No, Jeffrey, the penis for my sculpture."

"Ohhh, I see." Peggy Guggenheim had asked Marino to make a special cast of an erect penis so that she could affix it to her bronze in Venice. She deliberately wished to offend the nuns traveling down the Grand Canal. I composed myself and promised Ray that I would look into this "endowment" situation for him. On my next visit to Milan, I asked Marino if he would make an additional cast of the Guggenheim penis for the Stark sculpture.

With a twinkle in his eye, Marino responded, "If Mr. Stark wants one, you will have to cut off your own and give it to him." Despite his fears for the universe, Marino was often very playful, and this incident was no exception. So, while the sculpture was an edition of three casts, the appendage was an edition of one, specifically for Peggy Guggenheim. I had to call Ray with the disappointing news that his work would remain of indeterminate sex. I later heard that Stark commissioned a local artist in Los Angeles to cast a special bronze phallus resembling the one Marino made for Peggy Guggenheim. I am not sure if it is still part of the sculpture, which Stark eventually bequeathed to the Los Angeles County Museum of Art. It may be worth a visit!

CHAPTER SIX

GIACOMO MANZÙ

INVENTION AND CLASSICAL THOUGHT

"Art is not what you see,

but what you make others see."

– EDGAR DEGAS

T he Maestro, as Giacomo Manzù was affectionately known to
his friends and family, and his beautiful, compassionate ballerina wife, Inge, were friends of mine for almost three decades. I
began visiting them in Italy in 1968, the same year I met Marino Marini.
They had recently left Rome for the seaside town of Ardea, about twenty-five miles south of the capital's crowded, bustling streets.

The Manzù estate in Ardea was named Campo del Fico, which
meant grove of fig trees. Long before reaching its breathtaking
vistas, guests passed through two imposing blue gates that marked
the entrance to the compound. Between a point just inside the
gates and the elevated mountain peak on the distant horizon lay
an abundance of brilliantly mixed natural gardens, landscaped to
blend with the sculptor's art and his handsome house, with its
intricate wood and tile façade. Flower gardens comingled with
architectural details. Olive trees, which produced sensational olive
oil, were grown in the true Italian tradition, together with rows of
fig trees. Luxuriant tropical foliage and various species of cacti,
as well as other succulent plants, lined the curved and unpaved

ABOVE: *Campo del Fico, the Manzù home, in Ardea.*

road leading to the ubiquitous lemon trees, which were juxtaposed against recently completed sculptures. Each time that I visited, we discussed new plantings. Manzù's gardens, lush with vegetation, were a vital part of his life.

The floral imagery with which he surrounded himself also found its way into his bronzes, particularly in the series of *Still Life with a Chair* and *Still Life in a Basket*, works that also paid homage to the sixteenth-century paintings of Caravaggio. (Indeed, the Maestro often told me that these delicate sculptural baskets and chairs were merely props to express his deep affection for Caravaggio.) The fruits and vegetables, combined with branches of foliage, also captured his appreciation of the intimacy found in the surrounding natural world. He once confided that the chairs represented in his *Still Life* sculptures reflected his Bergamo family background. There were eight family members, and his only inheritance from his family was a single chair, which he hung with a single nail on a wall in his studio to recall his childhood. This cherished piece of family furniture figured prominently in the iconography of his art.

The house was sited to maximize the estate's breathtaking view. From its elevated front, you could clearly make out the horizon, that wonderful gray line where the expanse of the sky met the Mediterranean Sea about two miles to the west. Giacomo and Inge were gracious hosts; inevitably, they would be waiting outside the large glass front door to greet their guests. Inside the house, shelves of amusing hats flanked both sides of the entrance foyer. Regardless of the occasion or circumstances, the Maestro always wore a hat. Even in his non-air-conditioned studio, during the intense Italian summer heat, he could be found working beneath one of his trademark hats. Guests, to their delight, were often invited to try on the hats. I once photographed an adorable young child in the living room, playfully adjusting the artist's favorite black hat on top of her head, which she had taken from a table at the other side of the room. I still treasure that image.

Typically, within moments of my arrival, Giacomo would eagerly suggest that I visit his large studios. They were two grand, separate but joined spaces, one for working and the other for exhibiting the finished works. I always wanted to see both studios, and he was proud to show them off, but my visit often had to wait. This was Italy after all, and few things took precedence over a magnificent lunch, which was always served in the large dining room at the far end of the house. The Manzùs' private quarters were located at the opposite end, down a long corridor lined with drawings and sketches of subjects similar to his finished bronzes.

Early in the 1970s, during one of our lively conversations about food, I expressed my love of spaghetti. Throughout the many subsequent years of visiting their home, Inge would always serve a delicious plate of spaghetti to welcome me, topped each time with a different sauce, each one more delicious and creative than the last. And that was just the first course! Giacomo would sit at one end of the dining table, facing Inge at the other end. He would always offer an exuberant toast to her culinary accomplishments. Lunch in Italy can last several hours, and the Manzù table was no exception.

Meanwhile, I could scarcely wait to see any new work in the studio. My visits were almost like time-lapse photography. Outside, in the open air near the two spaces, there was often a larger carving in progress. On each occasion, I saw the progressive emergence of an outdoor carving, as if by magic, from a single large block of white Carrara marble.

The creative genius and impressive range of work emanating from Manzù's compound earned him a worldwide reputation. He always appeared to me to have great confidence in whatever he was doing in his studio. Whether he was working in plaster, eventually casting his many unique bronze sculptures; or when he was carving in wood, stone, marble, or alabaster; or even working in a broad range of precious metals, the Maestro's hands and vision displayed invention and

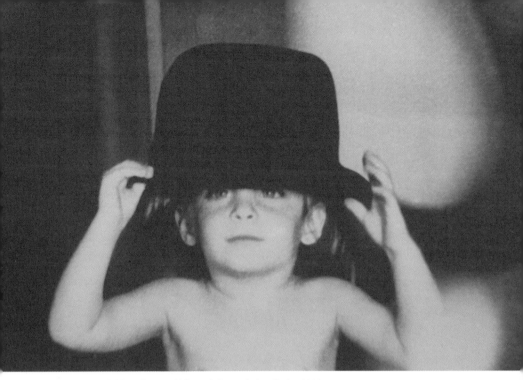

ABOVE: *Young child with one of Manzù's hats, Ardea, Italy, 1982.*

skill. He was also a remarkable master draftsman. The spontaneity of his sensitively drawn subjects was no different from his treatment of the incised surfaces of his sculptures. In this regard, Giacomo Manzù deserves the comparisons to Rodin, Michelangelo, and more recently Giacometti and Moore, all of whom initially clarified their sculptural visions in preparatory drawings.

The Maestro was clearly born with special gifts. His discerning eyes and his gifted hands created fresh and direct ideas, in whatever medium he was working. He often allowed me to witness those incredible hands at work. The front-row seat to watch this artist at work was as good as any premier seat for a Broadway production or sporting event. He was engaging, no matter what he was creating.

He also embraced a perfection of form and grace, equating the secular beauty of nature with a spiritual affinity for the ethereal. Everything about his world was constructed in a manner that revealed a reverence for life and for the legacy of the past. Form, above all, directed his discipline. He was a sculptor to his core.

His many iconic *Cardinal* sculptures, depicting the most senior members of the Catholic Church's clergy directly below the pope, became an image immediately recognizable as a Manzù creation. He began sculpting cardinals in the 1930s and continued throughout his life. Whether seated or standing, always under the silhouette of an enveloping robe, these solitary clergymen embodied a purity and beauty of form that almost seemed to exist on a plane beyond human touch and exhibited a reverence for a higher creation. Each work, though instantly identifiable as Manzù's, was unique, as was he. He also chose a wide range of images for his subjects, including lovers, tender nudes, children, still lives, and dancing figures, and at various points, crafted multiple images of his family, whether of Inge, his children, or even the children of friends.

When I purchased his large sculpture *Striptease*, Giacomo explained to me that he saw the work as more than just a young woman teasing the viewer by the mere act of lifting her dress. Instead, he explained the ironic conflict between the title, which describes a provocative performance, and that performance itself, when molded, sculpted, and converted into a sculpture. Having him interpret his work was invaluable. He explained that the sculpture was the embodiment of the female form. For him, the woman and the clothing were both static and yet vibrating slightly at the same time. He also felt that this duality spoke to the notions of feminine pride, at the very moment the young woman is escaping the norms imposed by society. I admired the work greatly for its defiance of the conventions demanded of women, forever a timeless subject for discussion.

But beyond the intellectual meaning of his works, the emotional and physical energy of his craftsmanship and his creative process seemed to translate effortlessly into all his finished forms. His works were also imbued with an abundance of love, with a deep sense of humanism, and with an astonishing versatility. These empathetic emotions, which he translated into his art, were also at the center of his magnetic personality. In this way, he was like Henry Moore, a very gentle soul. He possessed a deep reverence for life, which was always evident in his conversations, and these layers of sensitivity were embodied in his work.

As a profound observer of nature, Giacomo would sometimes finish a cast of a unique still life with a twenty-two-carat gold patina to express the reverence he had for the beauty of the world and the objects he created. He eventually had to stop using these patinas on his sculptures because the mercury fumes from the process became increasingly dangerous to his health—eventually this process was outlawed in Italy. I once asked what impelled him to devote such diligence to his still lives, focusing on delicate and intricate details. I remember he looked at me with a wide smile, gestured at the sculpture, and said simply, "Because nature is there for all to see. Just look." Of course, that is true, but it is the details of his interpretations, his art of reimagining nature's art, that reminded me not to take simple beauty for granted but instead to "just look." Another lesson in using one's eyes!

Manzù is the only known atheist whose work was commissioned by the Vatican. He was selected by Pope Pius XII to create a set of bronze doors. The doors, which he sculpted and cast during the reign of his good friend, Pope John XXIII, are known as the *Door of Death*, not only because they were the exit point for funeral processions but also because they capture the Christian meaning of death in ten episodes. Located at the far-left entrance to Saint Peter's Basilica in the Vatican, the panels contain multiple interpretations of biblical events, including the crucifixion and the death of Mary, but also the juxtaposition between the violent death of Abel and the serene death of Joseph. Heralded as a spiritual tour de force, the doors took him sixteen years to create, and Manzù signed them with an imprint of his right hand. I try to see them each time I visit Rome.

———

His *Cardinals*, however, remained his most revered theme. I studied his imagery during my college years, and I can still recall the excitement and anticipation I felt in being able to see the real works two years later on my first visit to his studios. Through the decades that followed, I saw how his *Cardinal* figures were born, reborn, renewed, and rediscovered. Some were more detailed than others. Hands and feet appear on some and not on others. Many of his *Cardinals* possess blank faces, while others yield a more pensive and expressive narrative. The clerical clothing and the tight classical folds of the robes of his subjects were rarely as detailed as those actually worn by the clergy, and they varied from sculpture to sculpture. The works were often defined by the play of light on the surface of the incised and rounded forms. Most often, as Giacomo once explained, the materials he was exploring dictated the forms of his *Cardinals*. Those forms were brought to life by his skilled use of the impact of natural light upon them. Curiously, he never repeated these folds from sculpture to sculpture, instead always seeking to create a new tactile and unique experience.

As I watched him form many of his *Cardinal* sculptures, Giacomo's own face was as intense as the facial expressions on his figures. He was always concerned with the gentle modeling of the draped material that surrounded the body. His abiding concept was always about form and volume and an adherence to nature, as well as his admiration for classical thought. As he often said, "I am not describing the church. I am looking at form." This distinction was crucial.

He also surrounded himself with classical carvings from ancient Rome and Greece and displayed them in his house with great reverence. He always intended to convey peace, tranquility, and a genuine respect for the classical past. Through the years, the *Cardinal* sculptures evolved to become more abstract. During his nearly fifty-year exploration of his subject, he truly carved his own path, working independently from any school of thought or popular movement. He penetrated the souls of his figures with a fidelity, passion, and gentle intensity that always resulted in works that seemed timeless.

On one visit, I was overwhelmed by the sight of a larger-than-life carving of a *Seated Cardinal* in ebony, nearly completed in Manzù's working studio. I learned early from the Maestro that ebony is a very difficult material to carve. Articulating it into a large figurative form meant fitting different shapes and sizes of the ebony to complement one another as well as to make the sculpture come alive. What made success even more difficult was the fragility of the material, which he always took as a challenge. Yet, it was a puzzle he always solved. I was especially touched when I realized that the Maestro had made the large ebony *Seated Cardinal* for me, and he was very proud to unveil it to me. I recall thinking how easy it was to view the work in its finished state, regardless of the vast studio space surrounding it. Giacomo's ability to render a massive sculpture with nearly abstract features was impressive. His work commanded attention in any environment.

Indeed, the scale of his larger studio, with its very high ceilings and bright white walls, created the necessary setting for carving a substantial image in space and served as a testing ground for the forms he created. The work was forced to compete for attention and to prove itself and its purpose within this enormous environment of conception; otherwise it would simply languish as a block of stone. The Maestro's creativity, like his mind, was immensely fertile.

I don't ever recall seeing a failed attempt come out of his studio. On the contrary, I saw only superbly successful forms, quietly drawing attention away from everything else around them.

———

In the spring of 1976, I asked the Maestro to create a marble carving of a seated cardinal. I had only one condition: he had to do the carving himself, without any assistants working with him. He agreed. I waited patiently for word of progress. On a Thursday morning in late 1976, he called to say that the work was completed. Three hours later, I was at Kennedy Airport on my way to Rome. One of the unspoken guidelines in the art world is to never leave a work in an artist's studio once it has been completed, especially over a weekend. I never wanted a weekend visitor to convince the artist to sell it, and I was determined to be in Ardea on Friday morning to see it.

I landed and went directly to Manzù's house. As always, he greeted me on the front steps. He had a big smile on his face as he extended his cut, bloodied, and bandaged hands. He exclaimed, "You asked me to do all the carving myself. I did, as you can see!" We embraced and quickly went off to view the carving in his studio, breaking our longtime tradition of having lunch first. Later, we did celebrate with a special Inge creation. But the excitement of seeing this particular sculpture took precedence.

I was surprised when I first saw the work because I was anticipating a piece carved from white marble. This was not the case. The Maestro could see the quizzical look on my face. As if he could read exactly what I was thinking, he quickly explained, "It started as a white stone, but it is beige now and the base is irregular. I wanted the piece to have the feel of an ancient carving." To achieve that look, he had soaked it in Italian coffee for a week, and the coffee stain had penetrated the porous white stone to create an unparalleled masterpiece, completely different from anything else of his that I had ever seen.

After lunch, I asked him to sign a photograph for my archives documenting the work, which he obliged. When I looked at the signed photograph, it said "Manzù, 1967." I reminded him that the year was 1976, to which he humorously replied, "Let the damn art historians figure it out." I smiled and thought to myself, *It's simply a magnificent work from a magnificent human being and a superb artist.* As much as he was joking, he also confirmed my belief about his work. There is no date that can change the timeless feeling which that sculpture exudes. I have since donated the work to Yale, where I first discovered the artistic genius of my friend, the Maestro.

ABOVE: *With the Maestro, 1975.*

CHAPTER SEVEN

ROY LICHTENSTEIN

GOING FOR BAROQUE

"Art is either plagiarism or revolution."

– PAUL GAUGUIN

Roy Lichtenstein's name and work will always be synonymous with Pop Art. He invented a new language, and in doing so, he brought us closer to understanding all art. His broad range of works have reached across cultural boundaries and saturated our visual recall, while still leaving us with the desire to see more.

Although Pop Art was technically a short-lived movement, it has never really gone away. By 1962 and 1963, Pop Art had become the new American modernism, and Roy, perhaps equally with Andy Warhol, was the movement's brilliant, controversial master.

When I had just started buying art for Sears, I was offered the opportunity to meet an unnamed artist. I was too busy and put off the opportunity. By the time I followed up a few months later, I was told that "Roy Lichtenstein already has a gallery representing him." Roy and I did finally meet and become friends, and we had a good laugh over my missed opportunity story.

On a personal level, Roy is one of my favorite American artists of the twentieth century. He looked to recognizable sources from the past and present to formulate his own vision. It is no secret that Pablo Picasso (my other favorite painter) strongly affected his work. As early as the mid-1950s, Roy's art displayed Cubist influences,

OPPOSITE PAGE: *Roy Lichtenstein in his Southampton, New York, studio, circa 1977.* **87** which made his work even more removed from other dominant art movements in America at the time.

By the late 1950s, when he did begin to flirt with abstraction, Roy simultaneously appropriated comic book and animation characters such as Mickey Mouse and Donald Duck. His work was new, brilliant, and inventive and even willing to explore subject matter taken from our mass-produced urban culture. The idea of depicting this kind of subject matter was so new that it was considered inappropriate for the high art of American modernism, Abstract Expressionism.

In the early 1960s, he decided to try the more literal idea of a cartoon, focusing solely on the figural image and omitting the obvious brushstrokes that so prominently defined Expressionist backgrounds. In the middle of that intense focus, he included the mechanical patterning popular in commercial mass-produced printing, namely Ben-Day dots. When enlarged, the dots took on a pronounced meaning and became the signature element of his art. This novel look became a crucial part of Roy's trademark vision, defined by black outlines, primary colors, and other cartoon forms. Roy's Pop Art of flattened surface imagery reflected popular culture's identifiable iconography and thoroughly challenged the notions of "high art."

Roy's comic book appropriations, his images of consumer products, and his renditions of familiar works by other artists transcended more than his own works; it became a new visual language, confronting all that preceded it. He understood better than anyone the ironic appropriation of imagery. At the same time, Andy Warhol was also creating his own statements about the way commercialization affects our perception of imagery.

I learned that Roy became part of the eponymous Leo Castelli Gallery after showing his comic paintings to the legendary art dealer. Very shortly afterward, as the story goes, Warhol arrived at the gallery to show Castelli his "new" paintings that had been inspired by comic books. Castelli informed him that he had already committed to an artist doing similar work. Warhol subsequently reworked his imagery and iconography and eventually joined the gallery. The account seems plausible, although I have never verified it, but it is interesting when considering the origins of Pop Art. Apocryphal or not, the moral of the story is that there was room for only one Roy Lichtenstein.

I had the pleasure and good fortune to visit Roy's studios in New York and Southampton beginning in the mid-1970s. Each studio had just about every creature comfort suitable for an analytical, investigative, and curious mind. The studio in Southampton could easily have been the prototype for the modern "man cave." It contained all that the owner could want, and he never had to leave. Roy could accomplish his thinking, analyzing, painting, and sculpting in a world of his own design. Every wall was tacked with potential material for his next painting, including newspaper and magazine clippings, photographs, and other objects he regarded as useful sources. Something of interest to him occupied every space, including the many flat surfaces. Yet even though it was busy, it was organized; the very few areas of disorder maintained a semblance of Lichtenstein clarity and sensibility and meaning. Later, he perched a saxophone near his desk—his remarkable wife, Dorothy, had given it to him as a birthday present.

The only real difference between the modern-day man cave and Roy's studio was Dorothy's occasional presence. I had the pleasure of observing her brilliant, upbeat, enthusiastic, and disarmingly charming place in Roy's life. Fittingly, they met when she was working in the Paul Bianchini Gallery, one of the early leading purveyors of Pop Art. Her devotion to his legacy was unwavering, and their partnership remains an inspiration to me. When I joined them over the years, I always witnessed mutual admiration and good humor. The encouragement she offered helped provide the equilibrium and focus he needed.

Roy was often working simultaneously on multiple paintings, drawings, and constructions for sculpture. The enormous wall on the studio's south side faced the Atlantic Ocean. Natural light streamed in all day. His painting wall was outfitted with a free-floating system of wooden pegs that he could adjust to hold canvases of any size and shape. It was a brilliant bit of engineering that very much resembled a Lichtenstein sculpture: clean, with enlarged, cartoon-like pegs.

It was clear that Roy had a natural understanding of order and assembly, which is what enabled him to juggle several works at one time. Many of them dealt with aspects of Synthetic Cubism (derived from Picasso), which was about managing elements of collage and eventually finding the order of a finished work. I would sometimes walk over to whatever work he was contemplating and typically ask the same question: "Roy, what is going on here?" In a very kind and inviting way, he would frequently say, "You'll have to come back and see." Curiosity usually got the better of me, and I returned to see the progress.

I took great pleasure in the times I met with Roy in his studio, and it influenced me in creating my own private space. I learned to take comfort in an environment where the things that supported my interests could be both relaxing and inspirational. We all need a comfort zone where we can think through our dreams and ambitions, without feeling guilty for taking what could otherwise be perceived by some as time off from work.

———

I have a clear memory of Roy working in 1978 and 1979 in Southampton on an important painting that a collector had commissioned. The image of this painting has stayed with me. It was a nine-by-fourteen-foot painting conceived to fill a large wall in a home that already contained a collection of Surrealist art. I was present when the painting was begun, with Roy executing a beautiful preparatory drawing, which he kept nearby for reference. I asked him about the risks of such a commission. It would have to relate to all the collector's art and yet not in any way detract from the other works by mirroring their imagery on a huge canvas. He said it was a "challenge," which he welcomed when he examined the collector's space. When I returned a few months later to see his substantial progress, I immediately thought of the famous Belgian Surrealist painter René Magritte. While reflecting on his well-known image *The Son of Man* (his self-portrait with an apple floating in front of his face), Magritte famously said, "Everything we see hides another thing. We always want to see what is hidden by what we see."

In Roy's painting, every recognizable element was rendered incomplete by the insertion of another visual element. Only half of a woman's head, facing left, is visible. The other half is interrupted by what looks like a large page from a sketchbook with an image of Swiss cheese. Like the apple in front of Magritte, I saw the Swiss cheese as a surreal surrogate for Roy's self-portrait.

On the right side of the work, the imagery is interrupted by a blue-and-red paisley figure, which suddenly leaps to the foreground, displaying curving forms not seen in the rest of the canvas. The figure is covered with his trademark Ben-Day dots as it sits on a chair decorated in Yves Klein blue. Interiors and exteriors are fragmented by other layered elements of moving forms and shifting perspectives, and there are additional elements as well. There is a reference to a Surrealist Max Ernst bird and a star rendered in the mode of the sculptor Jean Arp. There is an image resembling a shadowy Salvador Dalí landscape, appearing behind part of a Pop Art file cabinet. I always saw this cabinet as a symbol of the multiple sources for this inclusive work.

But the cabinet also directs our eyes more deeply into a landscape beyond the visible side of the woman's head. Here, Roy even appropriated a fragment from a de Chirico painting entitled *The Astronomer*, effectively making a surreal statement about the endless parameters of space. His tongue-in-cheek title for the painting, *Go for Baroque*, is an obvious play on the expression "go for broke," a slang term used in the dice game craps and also the motto of the US Army's 442nd Infantry Regiment in World War II, as well as the title of a 1951 Hollywood war film. In the end, Roy made the painting work.

By the close of the 1970s, on one of my visits to Southampton, Roy had completed the big painting. I noticed he had included a

ABOVE: *Roy Lichtenstein,* Go for Baroque, *1979, oil and Magna on canvas.*

lone triangle of green paint, defining the area adjacent to the Ernst-style bird. I could not resist asking, "Roy, why the lone triangle of green? It seems subtle but deliberate." Roy smiled and said, "I have always used green. I guess it is something to set off the primary colors." Then he added, "Picasso used it for similar reasons. Maybe the one area of green is a reference to Picasso. There is always a point of reference." Then I recall that he laughed and said playfully, "Or maybe I just needed a green triangle there." That was Roy. He was enigmatic, and he rarely gave me a definitive answer. He left the door open to interpretation. He allowed me to consider that great art can be as much the result of planning as it can be a moment of uncertainty. I admit that it is a perfectly placed green triangle and now, lodged forever in my mind, it also remains a point of reference. It is a reminder of Roy's continual generosity in sharing his time and his visual vocabulary with me.

It is no secret that Picasso inspired Roy. What is most fascinating is that Roy never permitted Picasso to overshadow him. Instead, he addressed Picasso by using his "Lichtenstein" visual code and, in doing so, always retained his independent expression. Even the green triangle in *Go for Baroque* is tied to Roy's own universally recognizable vocabulary. In every detail derived from Picasso, Roy's gift was to make his images truly his own and accessible to everyone. I feel that for all the signature iconography that Roy has contributed to the language of art, there is still a reserve embedded in the things he didn't show us: the process.

It is almost as if Roy employed a pathologist's approach when deconstructing his sources and his perspective. As in *Go for Baroque* and other finished works, he excludes any evidence of his effort. It is in this finished context that he differs from the Abstract Expressionist movement preceding him, where artists like Pollock and Franz Kline left their process and angst on the canvas, expressed through their gestural brushstrokes. A clean and polished look is an important part of the Pop Art attitude and is embodied in all of Roy's creations. But this characteristic has the effect of veiling the ironic humility beneath.

Because we don't see Roy's struggles on the canvas, we can easily forget that his finished work is the result of countless hours spent in his studio; we only see the perfectly crafted, instantly recognizable art. The artist's humility rests in the unspoken, untraceable hours of study, in creating methods to convert his ideas into images, which our eyes simply take for granted. Roy might disagree. He was very modest. I do, however, believe that he was like a scientist who studies the invisible and translates it into material that everyone can read.

In 1993, I saw *Go for Baroque* again, this time at Roy's retrospective at the Guggenheim Museum in New York. The green triangle was still there. The life and the images that an artist creates become part of the concept of a masterpiece, which of course endures forever. That longevity has the power of influence beyond our individual lives. I never tire of looking at *Go for Baroque*, either in books or as the poster published for Roy's 1993 retrospective. The painting does not look busy or complicated. Roy has filtered all his detail, movement, imagery, and excess through his comic book vocabulary, then reassembled fragmented moments into a painting, incorporating multiple historical art images. The Guggenheim chose *Go for Baroque* for the cover of its catalogue, probably for the same reasons Roy originally created the work: as a summary representing his larger body of work.

———

Roy achieved greater fame as a painter, but his sculpture also demonstrates his range of artistry. One of his creations was a limited edition titled *Modern Head*, a thirty-one-foot design cast in brushed steel that explored his interest in creating human figures resembling machines or machine parts. I helped place three works, one in Japan, another donated to Yale, and the artist's proof donated to the City of Jerusalem, where it stands in Daniel Park next to City Hall in memory of Prime Minister Yitzhak Rabin. Roy also completed a separate cast of *Modern Head*, which he painted a vibrant blue. For five years, it was on loan in Battery Park City, installed one block from the World Trade Center.

On September 11, 2001, when the Twin Towers were destroyed in the horrendous terrorist attack, *Modern Head* survived undamaged except for a few scratches, although it was covered in charred debris from the fallen buildings, the vibrant blue literally shrouded in physical loss. For weeks, federal agents working at the trade center site taped messages for each other along the sculpture's base. The work was removed and restored. In 2009, to honor Roy and his wife Dorothy, I gifted the sculpture to the Smithsonian American Art Museum at Dorothy's request. It now stands in Washington, DC, a testament to the breadth and expression of Roy's creative vision and skill and to the resilience of art that can literally rise from the ashes after a tragedy.

———

The times that Roy graciously made his studio accessible to me have been part of a life experience that expanded my visual and intellectual horizons and challenged some of my preconceived perceptions. Seeing simultaneous projects, all in various stages of completion, was a distinct privilege. What consistently amazed me was not so much the magic of his imagery but rather the more enduring way his iconography instantly altered the way I looked at everything else.

Through a simple set of tones and codes, Roy observed the widely recognized imagery of comic book art. He appropriated and expanded this visual grammar. With that new vocabulary, he was able to redraw, repaint, and even reassemble the work of artists that preceded him in a refined and economical way. He brought clarity to much of the intangible in art and exposed it to a worldwide audience, which embraced his art.

Part of Roy's genius was the irony found in his visual vocabulary. His art sometimes appeared to be cold and removed from individual expression. But those comic book shortcuts that idealize classic representations inevitably link everything to his distinctive style. This is no different from any other great artist in history.

Artists have always acquired signature attributes that make works identifiable as their own. Raphael borrowed from Leonardo to help formulate his distinctive work. Vermeer's paintings were instantly recognizable—generations have admired him for his stunning consistency, particularly the way he appropriated light. With Picasso, the range of appropriation and invention was so changeable that we often distinguish his works by the periods they describe. Roy extended the notion of a signature look by honing a very efficient visual vocabulary to define a broad range of images and subjects. The only repetition I can discover in his work is the repeated brilliance he used to redefine artistic elements and make them at once both familiar and new.

Of the Pop giants at the end of the 1950s that we know today, if I were to choose one whom I believe was the real genius of Pop Art, it would have to be Roy Lichtenstein. Like any great genius, he didn't only paint Pop Art into our culture; he created a world beyond Pop, beyond his initial influences and appropriations. Perhaps this might seem like too big a leap for some, but if there were an American equivalent to Picasso, it would be Roy Lichtenstein.

Like Picasso, Roy evolved his work with significant changes that allowed for a traceable thread and a continued production of exceptional art. He advanced the language of art by incorporating imagery and iconography, thereby making even the most sophisticated ideas and compositions universally understandable. It seems impossible to imagine painting and sculpture today without Lichtenstein's influence.

It has been more than two decades since Roy died. Because of him, I have continued to look at objects and my environment differently. The remarkable visual experience he offered me, and indeed everyone, abides forever.

CHAPTER EIGHT

LARRY RIVERS

THE RIVERS EXPERIENCE

"I like to pretend that my

art has nothing to do with me."

– ROY LICHTENSTEIN

There's a myth that Pop Art in America was born overnight with Andy Warhol and Roy Lichtenstein. It wasn't. Over the past few decades, critics and historians have been more inclined to recognize Robert Rauschenberg and Jasper Johns as the key artists who challenged Abstract Expressionism (Ab Ex), opening the door for the eventuality of Pop Art. A few critics may occasionally mumble another artist's name, but often with a certain degree of reluctance. That other name is Larry Rivers, the wild-card artist who in 1953 made a work of art that challenged Ab Ex's numerous tenets.

Larry was an unmitigated genius and an equally difficult and problematic figure. He was not art's shining humble equivalent to Jackie Robinson (despite his proclamations that he wished he were Black), but he most definitely was, in his field, more than equaled in talent and ability, and for most of the 1950s, Rivers was an art star.

I met Larry around the same time in the 1970s that I met Roy Lichtenstein. By 1970, Rivers's influence in the art world was not what it used to be, but everything about the man—his talent, his outrageous personality, and his ability to be a provocative influence—had not changed one bit. When I first met him in a local, gritty Southampton club where he was playing his saxophone, I could have easily assumed he wasn't really that serious about his art. He was believed to be a wild man with a radical, undisciplined, and irreverent personality. His public antics and unconventional lifestyle had earned him that reputation.

We established a friendship that lasted until his passing in 2002, and for years, I spent countless hours visiting him in his studios, where he spent most of his time. In truth, Larry was in that studio every day from early in the morning into the evening. When his routine was interrupted, he always found his way back to the studio to make up for his absence. Everything else was merely part of the show. He would say and do just about anything to shock and provoke, but despite all the antics, he was absolutely dedicated to his art.

Larry continually changed and experimented. He wasn't interested in being affiliated with any one school of art; rather, he wanted the freedom to create whatever he felt like creating, whenever he felt like it, and while he certainly hoped that his deviations from the obvious genius in his paintings and his extraordinary ability to draw would be appreciated, he never let his critics hold him back. Larry once told me, "Art is the only profession where you can succeed without being successful." He meant that if you remain creative and determined, the results of your creativity may not win you great fortune or public acclaim, but they can affirm your intent and validate your purpose. For him, producing a work of art was a concrete affirmation of his purpose. Time outside the studio was time spent searching for affirmation that he ultimately knew he could only truly get when making his art. In art, Larry had many ups and downs, but he always succeeded.

During his life, Larry displayed more controversy, drama, humor, and genius than the script of any Hollywood movie; he could make me laugh or feel more alive by simply being around him. In his art and in his life, he was a revolutionary who found a way to liberate his vision by embracing his own inner conflicts. Rivers craved attention. He was famous for the art he created but equally celebrated for his larger-than-life personality. He also had a way of altering the truth to fit his immediate needs. It often seemed to me that everything he said and did had more than one meaning, and those meanings were often diametrically opposed.

Beginning in the nineteenth century, New York artists often sought to avoid the summer heat by escaping to the townships collectively known as the Hamptons on the east end of Long Island. The quality of light was a main attribute in luring artists to this area. I too came for the light and quiet. This would put me in greater proximity to several artists, including Larry Rivers, Saul Steinberg, and Roy Lichtenstein.

Whether it was playing his saxophone or creating his innovative art, Larry sought the spotlight. He was a social butterfly, floating freely across social groups and mingling with poets, musicians, artists, and actors. In the visual arts, he embraced the idea of provocation as a way to engage the mainstream of the art world. The stars of the art world of the late 1940s and early 1950s were predominantly Abstract Expressionists. Larry's friendships with many of these artists inspired his aspirations to greatness. Once, while in his studio, we were looking at some of his early works from the 1950s, and he remarked that if he was going to get the desired attention, he would have to distinguish himself from the others. As a result, he intentionally created a painting in direct opposition to Abstract Expressionism.

In 1953, his contemporary version, or revision, of *Washington Crossing the Delaware* (now in the Museum of Modern Art in New York City) sent a shock wave through the New York art world. While it garnered great attention, the painting also attracted strong criticism from the very ranks he sought to join, although one of the main stars of Abstract Expressionism, Willem de Kooning, defended Rivers. Larry told me that essentially de Kooning had said, "Looking at a Rivers painting was like pressing your face in wet grass."

Washington Crossing the Delaware was conceived to be something similar in painterly style to Ab Ex—but where Ab Ex artists believed that they had elevated art above the representational, this work reveled in it. It utilized imagery that wasn't merely recognizable but was also Larry's appropriation of a famous American patriotic narrative—inspired, he noted, by his reading of Leo Tolstoy's classic *War and Peace* during what was also the early phase of the US-Soviet Union Cold War. To the Abstract Expressionists, a painting that illustrated Washington's historic crossing in a raw, semiabstract way would not simply be a betrayal of the Ab Ex philosophy, it would be an absolute insult to the practitioners of the art form. Anything representational defied both their principles and their fundamental way of looking at the world.

It may not sound like that big a deal now, but in 1955, when the Museum of Modern Art acquired Larry Rivers's version of *Washington Crossing the Delaware*, it was a true validation that opened the door to a flood of artists who suddenly felt liberated to let the radical nature of their provocative and recognizable subject matter step out of the shadows of Abstract Expressionism. The art world is replete with historical narratives that describe the way art has evolved over time, yet there are also important contributions to that narrative which are always at risk of being edited out of the history books because they don't easily fit. That, in my view, is exemplified by Larry Rivers.

By 1959–1960, Rivers was giving commercial imagery high art status with his paintings of cigarette labels and automobiles, paintings such as *The Last Civil War Veteran*, and more. All employed Pop iconography before America had ever heard the term Pop Art. Like it or not, artists as great as Andy Warhol and Roy Lichtenstein might not have evolved in quite the same way without Larry Rivers breaking open the door to Pop Art.

When I met Larry, I had already seen many of his greatest works from the 1950s and 1960s. But it was his distinctive draftsmanship that first attracted me to his work. Watching him work as often as I did was a privilege. It also gave me insight into his character. He could transform and channel his quick wit and salacious innuendo into genuine creativity. When his pencil or charcoal or brush touched paper, a new energy came over him and a crooked smile would fill his face with childlike delight. His artist's tools liberated him. Of all the draftsmen that I have watched work, Salvador Dalí and Larry Rivers were unparalleled.

Dalí could complete a perfect composition by drawing with a single line, without ever lifting the pencil away from the paper. Larry, by contrast, had a rhythmic approach, drawing his lines at great speed with certainty and confidence. He employed the techniques of great drawings. He used a heavy hand both to render and to erase. He would tear paper and tape it back together. He also smudged his lines, often muddying the edges of the paper. He would remove what anyone else would consider important and definitive, like the eye of a figure. Yet when he had finished and stepped back, he had genuinely captured the likeness. Larry's works were imbued with emotion and a truly expressive existence. I observed his magic when he did two portraits of my father.

Larry's open and accessible personality made it easy to approach him. Within minutes of our first conversation, he had invited me to his nineteenth-century shingle-style home and studio at 92 Little Plains Road in Southampton. On arriving, I realized at once that I was meeting a genuine bohemian artist. To be generous, I would describe the furnishings as "pragmatic eclecticism." Larry was by no means a hoarder, but there was a sort of Collyer brothers logic to the arrangement (referring to two brothers who had lived in Manhattan and amassed 140 tons of objects in their brownstone). The only clearly visible path was from the living quarters to his studio. Clutter was everywhere. It defined his environment.

I remember an African bird sculpture, with its legs removed, that hung upside down from a string and was used to turn on the guest bathroom light. Rivers used duct tape on a ripped sofa. In fact, duct tape, string, and staples held most of the things together in the house. In contrast, his library was rather well ordered. He had a voracious appetite for reading, but even the books were subject to his odd nature. I remember I saw an open book on a sofa with some pages cut out, which were stapled and taped elsewhere in the house. Larry did not have a planned aesthetic. Instead, his aesthetic musings were channeled into his art.

One thing I perceived when I first met Larry was that his showmanship might easily overshadow his art. He had a movie star appearance, with strong features and piercing eyes. If his natural intensity didn't seize your attention, he made sure to dress in a manner that did. His typical casual summer wear might include red suspenders holding up bright green shorts over a black muscle shirt. I remember once seeing him in a purple button-down shirt with a scarf, sporting Picasso designs, wound around his neck, his version of more formal attire. His shoes were equally bizarre. He had a favorite pair of bowling shoes with the toes cut out so that his exotic, colorful socks could be seen there as well as on his legs. His copper-painted sneakers were a sight to behold!

Larry had a booming voice that could seem abrasive, but he balanced that impression with a remarkable graciousness. He was quick to offer a snack or a drink. He was equally generous in ushering me into his studio, where a piece of paper, a canvas, or elements of collage created a fleeting image in scraps on the floor. There were tables with tools, knives, tape, glue, a staple gun, and charcoal, as well as another table with dozens of tubes of paint. I noticed an abundance of red paint, my favorite color. On those few occasions when he would ask me what I thought of a painting he was working on for me, I would make certain to casually mention the tubes of red paint, hoping he would include the color in his work.

His studio had skylights, but Larry had permanently affixed shades to cover them. I never asked why, but I always assumed that he wasn't there for the Hamptons' special light. He just liked being there.

———

Larry was from a generation of artists who rarely used an easel. Big works were either tacked onto the wall or laid out on the floor. He preferred the wall. To accommodate his large paintings, he had con-cocted an elaborate mechanism that he was very eager to explain. The system involved a long wooden slat running parallel to the floor, sus-pended from a pulley system that could move it up and down on the wall. On one of my first visits, he ushered me over quickly and, like a child with a new toy, eagerly described his invention. "Jeff," he said, "come here. I want to show you something. You see that strip of wood going across my wall? It is attached to this rope which I run though these pulleys with a canvas stapled to the wood." He was able to pull the canvas close to me so I could see how it was attached to the wood. "I just raise and lower the canvas by pulling on the rope. When I get it to the height I need, I go back over here and tie the rope back to the cleat. Then I just staple the canvas in place right on the wall, and it can't move! UNDERSTAND, MAN?!"

"But Larry," I had to ask, "what is this long, narrow, seemingly very deep trough going down into your concrete floor for?" Larry stopped, looked at me, and with great humor said, "That's where we send the people who don't buy my work. Watch your step. Don't fall in," before adding, "Actually, for the very large canvases, taller than this wall, like something you might want, I need to be able to lower the canvas enough to reach the top without folding it on the floor and smearing the wet paint." Ultimately, it was a perfect solution for what would become my first "Rivers commission," *Golden Oldies 50s* and *Golden Oldies 60s*, which he began in the late 1970s.

The artists who became my friends have all gone through various stages; they have good days and bad days, good years and not so good years. The reasons may be very personal. When artists, entertainers, sports figures, or anyone practicing their craft in the public eye are off their game, it leaves a very public record. As an audience, we tend to pass judgment quickly. I didn't have a great deal of patience when my baseball team was on a losing streak or when an artist that I admired for a certain set of skills suddenly dropped those skills for something new and uncertain.

The privilege of having a front-row seat to observe Larry gave me a different sense of responsibility. It was never my place to tell him that he might be going down a treacherous road. I am sure he knew that, but if he didn't, who was I to tell him he was wrong? Would it do any good to tell a power home-run hitter, who hasn't hit a home run in a while, that he simply needs to step up to the plate and try and hit one?

If there is a magic spell to revive a creative person's spirit and talent, I imagine that it would have to do with recapturing a time when things were working well. Often, the best thing is to be supportive. I did that with Larry when he seemed to want encouragement. I had a keen interest in his works that had already been placed in museums and were clearly not available for acquisition. One day, in the late 1970s, I said to him, "Larry, you're right about my interest in a large painting. You've made brilliant works based on historical subject matter. How large would a painting about your own history be?"

"Too big to start out here on Long Island," he said. So, we postponed what would eventually become *Golden Oldies 50s* and *Golden Oldies 60s* and three later large-scale commissions until he was able to paint them back in his New York studio.

In Manhattan, Larry was a Lower East Side guy. He lived and worked in an enormous loft that spanned an entire city block, stretching between 405 East Thirteenth Street and 404 East Fourteenth Street, just off First Avenue. Larry co-owned the building with a dry cleaner located on the Fourteenth Street side. Today the dry cleaner is gone, and there is a McDonald's in its place.

When I visited the studio, I would enter through a small door on Thirteenth Street, which was rather desolate and grimy. The long hallway leading to the elevator looked as though it served as the office for a drug dealer. The chemical aromas emanating from the cleaners were not pleasant, and the long walk from the Thirteenth Street entrance led to a large self-service elevator, a contraption from another era. It had to have been designed before the invention of the personal injury attorney. The elevator consisted of an enormous platform lift that traveled up and down in a large, open shaft. There were no doors and no ceilings, and Larry lived and worked on the top floor.

It was necessary to stick your head into the open shaft to locate the elevator from above and to pull the ropes firmly if you wanted the elevator to arrive at your floor. Doing it hastily or incorrectly risked possible dismemberment at best, decapitation at worst. The entire operation was one wrong move away from death. The elevator resembled an enormous mechanized version of Larry's Southampton studio device, except the passenger was the equivalent of the canvas. One wrong pull could land you in the deep, open trough at the base of the shaft.

The first time I stepped inside and onto the platform to go up to the studio, Larry turned to me and said, "Don't look up." I smiled and said, "Why is that?" He answered, "Because you might get oil in your eyes." The ceiling-less elevator was well lubricated. From then on, whenever I visited Larry in New York, I made sure to wear a baseball cap to avoid any oil from above.

When Larry and I arrived at his fifth-floor loft and studio, we stepped into an open living area. It felt like a nightclub when someone says "closing time" and all the lights come on. It was rather seedy; there were always a few stragglers hanging around, often a couple of beautiful women, and one or two assistants. From the floor to the exposed ceiling that ran through the entire loft was a distance of about fourteen feet. I could see the water pipes and all the electrical wiring, and the place looked as though it had last been painted more than fifty years ago. The maroon carpet was stained, doubtless the result of drippings from above. Across the room, I could see a mixture of three-dimensional works surrounded by a sparse assortment of peculiar furniture.

The clashing colors and odd objects, indiscriminately tacked to various surfaces, also gave it a nightclub atmosphere. But the clincher was the scene dividing the living area from Larry's sleeping quarters. Larry had constructed a full-blown stage for a band, with a banquette of lights and a piano and a professional drum kit. At the front of the stage, as if it were the star of the show, sat his saxophone, at the ready.

On that initial visit, Larry offered me something to drink before we headed in the opposite direction toward his studio. I followed him down the hall where photos and poems were tacked to the walls, imagery that touched all aspects of Larry's fascinating life and experiences. I remember wanting to keep up with him, but the display slowed my progress.

I have never forgotten that first visit, and the mixture of excitement and uncertainty, but I think that was always the feeling whenever I was around Larry in his studio. I was fortunate to spend a great deal of time with him. He became a sort of extended member of my family. He even took an interest in the lives of my family. He was always very inquisitive and asked numerous questions; it was as if Larry was constantly doing research. We spoke about my experiences with Vincent Price and how much I valued having him as a mentor and friend. Larry understood that bond because he too had a deep appreciation for the value of relationships in changing one's life. Curiously, both Vincent and Larry had been contestants on the popular television show *The $64,000 Question* in the same year; Vincent won the grand prize, while Larry made it to the final round but opted to take $32,000 and stop. He often asked me about my upbringing and family. We even talked about my close connection to my father. I remember Larry asking me to bring him to the studio some time, and on one visit, I surprised him by bringing my father along.

My dad dressed appropriately for the occasion, sporting a bright striped white shirt. He also wore his favorite fisherman's hat, a black model that would protect him from the elevator's messy lubricant. Larry took the time to speak with my father in depth and genuinely seemed to enjoy meeting him. During a later visit, Larry made a point of asking about my dad. I decided to ask if he would consider doing a drawing of my father. I remember him pausing and saying, "Your father is very tall. I'm gonna have to have him sit." That was Larry's cryptic way of agreeing not just to do a drawing of my father but to create a memorable experience and image.

Until about 1965, most of Larry's portraits were done from life. But after 1966, having felt that he had more than proved his artistry and technical proficiency, he decided to employ different technologies to expedite the demand for his work. Very often he began his drawings with photos. For the portrait of my father, drawn in Southampton, Larry made the extra effort to draw it from life. But rather than saying so, he simply blamed my father's height for his desire to have him sit for the portrait. Larry ultimately drew two portraits. In the picture where my father isn't wearing his fisherman's hat, Larry transferred all his own personal drive to the sheen that emanates from my father's face. The light glowing from my father in that drawing is absolutely exquisite. My father was the guiding light in my life, and Larry got it!

The greatest insight I had into Larry Rivers was watching him complete a series of works that I commissioned, starting with a request that he paint his own history in art. I still recall the moment in New York when he said, "Jeff, come with me! I want to show you something. I started working on what could be your big painting." I followed Larry into his enormous open studio. Unlike in Southampton, the path was wider and the tools and the paintings, some in progress and some completed, were further from the main thoroughfare. As we got closer, I saw what appeared to be new versions of some of his most famous images from the 1950s. "This will be a series of works that I am going to call *Golden Oldies 50s* and *Golden Oldies 60s*," he said. "I have decided to look back at about twenty-five years and select works that I think identify my history."

I told him, "I see *Nude with Boots*, sketches from *Washington Crossing the Delaware*, and that's *Cedar Bar Menu*. So, this one must be *Golden Oldies 50s*." "Yes," Larry said. "But I am only partly characterizing the '50s. It really only touches the tip of the iceberg." He explained that he was also "trying to include some of the spirit of my drawing."

I had never seen an artist respond so quickly to a simple cue and work so seriously and quickly. His process, in all the large works he did, was to produce an exhaustive group of studies to prepare. He revisited his most famous works from each decade. It was classic Rivers in every sense of the word. He was addressing history, and in this case his own, as if reading a diary and commenting in the margins, providing a new context for evaluation. I don't recall ever watching an artist review his own work like this, and it was astonishing to think that I would be able to own these paintings. It was equally remarkable to know that I had something to do with the direction Larry took.

Ultimately, he decided to focus on two nine-by-twelve-foot works, *Golden Oldies 50s* and *Golden Oldies 60s*. We thought about doing a *Golden Oldies 70s*, but in the end, Larry felt that he needed more time and more perspective to reevaluate that decade.

The *Golden Oldies* series was the first of many inspired projects that ensued during the years. With each new work, I learned more about Larry and his creative energy. He loved research. Before tackling any project, Larry would read as much material as he could. His monumental mixed-media construction, *The History of the Russian Revolution: From Marx to Mayakovsky* (now in the Hirshhorn Museum), created during the heightened tensions of the Cold War, was a bold work. It involved countless hours of research, artistry, and engineering. I saw the work when it was exhibited at the Jewish Museum in New York, the final venue for his 1965 traveling retrospective. The show left an impression. A few years after the *Golden Oldies*, I asked Larry to try to do something similar with Jewish history. But Larry said he needed time to consider the magnitude of such a project. The man with the big ego and reputation as a fearless provocateur was, in this case, intimidated. The responsibility of undertaking a project connected to his ancestry gave him pause. Ultimately, he accepted the challenge. Larry began thinking about the project in 1980. Work on it took about three years and spanned three individual ten-by-fourteen-foot canvases.

History of Matzah: The Story of the Jews required expert advice on the subject, and Larry sought it out. He consulted with Jewish Museum curator Norman Kleeblatt and hired the museum's researcher, Anita Friedman, to work with him on selecting resources for the project. He invited Joel Carmichael, a historian from Columbia University, to help formulate a plan for the work. He sought the help of his friend, the writer Irving Howe, numerous times. In preparation, Larry also read countless publications. Two important sources were

ABOVE: *Larry Rivers's painting* Golden Oldies 60s, *1978 (detail).*

Howe's *World of Our Fathers* and Chaim Potok's *Wanderings*. For his first canvas, he decided he needed a model to represent Moses and found the perfect sitter in his aging cousin Aaron from the Bronx.

When looking in retrospect at Larry's work immediately following the *Golden Oldies* series, it seems evident to me that these paintings helped him reset his direction. Larry ultimately put aside his late 1960s and early 1970s experiments with materials and techniques that differed from his distinctive earlier painterly style. Once again, his draftsmanship and painterly qualities reemerged. He began to create new versions of old themes, which, although they were quite independent of the *Golden Oldies* commission, clearly found inspiration in those works. During the process of revisiting his old themes, he used classic materials and made no effort to conceal his naturally brilliant hand.

For the next two decades, Larry demonstrated a stunningly broad range of technical proficiency. His innovative compositions revealed a more abstract version of his renowned images, and the range was astounding. Larry was clearly reenergized with a life force that seemed to have been temporarily derailed during the 1960s. I recall an artist (perhaps Picasso) saying in effect, "When you are stuck in a rut or don't know where to go with your work, go back to what you know and let the work evolve from there." That is what the *Golden Oldies* did for Larry. By 1983, when we had started talking about another commission, Larry was back in full swing and ready to create some of the most ambitious projects of his career.

My good friend Danny Berger ran the Mezzanine Gallery at the Metropolitan Museum of Art in New York. Danny knew that Larry was a friend and asked if I would approach him about making a print for the Met's gallery. Without hesitation, Larry agreed. He produced a memorable drawing of one of his most famous themes, the *Dutch Masters* cigar composition. In 1963, just as Pop Art was emerging (due in part to his ideas), Larry borrowed the image from a cigar company that had, in turn, appropriated Rembrandt's masterpiece for its label. The painting that resulted was a brilliant commentary on high and low art. For years, Larry repeated the theme many times, but always changing aspects of the imagery to create a new twist. In this instance, he made it clear that his contribution was specifically created for a museum dedicated to great artists like Rembrandt. Larry's emphasis was not on cigars but on Rembrandt's figures.

Several years after Larry completed *History of Matzah*, I asked him to address the history of Hollywood. He approached it with the same enthusiasm and sense of responsibility as his other history projects. He was the writer, director, editor, and producer. He spent hours producing nearly fifty studies for consideration as he worked to connect defining moments in Hollywood's history across several eight-by-ten-foot canvases. Larry's generosity and his appreciation for the value of relationships was evident again when he featured my early mentor Vincent Price prominently in one of the paintings and created an extraordinary preparatory drawing in charcoal for the work. Larry valued my story with Vincent and used it as a way to connect me personally with *The History of Hollywood*. I didn't ask him to do it. It was just Larry being kind and imaginative.

Larry always produced paintings that far exceeded my wildest expectations. For my end of the bargain, I always paid him promptly, which usually involved also receiving some kind of special request from him for the funds. No transaction felt quite right unless I received one of Larry's messages. It would have almost been worth it to delay a payment just to hear his additional pleas, but I never did that. He started making his case almost from the moment when the brush left his canvas for the scrub sink. I still have a handwritten letter from Larry asking for immediate payment on one of the last works he did for me. It read: "Jeff, P-Day hath arrived! With a daughter's wedding behind me and the government in front of me I want the money..."

This exchange involved my last commission about art and the artist, entitled *In Their Time*. With his first canvas completed, Larry added one more reminder for the money: "While I wait, both for the promised photos and the bread, I'll start with what I got." He then went on to suggest that I try to get out to Southampton to see him so that "we can at least get a better idea of what will go into *In Their*

Time II." Beneath his signature, Larry added a third subtle reminder. He had drawn a quick sketch of a figure that appears to be swinging a baseball bat. It was extra insurance to make sure he was communicating with me in a language I would understand, suggesting that his letter was a pitch and I needed to hit something back. In this regard, Larry looked at art as if it were a team sport.

If you were fortunate enough to know Larry Rivers, you valued his generosity, while also forgiving him for his shortcomings and his frequently embarrassing need to shine. You understood the way that he transferred light into his art to ignite dialogues and extract the sublime. Initially, he came to the Hamptons for a reprieve from his own inner darkness. Yet year after year, he returned, not to assimilate the natural light surrounding him, but to challenge it.

In the end, Larry even sought to compete with the sun.

ABOVE: *Handwritten letter from Larry Rivers to Jeffrey Loria, summer 2000.*

CHAPTER NINE

CLYFFORD STILL

AN UNYIELDING GENIUS

"An artist must be free to choose

what he does, certainly, but he also must

never be afraid to do what he might choose."

– LANGSTON HUGHES

T rying to anticipate or chase trends in the art world can be risky. Fashion is fickle; a work of great art may be timeless, but it is not always commercially popular or sought after by collectors. The other inescapable fact is that not all art *is* great; fashion, trends, and chasing both can deceive the eye.

In the 1970s, as the crafted art object was challenged by the rise of conceptual art, which weighted the value of ideas over process of production, ultimately resulting in anything that might be considered a form of expression, I remained focused on art as a tangible object. While I was curious about conceptual art, I stuck to my core belief that great art and great artists are timeless.

As a first-generation Abstract Expressionist, Clyfford Still was one of the movement's original practitioners. Even before Mark Rothko and Jackson Pollock, as early as 1938, Clyfford Still had already made a transition from recognizable imagery to abstraction. By the time we met and became friends in 1970, Still was no longer living in New York, and while he remained completely dedicated to his vision, Abstract Expressionism was no longer dominant on the art scene. That's not to say that Ab Ex was dead—it remains very much alive today—but in 1970, Pop Art had surpassed Ab Ex as the new sensation. For me, none of that mattered. I was always interested in Still's work and happy to travel to Maryland to meet with him. We bonded over similar tastes, important art, and eventually the realization that we shared a passion for baseball.

Clyfford Still's enigmatic persona was impervious to probing by even his most intimate friends. He craved isolation and solitude, and he favored distance from the mainstream art world. But his choices should not be mistaken for an antisocial attitude. As I saw firsthand in the decade that we knew each other, the most important thing to him was his work.

One essential truth about Clyfford Still was that he was not swayed by changing trends. Observing his personal dedication to an unyielding vision helped me reaffirm my own beliefs in following my instincts and not being unduly influenced by others' views. The reason he left New York City in the 1950s was so he could concentrate on his work without the distractions of city life, even though he always considered New York his home and visited often. In one of our many memorable meetings, he explained that he did not simply abandon working in New York in the 1950s without cause. Rather, he realized that he needed a new and positive environment so that he could be true to himself and his work. He didn't want to be bothered by the chatter of art talk or gossip; he once described to me what he saw as the fruitless dialogues of his contemporaries in the art world and deemed it "noisy activity," as he laconically put it. He also deeply disliked "the pretentiousness of the self-promoters" in what he saw as the "New York art factory." To his mind, such discussions only served to waste time better devoted to the pursuit of his art. "They would have destroyed my work had I succumbed," he told me.

Still did not need to be in the center of the art world; he didn't need to focus on whether Pop Art was overtaking Ab Ex. He just needed to forge ahead and exercise his creativity with the same unwavering genius that guided his art throughout his life. He was his own man, remaining that way until his death in 1980. Time has proven the wisdom of Still's approach, that conviction combined with determined greatness cannot be denied.

Whenever we were together, I always felt that the intensity and commitment he brought to his work was a function of the privacy he guarded carefully against all competing demands. That was partly why "Mr. Still," as his devoted and protective wife, Patricia, always called him in my presence, endured as one of the giants of twentieth-century Abstract Expressionism. I didn't know Jackson Pollock, who had died tragically in 1956, or Mark Rothko, who took his own life in 1970. But Still often talked about his relationships with both of them.

In fact, a week before Pollock died in a car crash, Still had visited him in East Hampton, Long Island, where he pleaded with Pollock to take some time off and join him in Minnesota, his next destination. Still hoped that Pollock might be able to curtail his drinking. Pollock, however, did not take him up on his invitation, and a week later, Still saw in a local Midwest newspaper that his friend had died in a car accident, attributed to his driving under the influence of alcohol.

Still also enjoyed Rothko's friendship. Because of the reverence he felt for Still and his paintings, Rothko even wrote a foreword for the catalogue of an early Still exhibition at Peggy Guggenheim's Art of This Century Gallery in New York.

In our years of friendship, I too knew that "Mr. Still" was unique. At the beginning of the 1970s, I wrote him several letters suggesting that we meet. Initially he did not reply, but one day he responded, offering to have lunch in Baltimore. I remember my excitement at the thought of meeting one of my heroes in the art world. Our first encounter was at a small restaurant specializing in local crabmeat. (I will confess without shame that in 1993, when I considered purchasing the Baltimore Orioles baseball team, the thought of being close to the best crabmeat in the world certainly crossed my mind.)

After we lunched in Baltimore while bonding over our shared passions for art and crabmeat, a mutual friendship commenced that endured for a decade. For our next meeting Still invited me to his home in New Windsor, Maryland, a quaint, rural town fifty miles west of Baltimore. Those fifty miles seemed to consist of endless farmland, which I always thought played a role in his work. Not only did the sweeping vistas inspire him, but the liberty suggested by the land did so as well. Clyfford loved that sense of freedom.

My first expedition to his home resulted from a reply he wrote to me in October 1972:

> *Dear Jeffrey Loria,* [He often called me by both my first and last name.]
>
> *It was most gracious of you to send a note reminding us of a pleasant lunch in Baltimore with you.*
>
> *As I recall your desire to visit New Windsor, I must again warn you that all but a very few of my works are packed and stored, and those few are familiar pieces of my own permanent collection. If, however, you drove down, the landscape alone at this time of year provides a visual treat that would merit the effort.*
>
> *I, of course, found you a very tolerant and personable young man and enjoyed our exchange of reminiscences. If you care to risk the drive, I propose Wednesday the 25th of the month. We will look for you to arrive by mid-afternoon and could have an early dinner at a nearby town.*
>
> *If this does not meet with your convenience, drop me a note.*
>
> *Best regards,*
>
> *Clyfford Still*

ABOVE: *The Still home at 312 Church Street, New Windsor, Maryland.*

That first visit to New Windsor went well and was followed by many others. Thereafter we always met at the Still residence. But fixed in my memory is the first time I drove up to his house, perched on a quiet street. What struck me most were the grand columns enveloping the front door. Despite their height and grandeur, they were very inviting. Clyfford was standing outside and graciously welcomed me. Inside the door was a large living room populated by his private collection, probably twenty-five or thirty paintings in all, rolled up and placed around the room. The paintings were stacked vertically on their edges, some six to eight feet high, apparently at random distances from each other and occupying the entire living room and the adjoining room. The curious scene had the mysterious otherworldliness of Stonehenge.

In the middle of my Stonehenge moment, Still began the first of many conversations about his need to move away from the pressures of Manhattan, which he found stifling and inhibiting his ability to paint. Over the years, he repeatedly told me how he never wanted to be considered part of any school or movement because he viewed his art as an extension of himself. He always spoke with the same clarity, logic, and careful reasoning that were so apparent in his letters. In person, his words somehow suggested a deeper confidence, making the interaction even more meaningful. I always felt honored to be in his presence.

During that first visit, when he unrolled one of his never-before-seen canvases, it was a unique revelation to me. The canvas he so delicately unveiled captured a depth and breadth of shimmering, jagged edges, displaying a unified color and texture much like the Maryland landscape I had just seen during my drive. He favored elongated, towering compositions, free of excessive ornament or distraction. I remember thinking that the overwhelming spirit they represented came from the hand of a pure genius. The reason why innovation should not be denied but nurtured was staring me in the face.

Still rarely sold his works privately, preferring to keep them, unless necessity dictated otherwise. By the time I left several hours later, he knew I wanted to acquire a group of his works. My train ride from Baltimore to New York was nothing short of euphoric; the impact of the day was extraordinary.

In early 1976, I received a package of photographs of three paintings. One photograph was of a magnificent painting, which we had looked at together that day in New Windsor. The other two paintings he was offering to me were equally stunning. It didn't take me long to respond with my most sincere gratitude. I acquired all three of them.

Clyfford's package of photographs was equivalent to today's ubiquitous use of modern technology (e.g., JPEGs and TIFF files). When I started my career, I relied on photographs and transparencies sent via the United States Postal Service. Even fax machines did not yet exist. The high-tech communication of the day was the landline telephone. Micro-dialoguing with electronic attachments was inconceivable. But that old-school technology of photographs in an envelope, with an accompanying letter, carried a different kind of weight and tone of importance. A leisurely exchange of information does not suit today's business environment, but there have also been losses generated by our desire for speed and rapid turnaround. The nuances of meaning reflected in Still's letters often do not exist in our current communication. Today's messages rarely if ever bear the artistry and thoughtfulness that were conveyed in his handwritten letters.

When it came time in March 1976 to deliver the paintings to New York, Still wrote:

March 8, 1976

Dear Jeffrey Loria,

Knowing you expressed a desire to see the work as soon as possible, I chose a stretcher already assembled which had been made by Albright Art Gallery for a picture of the same size which was shown in their 1959 exhibition, and mounted your work on it.

As a parenthetical explanation, I must add that when I have the urge to work, I seldom take the time to concern myself with the stretchers beyond that which will properly hold the field I am about to deal with. The mechanics of perpetuation come later and are relative only to conditions I dare not be concerned with at periods of execution. In other words, I am not a manufacturer of products. I am sure you will understand.

To protect the paint surface of the pictures from contact with each other while being moved from New Windsor to your designation, I have tacked a quarter-inch trim around the four edges of each. This is simply a protective device and not intended as a frame. They can easily be removed with a screwdriver or chisel when no longer necessary. Insomuch as these pictures are not windows, I find frames disturbingly limiting to their implicit extensions.

They have been selected to go out of my studio because I trust the sincerity of your interest and the caliber of your understanding.

You have more than our best wishes.

Yours,

Clyfford Still

———

Our friendship would have been deep and rich if it were based solely on art, but we shared another passion in common: baseball. He was a genuine enthusiast, even a fanatic. We often spoke about the Yankees icon Roger Maris; both Still and Maris had lived parts of their lives in North Dakota. They represented a Middle American purity and work ethic, which they carried with them through their careers.

One summer, he wrote to me:

> *Dear Jeffrey Loria,*
>
> *Your response to the photograph, which I am pleased for you to have, carried a suggestion which I may have been subconsciously hoping for—namely, a chance to visit a Yankee game with you. I sincerely enjoyed the evening and the game at Shea Stadium—including the airplanes. Be assured I will time my next visit to New York to coincide with a chance to see the Yankees in action. They have always been my favorites chiefly because they demonstrate how baseball should be played by professionals.*
>
> *Of course, should your duties bring you into this area, feel free to give us a phone call. You are always welcome to visit us.*
>
> *Yours,*
>
> *Clyfford Still*

A few weeks later, he wrote to me again, after I sent him a Yankee yearbook:

> *Dear Jeffrey Loria,*
>
> *The handsome Yankee Yearbook will not be denied! We plan to be in New York August 2. If your plans permit, we would very much like to see the Yankee-Detroit game on the evening of that date with you.*
>
> *Drop me a note if you are free on that evening.*

We did see that Yankees-Tigers game together. I remember the details vividly. A Yankee player hit a home run to put the Yankees ahead. Still, who was very tall, was up cheering the home run before I was even able to get out of my seat. The temperature in the ballpark was in the nineties that night, and the humidity was stifling. But Still, who detested air-conditioning, asked me to turn it off for our car ride back to the city. With the air-conditioning respectfully silenced, I quietly melted while Still rode bundled up in a scarf, perfectly content and thoroughly enthralled with a wonderful evening at the ballpark. On that drive, I asked why he rooted for the Yankees so energetically. He confessed to being a "New Yorker" at heart.

Early in 1980, I received a letter asking me to come to New Windsor. Of course, I went right away. On that visit, mixed among our regular conversation, Still made a few rather vague and random mentions of his lifetime desire to own a Lincoln automobile and also of his determination to secure his wife's financial future. I soon learned the devastating and sad news from Mrs. Still that he had cancer, and he wanted to settle his affairs in a private and expeditious manner. The evident trust he put in me was deeply gratifying.

This was about the time the Metropolitan Museum of Art in New York was staging a major retrospective of his work. He suggested I visit the exhibition, which I had already viewed several times. From this dazzling exhibition in May 1980, I purchased three additional paintings. This time, there was no letter from Mr. Still defining the works. Instead, Mrs. Still relayed his warm regards and his request to tell me how much they'd enjoyed our most recent afternoon together in New Windsor. His health was failing. The last letter I received was a thank-you letter from Mrs. Still for my condolences after he died on June 23, 1980.

In retrospect, there were several reasons why I loved and admired this man. He was uncompromising in his principles, knew exactly why he was put on this earth, and was never deterred by the "noise" around him. He was unyielding in transmitting the fire and intensity he felt, which was reflected in his work. It may have distressed others around him at the time, but the living proof is available for all to see at the Clyfford Still Museum in Denver, Colorado, a testament to a monumental genius and a passionate baseball fan.

Clyfford Still

ABOVE: *"With my compliments to Jeffrey Loria for his commitment to the arts and the values uniquely inherent in their value. Clyfford Still"*

CHAPTER TEN

DINA VIERNY

FROM LIVING MODEL TO A LIVING LEGEND

> "The beauty one can
> find in art is one of the pitifully few
> real and lasting products of human endeavor."
>
> – J. PAUL GETTY

One of my most treasured friends and mentors in the art world was not an artist. Dina Vierny is universally recognized as the brilliant champion of the legacy of the French sculptor Aristide Maillol. She had been Maillol's model, and throughout her life, she continued to reflect the strength, persistence, energy, and, above all, the humanism captured in his sublime sculptures. But Dina was also a powerful, influential, and courageous woman in her own right; she stood defiantly strong in contrast to her diminutive five-foot stature. Throughout our more than four decades of friendship, I remained in awe of her life and achievements. Without fanfare, she rose from being a living model to becoming a living legend. At the urging of Henri Matisse, she became an important art dealer in Paris after World War II. During the war, she was an operative in the French Resistance and was imprisoned by France's Nazi occupiers.

I first met Dina in the spring of 1963 in her Paris gallery on 36 rue Jacob, which she had established on the Left Bank in 1947. The

OPPOSITE PAGE: *Dina Vierny at camp de Chalifert in 1936.*

135

gallery is still there today, overseen by her grandson. It is a small space, but emanating from it were and still are astonishing exhibitions and fascinating works by many prominent artists.

I remember the first work I acquired from her. It was a rich and beautiful drawing by the sculptor Constantin Brancusi, depicting the interior of his studio. Contained within the borders of this one drawing were studies of his definitive sculptures, arranged on their bases, as they stood in his studio. I would love to have that drawing today. Dina's rue Jacob gallery was a gathering place for artists, collectors, and serious critics who understood the magic of her vision. I learned something new each time we were together. She spoke, and I listened.

When recalling her years modeling for Maillol, Dina was always fond of telling me, "I came to pose for an hour and stayed ten years." Born Dina Aibinder to a Jewish family living in the Russian town of Kishinev, in what is now Moldova, her parents immigrated to France when she was a child. She began modeling for Maillol in the mid-1930s, when she was a fifteen-year-old schoolgirl and he was seventy-three.

She was initially a reluctant model who wanted to keep current with her science studies. She told me that her downward gaze in some of Maillol's early works was in part due to her studying her chemistry lessons, which required her absolute attention; she was glancing down at her textbooks. Her parents always demanded that she do well in school and knew little if anything of her modeling.

Dina, as a young and curvaceous beauty, was sought after as a model by many artists. She eventually posed not only for Maillol, but also for Matisse, Dufy, and Bonnard. Indeed, Dina was the woman who posed for Bonnard's last important painting of 1939, entitled *Dark Nude*.

As World War II raged, Dina joined Maillol in Banyuls-sur-Mer in southern France, near the Pyrenees, where he had a studio, and she served as his only model. From 1941 to 1944, the years leading up to his death in a car accident, Maillol produced his last sculpture, *Harmony*, which was in fact an homage to Dina. He took her striking features and transformed them into gloriously smooth surfaces, incorporating his passion for Greek, Egyptian, and Cambodian art into this work of idealized beauty.

ABOVE: *Dina posing for* Harmony *in the studio of Aristide Maillol near Banyuls-sur-Mer, March 1941.*

But Maillol's rural locale had another attraction: it enabled Dina to be in close proximity to the Spanish border. She had already been working with the French Resistance, the underground sympathizers who opposed the Nazis now in control of vast swaths of France. Joining with the American journalist Varian Fry, who led the Comité Fry group, and others, Dina helped smuggle refugees from a transit site at the Villa Air-Bel in Marseille into Spain, following a path to the border and crossing the mountains, thus saving many lives. When Maillol learned about her work with the Resistance, he shared his knowledge of local shortcuts and smugglers' routes, as well as herders' and animals' paths. Fry christened the secure smuggler's route across the French-Spanish border as "the Maillol Way."

After a few months, Dina was arrested by the French police—who were focused on her correspondence with artists but remained unaware of her daring refugee rescues. Maillol hired a lawyer to secure her release and then sent her to pose for Matisse, who was waiting out the war in the coastal city of Nice. But Dina didn't stay long. She returned to Maillol and eventually made her way to Paris. For a time, she worked with another Resistance fighter, Victor Waddington, an English art dealer, whom I met in the mid-1960s and admired greatly. She often recounted their joint exploits to me, and after the war, they remained close friends.

Dina's work with the Resistance meant she had to be available when help was needed. Early on, she always wore a red dress in the cafes of Marseille so she could be spotted quickly by those attempting to escape. But as is often the case, no good deed goes unpunished. She was arrested in Paris by the Gestapo in May 1943. Confined to prison in Fresnes for six months, she refused to admit either her role with the Resistance or her Jewish identity.

On the day she was arrested, Dina had scheduled a lunch with Picasso. Eventually, she managed to smuggle a note to him inside a used Camembert box, excusing herself from missing their lunch and telling him that she was in prison. When Maillol learned of Dina's incarceration, he asked for help from a friend of more than twenty years, Arno Breker, a German artist regarded as Hitler's favorite sculptor.

Breker agreed, but in return, he insisted that Maillol had to allow him to sculpt his bust and that the Frenchman pose for it. In 1987, the Breker bust of Maillol was sold at a public auction at Drouot in Paris. When I asked Dina why she didn't try to buy it, she looked at me quizzically and responded, "That Nazi? They put me in jail!" In a fitting bit of irony, the bust was acquired by Jean-Marie Le Pen, the polarizing, far-right-wing former head of France's National Front.

During our first meeting in Dina's Paris gallery, I was curious to learn how a woman in postwar France was able to open a gallery and survive in a milieu dominated by men. Dina graciously explained that Maillol had willed his estate to his only son, Lucien, a pilot in the First World War, whose passion was to become a painter. When Maillol died in 1944, his studio was filled with uncast plasters and bronzes, drawings, and terra-cottas. Because Maillol understood that his son wanted to be an artist, he had proposed that Lucien work with Dina. Sons of artists who follow in their fathers' footsteps traditionally do not become successful artists themselves; rather, they need to find a separate path in a different creative field. Renoir's son, Jean, became a filmmaker, while Matisse's youngest son, Pierre, became an important art dealer; both chose professions better suited to their personalities. Maillol recognized this, and hence his advice to Lucien to work closely with Dina in order to protect Maillol's achievements, legacy, and commercial viability as an important twentieth-century French sculptor.

For me, viewing Maillol's works shows the hand and mind of a gifted, intellectual sculptor, whose unique work reflected a deep reverence for the female form. All one has to do is see how he arranges and analyzes his subjects. You feel that you are actually seeing beneath the surface of bronze flesh. Whenever Dina handled his sculptures, it was always with a loving smile on her face.

Dina recounted on more than one occasion that, just as the war ended in 1945, Henri Matisse encouraged her to open a gallery. She always saw Matisse as not only her mentor but her protector as well. Matisse told her that she had a gifted eye, along with a passion for art. He observed she often perceived what others didn't see. Essentially, he told her, "You love art; then you must be a dealer."

A few months after Dina opened her gallery, she recounted how she and Matisse met again. According to Dina, Matisse said, "I give you one year, and you will be bankrupt!" Somewhat taken aback, Dina asked, "Why? You were the one who encouraged me to have a gallery." Matisse replied, "Open a gallery, yes. But you love the artists too much." With a certain amount of selfless wisdom, Matisse then empathetically stated, as if it were a bad thing, "You are on my side!"

From that point forward, Dina's skills as a businesswoman blossomed. She was able to make the transition from loving the artists to dealing with them in a businesslike fashion. Her gallery and her commercial acumen remained remarkable. She had the ability to ascend from an artist's model, immortalized by a distinguished sculptor, as well as by painters such as Matisse, into a champion of important causes and one of Europe's leading dealers. She was truly a courageous and intelligent woman, navigating what had been for decades strictly a man's world.

In 1951, as part of her new approach to balancing art and business, and following Matisse's sage advice, Dina sought out the work of fellow Eastern Europe émigré Serge Poliakoff for her gallery's first major solo exhibition. She had met him in a gypsy cabaret in Paris in 1950, when Dina, being the gutsy woman that she was, temporarily replaced a friend who had lost her voice. Poliakoff played guitar to earn a living, and that night, Dina spontaneously posed as a cabaret singer to accompany the strumming guitarist. Poliakoff eventually revealed that he was a painter as well. When Dina initially saw his work, she was fascinated and thought it was "sublime."

Dina told me that she didn't sell a single painting during Poliakoff's first exhibition. But she and Poliakoff remained friends for life. The fact that they had both left Russian-dominated territory for Paris contributed to their camaraderie. She continued to show and eventually sold his work in her gallery. Coincidentally, Poliakoff was the first artist I met in Paris, an experience I can easily recall more than five decades later.

OPPOSITE PAGE: *Portrait of Dina, 1936.*

I walked up a thin staircase to the top floor of an apartment on rue de Siene, where Poliakoff lived and had his studio. When I arrived, the landing was so narrow that it was nearly impossible to turn around without falling down the flight of steps behind. I practically hugged the door as I knocked. Poliakoff opened it wide, and all but thrusting his face into mine, his first words were, "Did you bring money?" My response was, "I have money if you have a picture I want to buy." I left that afternoon with one of my first paintings from a living artist. Ironically, the great Russian artist Marc Chagall spoke the identical words to me years later when I met him for the first time. He was half hiding behind his formidable wife Vava, who handled his art business, when he asked if I had brought money. Again, I replied, "Yes."

———

Even though I was not yet twenty-five years old, Dina generously welcomed me into her circle. She was always fond of telling me that I was like a third son. Indeed, her gifted elder son, Olivier, and I have remained close friends for the past five decades. We often speak of his mother's generous spirit and how she was anxious to share her knowledge and kindness. She loved to laugh. She had an amazing memory and an ability to recall visual details and experiences.

Early in our friendship, Dina surprised me one day with an unsolicited bit of encouragement: "Jeffrey, you are *something*. Keep doing it." To show how sincere she was, she always shared a great deal about the subtle nuances of Maillol's bronzes, terra-cottas, plasters, and the foundries he used to cast his work, as well as a wealth of memories. We made many trips to the Godard Foundry as well as the Susse Frères Foundry in Paris. The generosity of her observations and experience and her interest in sharing them with me became a part of my way of understanding. Matisse was right: Dina indeed saw what few could. As well as having a magical eye, she had a perceptual spontaneity and was able to brilliantly read people's most human intentions.

She dedicated the last thirty-five years of her life to enriching France's cultural holdings. With passion and commitment, she undertook to preserve the work and memory of one of France's most acclaimed sculptors and single-handedly created, built, and financed the Maillol Museum on rue de Grenelle, which I still visit regularly on my trips to Paris. The museum was officially dedicated by President François Mitterrand in 1995. Today, it is directed by her son, Olivier, whose organizational skills and imagination in bringing unique and exciting exhibitions to the museum are unparalleled.

In the Maillol Museum, one discovers the meaning of the expression "inveterate collector." Dina collected the works of Matisse, Dufy, and Poliakoff as well as Maillol. She told me that she started collecting objects in the antique shops in Saint-Germain-des-Prés at the age of fourteen, using her lunch money. She pursued a wide range of interests in strange objects. It was the Surrealist concept of the dream that led her to collect Mesopotamian and African weights, autographs, antique furniture, trompe l'oeil, objects from the Amazon, porcelain, Viennese ball notebooks, and much more.

Her fervor for acquisition culminated in her vast collection of nineteenth-century horse-drawn carriages and antique dolls. (All of these were eventually donated and dispersed to various museums.) She saw her objects as living characters and considered them human. In the early 1980s, still inspired by meeting her friend André Breton in Marseille in 1941, and also by her relationship with the Surrealist painter Victor Brauner, she started collecting the ready-made objects of Marcel Duchamp. The ready-mades were ordinary, mass-produced manufactured objects—such as windows, bicycle wheels, and toilets—modified and reconfigured by the artist to elevate them to the status of "art." Quietly, she amassed one of the most important private collections of ready-made objects.

Dina was always subconsciously committed to her Russian heritage. When the new avant-garde Russian artists of the 1970s were forbidden to show their work in the West, Dina went to Russia and found Enid Burlakov and Ilya Kabakov. She was startled by their work and told me, "I never saw such a thing like that in my life.

ABOVE: *Maillol sculpture,* Monument to Cézanne, *in the Tuileries Gardens, the Louvre, Paris.*

I met two geniuses in the same night." She managed to transport these works to her Paris gallery, where they were shown for the first time in the West.

Through her gallery, she also made two remarkable lifelong friends: movie producer Billy Wilder and actor Gregory Peck. They both adored her, and both collected the work of Maillol. When I met Gregory Peck for the first time, he couldn't stop raving about what a spectacular woman Dina Vierny was. In the early 1950s, Dina also exhibited the work of the primitive painter André Bauchant. She recalled that when Billy Wilder, along with his friend and fellow producer Ray Stark (later, my client with the Marini horse), came to visit, they both had an interest in Bauchant. They approached several paintings, each time asking for prices, and each time Dina would say, "Not for sale." Finally, they asked about a painting that was available and bought it, but not without leaving a note in the guest book as they departed: "Dina Vierny is an amazing woman. She keeps the beautiful paintings and sells the ugly ones." The three remained friends for life.

But Dina's greatest dedication remained to the work and memory of Maillol. For decades, she removed fakes and forgeries from the art market and unfailingly protected his image, his work, and his legacy. In 1962, the large marble sculpture *Monument to Cézanne*, which Maillol had carved in 1912 and which had foolishly and unceremoniously been refused by the city of Aix, was sitting outdoors in the Tuileries Garden. It had suffered extensive damage from years of neglect and urban pollution. Dina feared for its survival. Using her friendship with the sister of Charles de Gaulle, Dina was able to obtain an interview with the writer André Malraux, France's then minister of culture. She asked Malraux to move the work inside so that it could be protected, and she volunteered to pay for its restoration. Shortly after that encounter, Dina told me, Malraux called her and asked about creating an outdoor sculpture garden at the Tuileries. She replied, "Monsieur le Ministre, I am casting the Cézanne monument in lead, and we will make an ensemble of eighteen sculptures for the garden at the Louvre."

The dream became a reality in 1964. Maillol's sculptural master-pieces, including *The Mountain*, *The River*, *Harmony*, and others, still grace the world-famous Tuileries Garden adjoining the Louvre Museum. When I first saw it, I recall thinking that the garden was simply majestic, set within the Louvre and enriching the heritage of the French nation. In ways large and small, Dina's legacy still endures across Paris.

Her welcoming me into her world and her family enabled me to know one of France's most heralded women of the twentieth century. Each time I am in Paris, I am always grateful for all my memories of her. I miss her deeply.

ABOVE: *Dina in Paris, 1990.*

CHAPTER ELEVEN

FIRST IMPRESSIONS

BRIDGET RILEY
A VISUAL TRANCE

ALBERTO GIACOMETTI
THE MISSED OPPORTUNITY

"The most interesting thing

about artists is how they live."

– MARCEL DUCHAMP

During the course of a lengthy career, I rarely acquired art from a specific artist at the behest of a client. I bought art because the object was special in my eyes rather than for pure commerce. In this way, my attention could be focused on the artist, the object, and then later, the client.

When I consider the prospect of acquiring a work of art, there are some fundamental variables that contribute to my decision. But it always begins with something that I absolutely love. Of course, love is subjective; decisions based on that alone would be risky. What I love may not be what someone else loves. Still, it has to start with that intangible feeling. Next, the work needs to be able to stand on its own merits and maintain a high level of quality.

However, if a client were to ask for something specific, the object I selected would still have to represent a work of quality from an artist whom I respected and admired. One of my early (and few), client-focused acquisitions was a work from the British artist Bridget Riley, a leading proponent of the English Op Art and Color Field movements.

OPPOSITE PAGE: *Bridget Riley with her work,* Continuum, *in 1963.* **151**

Looking at a Bridget Riley painting or work on paper can lead one's vision beyond the surface level of perception to permeate our deeper mental focus. It is as if we can physically sense the movement of visual stimuli through the optic nerve into our brain. Simply put, it is not unusual to feel a little dizzy when looking at Riley's work. To regain balance, one needs to look away from the object. Still, the image is alluring, and the disorienting sensation is strangely stimulating. We don't want to look away. We are seduced into a visual trance, comfortable in the knowledge that regaining composure requires simply turning one's head. Her work emphasizes her passionate ability to entice and befuddle even the most grounded among us.

Knowing I would be traveling to London in late 1964, a client asked me to contact Riley on his behalf. At that time, Riley was still exploring the contrasting dynamics of black-and-white configurations designed to push the boundaries of our perceptual tolerance. She had dealt with color previously, and would again, but it seemed that working strictly with black and white enabled her to develop the dazzling structural geometry that was emblematic of her better-known Op Art work.

When I arrived in London and called for an appointment, she asked me to come by the next morning at 8:00 a.m. It seemed an odd time, but who was I to question the artist? I arrived at her studio early, as requested, and knocked on her door several times. When she finally opened the door, it was very clear that she wasn't coming from her studio but had just rolled out of bed. She was wearing practically nothing except a smile and perhaps a touch of rouge, entirely reflected from my own bright red face. It was, after all, 1964; I was still evolving from my relatively conservative and sheltered upbringing.

She invited me in and asked me to follow her up the steps to her studio. As she turned around, I quickly closed the door behind me. Fifty-one years after Marcel Duchamp's iconic *Nude Descending a Staircase*, I was experiencing something more accurately entitled as nude "ascending" the staircase! I was a shameless but invited voyeur, with Miss Riley, the very confident, clever, and talented artist, right in front of me. I tried to remind myself why I was present, and truthfully, beyond her particular fashion choice, the rest of her demeanor was very professional. She did not give me any reason to believe that this was about anything other than looking at her work. I thought to myself, *That's what you are here for, Jeffrey. You need to focus on the art waiting in the studio.* As we continued up the steps, I continued my internal dialogue: *Maybe you should look away, Jeffrey.*

I don't want to look away. I feel as if I've been seduced into a visual trance. I am already dizzy. What if I turn my head and stumble? I have to remain focused.

If you think you are dizzy now, just imagine what you will feel if you keep focusing on her. The visual stimuli will travel through your optic nerve into your brain, where somehow the internal noise will permanently disrupt you.

I remember that I started recalling baseball statistics to distract me.

We reached the studio. The walk was both endless and not quite long enough. Ironically, the optical illusions embedded in her art helped me regain my composure. While scantily clad, she was gracious and businesslike and confident enough to know that her art would always be the main attraction. Once she had put on a robe from a nearby room, she presented a selection of works that I could choose from. They were all mind-bending and thoroughly engaging. It would have been hard not to find a great one among them.

The entire experience gave me insight into the relationship between an artist's lifestyle and their passionate or impassioned work. I learned something about an attitude that can disarm and disorient us. Meeting Bridget Riley expanded my horizons beyond anything I had learned studying her work in books and classrooms. I left that studio with a brilliant Op Art work on paper and a wonderful memory, which, more than fifty years later, still hasn't quite faded.

ALBERTO GIACOMETTI
THE MISSED OPPORTUNITY

My initial opportunity to see an actual Giacometti work at an exhibition occurred during my third year in college when I visited the Wadsworth Atheneum Museum of Art in Hartford, Connecticut. I will never forget the visceral impact that Giacometti's sculptures had on me: rigidly static female figures, portraits, busts, and striking group compositions of men and women, some moving in different directions, all on a single base. Somehow, these stick sculptures, with their thin and attenuated figures, occupied the whole room. They gave off a presence larger than themselves. I have never seen another artist who approached the human figure the way he did.

These human forms also seemed consumed by a highly expressive spirit of loneliness. Giacometti's sculptures reminded me of mysterious trees set in a landscape. Not surprisingly, one of his most remarkable and celebrated sculptures is entitled *La Foret* (The Forest).

Giacometti's work always retained a certain balance between the real and the surreal. In the progression of sculptural evolution, his sculptures seem to come from nowhere. In short, the sculptor was an imaginative genius.

When I was beginning my career as a private art dealer, I attended a Giacometti opening at the Pierre Matisse Gallery in New York City. As I entered the gallery, to my great surprise, I spotted Giacometti in the distance, standing between his sculptures and a display of his drawings. He was easily recognizable with his full head of disheveled hair, an intense expression on his face, and his ever-present cigarette dangling from his lips. As luck would have it, we left the exhibition at the same time and rode down in the elevator together.

For more than an hour, in the lobby of the Fuller Building on Fifty-Seventh Street and Madison Avenue, Giacometti and I stood talking, along with his wife, Annette. I recall that we spoke at length in English and French about his art, especially about the role his brother Diego played in helping him cast and patinate most of

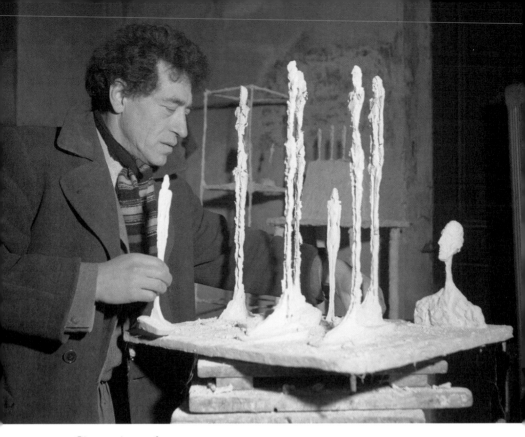

ABOVE: *Giacometti at work.*

his sculptures. He mentioned how he worked from both memory and a model. He explained that in general his paintings and drawings were mostly from life, while the sculptures were often, but not always, from his imagination. I remember him being exceptionally amiable and fascinating. At one point during our lively conversation, Giacometti invited me to visit him in his Paris studio. I immediately accepted the invitation. "Yes, yes, yes," I replied excitedly.

But after meeting Alberto and Annette and conjuring many expectations, I procrastinated, and he died before I could visit his studio in Paris. Not seeing him there remains one of the greatest regrets of my life. Even though I have placed many of his paintings and sculptures in private collections, it still pains me each time I pass by the building at 46 rue Hippolyte-Maindron, which housed his three-room studio. An almost perfect re-creation of his studio now exists less than a mile away from its original site. The cluttered, dark, confining, and uncomfortable-looking space, even lacking a toilet, is a revelation for those like me who never visited the original.

Alberto Giacometti created a new sculptural concept and style that challenged our perception of the figure and how it exists in space. No matter where one stands in proximity to his sculptures, they always feel extremely attenuated and distant, yet intense. The isolation of his elongated figures exists in his paintings and drawings as well. He was always searching for his personal representational view of the human image, with all its anxieties and vulnerabilities, in his iconic forms with their thinly stretched, gaunt, slender proportions, exhibiting only the barest sensation of movement. Yet he provocatively titled them *Walking Man* or *Pointing Man*.

His works are invariably very tangible. On closer inspection, they reveal the artist's manipulation of the clay and plaster, which he had pinched and prodded before eventually casting them into bronze sculptures. It is this human touch that reveals the artist's struggle. Despite their thin silhouettes, his works have a sense of weight and permanence, which always challenged my perception of three-dimensional sculptural volume.

OPPOSITE PAGE: *Alberto Giacometti, 1965.*

While Giacometti's art appears isolated and remote, the man himself was very different: he was looking to make a connection. Perhaps like Henry Moore, he was curious about my youthful interest. His invitation to visit his studio was genuine and offered the possibility of insight into the openness of the sculptor, as well as his lonely, remote art. What I lost from missing that invitation made me better as an art dealer, because it showed me the importance of opportunity and personal relationships. The opportunity to be with an artist in his own studio, where his creativity is most focused, enables one to see what really motivates them and provides the best opportunity to study a person's character, temperament, and gifts, because they are at their most vulnerable and most revealing.

Dedicated artists working in their studios are immersed in a self-imposed, challenging atmosphere. In Giacometti's world, the images he formed always seemed to be at the edge of his control. To achieve his definition of perfection in his paintings, he would layer paint until the work displayed a nearly three-dimensional sculptural quality. His sculptures juxtaposed the seemingly incompatible qualities of the ethereal and the intensely rooted. The act of creation, of making something from nothing, requires confidence and conviction. And the best place to understand that is inside the "workroom" of the artist.

CHAPTER TWELVE

THE SURREALISTS: ILLUSION AND INTRIGUE, PART ONE

SALVADOR DALÍ
THE CONSUMMATE PROVOCATEUR

> "The most seductive thing about art is
>
> the personality of the artist himself."
>
> – PAUL CÉZANNE

The 1960s emerged after a decade and a half of a population boom that helped to fuel an accompanying transformation in culture. The abstract imagery of postwar American Modernism, so dominant during the 1940s and 1950s, was rapidly losing favor to a new, burgeoning art movement representative of a broader group of people and their immediate interests. Consumerism emerged as the new gospel. Diverse status symbols arose as defining marks of social ambition and accomplishment. Seen from this perspective, the earlier Surrealist movement seems to stand against the tide of depicting ambition and achievement through objects. And yet, in the latter half of the twentieth century, right up through today, Surrealist objects became among the most compelling I have ever seen.

When you walk down the road toward Surrealism, you think that you can feel the rocks beneath your feet, but as you approach your destination and look down, you might find that instead, you've been walking on a cloud, floating on the air. That's often how I felt when I entered the world of a Surrealist artist. They were builders of illusions. They were the artists most responsible for allowing me to see that an imagined world could become reality, and their works became some of my greatest searches and my greatest obsessions.

Salvador Dalí was my first personal introduction. He turned crazy into an art form. He drew a squiggly line between utter genius and pure insanity, and because that line was drafted with such technical proficiency, he was able to cross it at will without ever succumbing to the allure of either side. Of all the artists I've met, only Dalí could both set and then immediately break the standard for thinking outside the box. A single Dalí work still remains for me "the one that got away."

Max Ernst was older and not as animated by the time we first met, but he nevertheless conveyed a concentrated intensity that could feel intimidating, if it weren't for the fact that he was so gracious. Ernst had piercing blue eyes that seemed to anticipate the avian imagery in his art. I often felt as though he was studying my micro-expressions as a bird of prey would to determine if I were friend or foe. I spent decades in pursuit of an elusive Ernst work that might have been attainable years earlier had I simply asked for it when I was in his home.

Roberto Matta, on the other hand, was incredibly animated and verbal. His age did not slow him down. His mind was infinitely fertile, firing off ideas and thoughts at a rapid speed, perilously close to sounding like a poem being tossed into a wood chipper. It could be hard to follow what he was saying as he chewed through language, but he wasn't crazy; he was simply brilliant. The images he created in paint often seemed like an extension of his unfinished thoughts. Even today, I can look at a Matta painting and immediately be transported to a place that makes me smile, recalling some distant open-ended conversation we had.

The experience of meeting and befriending these brilliant Surrealists provided me with my own freedom to realize that I too could dream.

In the early 1970s, I sometimes traveled with the New York Knicks basketball team—I was drawn to the sport and also friendly with the coach, Red Holzman—and I occasionally visited cities where the Knicks were playing. On one such trip to Atlanta, I bought a 1936 painting of Dalí's called *The Anthropomorphic Cabinet*. It was a reclining Venus de Milo in a landscape, with drawers protruding from her body. It was a small masterpiece, but at the time, I couldn't afford to keep it.

I remember going from the collector's home to meet Red and some of the players for lunch. When I showed them what I had wrapped under my arm, their overwhelming response was, "What the hell is that?" There were anguished looks on most of their faces. I kept the painting under my seat in the arena, to protect my investment. As I think back on it now, the act of sitting through a basketball game in a large public arena with a valuable Surrealist masterpiece under my seat was not only reckless but rather surreal itself. Maybe I did it because I knew that I could only possess this iconic work for a finite period of time.

For an art dealer, one potential complication to manage is the issue of personal involvement with and connection to individual works. After selling an object, one can feel deeply rewarded, but also compromised, despite any monetary gains. When I look from a professional perspective, I am able to rationalize letting go of those works that I would love to have kept. To embrace the role of conduit means to understand that there is a rich cultural value to exposing the work to a different environment, where it can continue to reach and influence a new and broader audience.

Today, *The Anthropomorphic Cabinet* hangs in the Kunstsammlung Nordrhein-Westfalen in Düsseldorf, Germany. It is a valuable work of art and an iconic Dalí image. But on occasion, it saddens me that I parted with it. It is a reminder that sometimes the best deals are the ones you don't make.

At the time that I purchased the work, I was still making frequent visits to Dalí in Port Lligat. I remember looking out his studio window and seeing the vistas of endless water, replete with a vast expanse of sand, which clearly inspired his unique landscapes. The images of local fishermen, placing their colorful fishing boats on the rocky beach, also found their way into his art. It was all there for his innovative eye, just below his studio window, and I was fortunate to witness it often.

On one visit, in 1972, I asked if he had any works similar to the painting I had just sold. He asked Gala to come into the studio with her drawing of *The Anthropomorphic Cabinet*, which he had given to her as a gift. When Gala arrived with the drawing in hand, I was excited to see the imagery so closely again. Of course, the drawing differed slightly from the painting, but it was as masterfully executed. I saw the opportunity to rectify my loss and acquire the drawing. Gala quickly put an end to my hopes. "You are not going to get this one, Jeffrey. This one is for me."

The next winter, in December 1973, when I met Dalí in the Saint Regis's King Cole Bar, he gave me another, very recent drawing of a nude as a surprise gift. I think it was out of sympathy for my being rebuffed by Gala. I gratefully appreciated the gesture. Dalí was now almost seventy, and I immediately observed that this drawing was from a different hand than the one that had drawn the 1936 image I had coveted. I don't think it is possible to maintain that form of elegant drawing skill into old age. Like an aging opera singer or an elite baseball player no longer in his prime, the tools evolve, their use changes, their application must become more judicious. It becomes harder to control the gift. When I first met Dalí, I would often watch him at work. He would draw with amazing speed and dexterity. He could complete a composition without ever lifting his pen off the paper. Clearly, the years had altered his abilities, which only cemented in my mind the perfection of the image in that original 1936 drawing.

Recently, I told several colleagues I know that I wanted to buy a Dalí drawing with subject matter similar to what I had cherished in *The Anthropomorphic Cabinet*. One day my doorbell rang and a colleague of mine presented me with the same drawing that I had

ABOVE: *Dalí,* The City of Drawers (Anthropomorphic Cabinet), *pencil on paper, 1936, former collection of Gala Dalí.*

seen forty-plus years earlier in Dalí's home. On Gala's death, she bequeathed the work to her sister, and when her sister died, it passed through two or three Spanish collections and ended up in the New York art market in the hands of another dealer. It seemed like a moment of poetic justice and only strengthened my belief that long-term passion and commitment will often prevail. As Dalí perceived, works of art can literally bend time (his melting watch!) and portray the unexpected. When I least expected it, I was finally able to acquire *The Anthropomorphic Cabinet* drawing.

CHAPTER THIRTEEN

THE SURREALISTS: ILLUSION AND INTRIGUE, PART TWO

MAX ERNST
PATIENCE, PASSION, AND PERSISTENCE
THE ARTIST AS A BIRD

"Art does not reproduce

the visible; rather, it makes us visible."

– PAUL KLEE

I n 1964, I was walking down the rue de Seine toward the river, deep in appreciation for the fresh air and sunlit afternoon in Paris. At the intersection of the rue de Seine and the rue des Beaux Arts, in the heart of the Sixth Arrondissement, a window poster announcing a Max Ernst exhibition at 41 rue de Seine caught my eye. I entered the gallery. Sitting at his desk in the back was a wonderfully dapper elderly gentleman who introduced himself as Aram Mouradian. He was Max Ernst's Paris dealer and, as I soon learned, also an expert in the works of the legendary Italian painter Amedeo Modigliani. As I walked around the gallery, my eyes immediately opened in wonder before the mysterious spectacle of Ernst's universe. Confronting me were the works of a visionary. Few artists have been able to combine both the imaginary and the real like Ernst. He filtered his images through his vivid imagination, and it was magical.

While in Mouradian's gallery, I was mesmerized by a painting adjacent to his desk: a famous and glorious 1928 work, *Le Chaste Joseph*. Mouradian explained to me that the title was a vague reference to the biblical subject of Joseph. This image featured two love-

OPPOSITE PAGE: *Max Ernst in his studio.*   **171**

birds, embracing and kissing, as a third bird hovered over them. The three birds are symbolic of an entangled love relationship in Ernst's life at the time, even as the two birds in the foreground stretch out their wings to represent his depiction of unconditional love, forming a harmonious combination of the imagined and the actual.

For a dealer, there is often more immediacy to acquiring a work of art than there is to developing a friendship with a client. It isn't unusual for the purchase to come first, and only then will a friendship possibly follow, although a mutual passion for art is a good place to start. When I approached Mouradian about the work, he said that he intended to keep it for himself. As I recall, I was already carrying a wrapped painting from an earlier purchase in the neighborhood under my arm, so he knew that I was serious—but so was he. Yet although he made it clear that the painting was not for sale, in that moment, we established a mutual respect for each other. My friendship with Mouradian endured until he died years later. In hindsight, I probably knew subconsciously that I would see the painting again once the show had closed.

The female figure in the painting represented the beautiful and strong-willed Gala, who later married Dalí and who was a central figure in the Surrealist movement and in the lives of several artists and writers. Her first marriage was to the French poet Paul Éluard. Her next liaison was Ernst. For about three years, between 1924 and 1927, Ernst, Gala, and Éluard were involved in a well-known love triangle. Indeed, that third bird, hovering above the two central figures of Gala and Ernst, represented Éluard. It was painted as more of a suggestion, fading into the distance and lacking the intensity and presence of the richly painted birds below. Somewhere, however, between 1927 and 1928, the trio dissolved. Gala and Éluard traveled to Spain, where they visited Dalí and created their own new threesome, until Gala chose Dalí and remained with him thereafter.

Le Chaste Joseph summarized in one iconic image Surrealism's multiple complexities. The birds represented biblical entanglements of human love with all of its foibles. I was drawn to the painting's significance, and I understood why Mouradian kept it for so long.

Completely enthralled by the work, I decided then and there that no matter how long it might take, I would acquire the painting. Little did I realize that it might take half a century.

I also decided that I had to make a determined effort to meet the genius behind it. Max Ernst's creativity was boundless, even though he never achieved the same global fame or pop-culture status as his Surrealist counterpart, Dalí. Doubtless, Dalí was the better self-publicist. But Max was every bit as great an artist. His influence is undeniable and can be discerned in the works of countless others. He was consequential in many ways, including his short but significant marriage to the philanthropist and collector Peggy Guggenheim; his creation of an artist's colony in Sedona, Arizona; as a pioneer in the Dada movement; and as a key figure who helped inspire Abstract Expressionism.

In the early 1970s, I sent a series of letters to Ernst, explaining my admiration for his work and my interest in meeting him. I told him I would be in Europe and asked if we could meet. After several attempts, I finally received a reply in 1973 that could be best described as coolly polite. The letter was from Ernst's third wife, Dorothea Tanning, who was also a painter. I remember that in one of my early discussions with her, I mentioned that I had been asked to help organize an exhibition of female artists. She refused to participate, saying, "I am not a female artist, I am an artist." Her letter essentially said, *We are very busy, and we are not interested in parting ways with paintings from our collection. But if you can make it to our house in Seillans, France, on Tuesday, May 22 at 4:00 p.m. we can spare thirty minutes.*

It was clear to me that this was not the warmest invitation, but my father's wise words echoed in my mind: *No is a temporary impediment on the way to yes.* Dorothea and Max could have ignored my letter or sent one saying they were not interested at all, but they did not. I acted immediately.

Curiosity was a critical component of my success. In my early years, I was always willing to toss myself into the world and take a chance. I will never forget that Tuesday afternoon in Seillans in the south of France. I walked into an imposing country home and was met by Dorothea, who escorted me into a downstairs room where Max was seated. He greeted me warmly with his unforgettably penetrating blue eyes. I explained that I wanted to buy a painting. After some polite conversation and drinks, Max asked Dorothea to walk me through their home to see if there was anything I liked. Certain paintings were already earmarked as eventual museum gifts. They included some of his early and important work. When we arrived on the second floor, in what can best be described as an upstairs gallery, there was a series of paintings hanging side by side. I could tell, based on the lull in conversation, that Dorothea was quietly observing me, gathering a sense for my reactions and preferences. I stopped in front of what was clearly a masterpiece, a joyful painting with an incredible orchestration of color, *La Fête à Seillans*. (It was eventually given to the Pompidou Center in Paris.)

One thing I have learned in my career is to notice the hidden gems, those works that are perhaps less obvious to an untrained eye. For a brief moment I thought about saying something, but I didn't. Maybe I was thinking too hard, trying to anticipate their reaction to what I might say.

The painting hanging immediately to the right of *La Fête à Seillans* was a work that also piqued my interest. *L'Illustre Forgeron des Reves* (The Illustrious Dream-maker), a picture painted mostly in muted blues, radiating with sea creatures and poetic invention. It struck me as a subtle and splendid representation of Max's work, a style that often appears to straddle two and three dimensions. Also visible were the faces that would be incorporated into some of his future sculptures, such as *Moon Mad* and *Apaisement*. When the sculptures appeared a year or two later, their images were strikingly reminiscent of the painting.

We looked at forty or fifty more pictures. I was careful to remain respectful and did not comment on many others. When we arrived back downstairs where Max was sitting, we continued our conversation. He seemed to appreciate my interest and asked me a few questions about how I responded to his work. At a certain point, it appeared I had passed some formal test that he had devised for me. Everything seemed to relax, and Dorothea suddenly said, "Max, Jeffrey loves *L' Illustrate Forgeron des Reves*." Without hesitation, Max said, "Well, then you can buy it."

He asked his wife to remove it from the wall so that I could arrange for its trip to America. He trusted me enough to wait to be paid for the work. Infinitely more important, he trusted my taste and judgment and felt I could represent his work to a discerning international clientele. This meant the world to me. That Tuesday meeting with Dorothea and Max taught me to be bold, and it cemented my belief to trust my intuition and my eyes as a dealer. In many ways, it was a landmark moment in my business career.

It might seem impossible to have hoped for better results from my visit with the Ernsts. In retrospect, however, part of me thought that maybe I should have. Had I expressed a reaction to *La Fête à Seillans*, as I did with *L' Illustrate Forgeron des Reves*, I wonder if that work would have been available to me as well—and I would not have to visit it in the Pompidou. This is not about wanting more, it is about learning a lesson: knowing how to be true to your instincts and to not overthink. I knew the first work was an incredible masterpiece, but I was too cautious. I would not forget the lesson.

But I had acquired a gem, and best of all, Max and I became friends. We saw each other in Paris from time to time, and he was always welcoming. He imparted valuable wisdom about art and about life. Thirty-five years after his death in 1976, I donated a sixteen-foot bronze Ernst sculpture, entitled *Habakuk*, to Yale. Max had created the original maquette in Germany in 1933, as Hitler was rising to power. The sculpture is a reference to the prophet Habakuk (sometimes spelled with an additional *k*), who is mentioned in the Bible. In one of those passages, he demonstrates his steadfast faith when responding to God's apocalyptic description of the end of the world. The work was Ernst's defiant response to Hitler's rise. Yale permanently installed *Habakuk* at a ceremony to honor the new university president, Peter Salovey, where he remarked, "The sculpture reminds us to stand by our righteousness." I cannot imagine a more fitting statement nor a more appropriate setting for Ernst's sculpture.

ABOVE: *Max Ernst with his sculpture,* Habakuk, *in front of the Kunst Museum in Dusseldorf, Germany.*

But there is one more piece of the Ernst story. I did not give up my quest to acquire *Le Chaste Joseph*. Aram Mouradian, the Paris art dealer, maintained possession of the work as he assured me that he would. From time to time, I continued to make him aware of my ongoing interest.

Somewhere in that relationship, I think there existed a kind of Hollywood movie storyline—a mutual admiration for the other's tenacity. In extended movie scenes depicting pursuit, there is often a reciprocal admiration between the chaser and the chased. Aram wasn't young when we met, and when he died, he left the painting to his daughter. I subsequently visited her many times. The painting hung in a guest room in her apartment in the Passy section of Paris. She had no desire to sell it, offering no excuses or explanations, and of course, she was under no obligation. I assumed that since she was so close to her father, she must have seen the painting as an important connection to him. No one should underestimate the emotional value of a painting.

Years later, *Le Chaste Joseph* passed to Aram's grandson, José Maria, whom I met in the late 1980s. Now a retired pilot, he is a very intelligent and wonderful young man, and a guardian of his grand-father's legacy. Like his mother and grandfather, he was unwilling to part with the work, and I was beginning to believe that my pursuit was a reflection of the biblical imagery in the painting. If I wasn't successful, I might become *Le Chaste Jeffrey*.

In the 2000s, José Maria called me for a recommendation for his children, mentioning a Camp Takajo in Maine. My nephews had gone there, and I highly recommended the summer camp. When they were in America, I spent time with his boys as well. They are great young men, and getting to know them cemented four generations of friendship with this family. More than another decade would pass until José Maria finally sold me the painting. In addition to patience, I guess I have had the luck of longevity.

Patience and passion are equally important; sometimes the most incredible objects begin as unobtainable, hidden works. I kept my eye on *Le Chaste Joseph* for fifty-two years. The painting is now ninety years old. It remains a tangible representation of my treasured memories of Max, and it is there for me to see as often as I want. Finally.

OPPOSITE PAGE: *Max Ernst,* Le Chaste Joseph, *1928.*

CHAPTER FOURTEEN

THE SURREALISTS: ILLUSION AND INTRIGUE, PART THREE

ROBERTO MATTA
ETCETERA, ETCETERA, ETCETERA

"There are no rules. That is how art is born,

how breakthroughs happen. Go against the rules

or ignore the rules. That is what invention is about."

– HELEN FRANKENTHALER

Roberto Sebastián Antonio Matta Echaurren, called Sebastian by his wife, Germana, was usually known simply as "Matta." He was doubtless the most intellectually brilliant and insatiably inquisitive artist I ever met. He loved life and all that it had to offer. The one common denominator was his passion, combined with his unbridled energy. In the archival photographs of the expatriate Surrealists who escaped to America during World War II, Matta is the youngest member of the group. He carried that youthful spirit deep into old age. He liked to laugh and would remind anyone who would listen that he was born on 11/11/11 at 11:00 a.m.

Matta had an etymologist's love for words. He was not as interested in the origin of words as much as he was pulling apart language when enthusiastically describing a particular subject. He used to say, "I undress words as one peels an onion"—something he usually demonstrated to me with his hands. He picked away at the meaning of what he was describing, using his multilingual skills and

OPPOSITE PAGE: *Roberto Matta in his studio, circa 1990.*   **183** frequently combining Spanish, English, French, and Italian in the same sentence in the course of explaining his ideas.

Matta was curious about everything. He was very well read and widely knowledgeable, which enabled him to expound broadly on politics, literature, and art. At the same time, he could easily drift off into his own universe, giving incomplete explanations, speaking in half sentences, and finishing a thought with an enthusiastic "Etcetera, etcetera, etcetera." I couldn't always follow his enthusiastic monologues. The confusion I felt at times in trying to follow Matta, as he darted through his own cosmic realm of descriptive analysis, was inevitably relieved by the ironic clarity of his concluding exclamation, "Etcetera, etcetera, etcetera." That's when I could take a moment to process his insights and maybe determine what he was saying.

There was rarely a time when Matta didn't appear to be engaged in lively thought. He often claimed that he slept very little because it interfered with his thinking. But his eyes didn't carry the weight of sleeplessness. They were bright and alert, as though he were on an expedition through art in order to unravel life's riddles. Perhaps that explains why he often claimed that he was not a painter, just simply an explorer of the mysteries in life. Everything about him was energetic. Even his movements were sharp and quick. He moved as quickly as a hummingbird in pursuit of nectar.

When I first met Matta in Paris in the mid-1970s, he had a small apartment on the top floor of a building set back on the Boulevard Saint-Germain. He eventually moved to a gracious residence on the rue de Lille behind the Musée d'Orsay, which had a large adjoining space for his studio and an exquisite garden in the back of the house. There, he immersed himself in his superb collection of tall figurative carvings of Oceanic art, which served as an inspiration and spiritual source for his creations. He also surrounded himself with them in Tarquinia, Italy, where he had another studio and often spent the summer. It was in the alchemy of his studio in Paris, however, where Matta pursued a constant exploration of what he called his "new space."

ABOVE: *Artists in Exile, New York, 1942: left to right, first row: Roberto Matta Echaurren, Ossip Zadkine, Yves Tanguy, Max Ernst, Marc Chagall, Fernand Léger; second row: André Breton, Piet Mondrian, André Masson, Amédée Ozenfant, Jacques Lipchitz, Pavel Tchelitchew, Kurt Seligmann, Eugene Berman.*

His Oceanic sculptures seemed to be not merely an influence but rather a source, reemerging on a grand scale, tall and elongated, in his paintings and drawings. He employed the carvings as symbols meant to criticize the horrors of conflict anywhere in the world. These images began appearing in the 1940s as agitated and even frantic depictions of creatures bent on devouring. Eventually, they emerged as spaceships late into the 1960s.

Matta would often stand in front of his paintings, narrating humorous stories about their iconography and frequently laughing at his own jokes. He might begin with an explanation of the painting, describing the interchangeable nature of his foregrounds and backgrounds by asserting his theories of geometry. Then he might ask himself a question that only he could answer. "Do you think the pig understands that this is *una pintura de nuestro futuro* [a part of our future]? He sees what you see, but you don't have a pig's eye. Only the pig knows the pig's eye, *comme le papillon* or *le rhinocéros* [like a butterfly or a rhinoceros]." With a twinkle in his eye and a laugh, he would of course conclude his thought with an "etcetera, etcetera, etcetera."

Through the years, it became apparent that Matta's thoughts were primarily focused on imagining the future as a way to examine past connections. Conversations were always about events of the day. Political commentary, both in Europe and America, excited him, as did philosophy and science, as well as the feelings people have about themselves and others. He would often pose the question to me, "How can I paint the connections we have with the eternal movement?" Well into his nineties, he was obsessed with the concept of how he could draw the contours of moving and yet invisible creatures.

Simply trying to keep up with Matta's torrent of thoughts and remarkable energy could be both exhilarating and exhausting. I'll never forget a walk we took in the Luxembourg Gardens near the Medici Fountain. It started to rain. Suddenly, Matta began leaping from leaf to leaf on the ground, in a way that made me worry that he would slip and fall. As he darted about, he described a recurring dream from his childhood. Actually, it sounded more like a nightmare: "There are wet leaves all over the ground. I have to keep moving. I have to keep running and jumping. *Rapido, rapido*, or else they will catch and imprison me."

This drive to keep moving became an obsessive pursuit, from the elusive nature of his imagery to the manner in which he walked in the streets of Paris. Even in his late eighties, he would walk briskly with his ever-present cane. If you dared turn your eye away from him, he would disappear. On the surface, it was like a kind of child's play, a game of appearance and disappearance. But the psychology of his recurring dream revealed that it was more about escaping his own early demons.

Much of Surrealism is about rendering images of the subconscious mind. Whether he was consciously or subconsciously conjuring such imagery, Matta was fully committed to that effort. It saturated his canvases. He would often say, "If you run with the movement, you become the movement itself." The ambiguity of his eloquence always made me wonder if he intentionally wanted his ideas and his imagery to appear vague and open to interpretation, so that perhaps he could not be pinned down to any specific point. That would seem to reflect the psychology of a person who was fearful of being imprisoned. Or perhaps he was simply grasping for answers to life's intangible mysteries.

———

I was fortunate to be present many times when the esteemed photographer Henri Cartier-Bresson made his visits to Matta's studio. The two would become engrossed in philosophical conversation on the elusive nature of inspiration. Cartier-Bresson explained his obsession with what he called the *instant décisif* or "the decisive moment." As a photographer, it seemed logical to try to capture on film in a split second the singular, most important moment of any situation, as well as the perfect forms, the geometry, and the lights and darks in a composition that cements and affirms that decisive moment. To make his idea clear to Matta's painter's eye,

Cartier-Bresson referred to the decisive moments in the meticulously composed paintings of the celebrated seventeenth-century French painter Nicolas Poussin. In his work, which adheres to a set of unvarying rules of composition, Poussin does create moments of heightened emphasis. Matta, however, was not interested in pinpointing specific moments. Rather he was concerned with what he called the "morphogenesis of objects and feelings."

As I recall, he explained to Cartier-Bresson, "I want to paint the movement." Matta tried to embody in paint the uncapturable imagery of movement. He understood the conundrum that, once caught in paint, movement was no longer moving. It was caught. Matta sought to liberate the frozen moment of movement by illustrating its kinetic energy. "By running with the movement, you become the movement," he continued to insist.

The privilege of knowing a Surrealist like Matta allowed a layman like me to see inside the Surrealists' motivation. On that rainy day in the Luxembourg Gardens, Matta gave me a basic psychological insight into the nature of Surrealism, partly rooted in Freudian theories of free association and dream analysis. As a result, I could better understand many of the unrecognized moments in Matta's art. His indiscernible space between foreground and background was connected to his terrified feelings of potential capture. I believe this explains why he never ended a thought with a sense of finality. It was as if Matta feared endings—and the imprisonment of conclusions.

If Matta's discussions and stories did not end with "Etcetera, etcetera, etcetera," they might end with the phrase, "*Aux ames citoyens.*" In English this can mean, "To the citizen," or, "To your souls." When I heard this phrase for the first time, I asked him what he meant. With a sparkle in his eye, he explained that it was a play on words from the first line of the refrain of the French national anthem, *La Marseillaise*. The line is, "*Aux armes, citoyens,*" which translates in English as, "To your arms, citizens." The line from the anthem is a call to arms, for all to join in the fight to defend the nation. Matta's play on and use of those words was aimed at inculcating a passionate call to a more contemplative humanity. It was an appeal to our souls, not to violence. When he used it to finish a conversation, I always found it to be an inspired and uplifting way to conclude with a sense of continuity and community.

In the late 1930s, while employed as a draftsman in the studio of Le Corbusier, Matta met the painter Gordon Onslow Ford. The two artists became immediate friends. Matta helped convince Ford to embark on his own path after Ford's brief apprenticeship with the artist Fernand Léger. As two of the younger members of the pre-World War II Surrealist group in Paris, Matta and Ford found an immediate kinship. Matta told me that they would vacation together and read the same books. They each encouraged the other to expand his perception and reach beyond the limitations of what one could see. Their influence on one another was profound. When Matta became a father to twin boys, he named one of them Gordon, after Gordon Onslow Ford. The other twin was named Sebastian, known as Batan. Around me, Matta half jokingly referred to the boys as Twin A and Twin B. Both Batan and Gordon set out to become artists. Sadly, in 1976, at age thirty-three, Batan took his own life.

Gordon's legacy is still not quite settled. He made an impact in the 1970s by cutting holes into walls and buildings to reveal forms of hacked-out interiors. It was an urban version of the Land Art or Earthwork installations done in the later 1960s and 1970s by various artists. While Gordon is probably most known for cutting into structures, he did explore other mediums and imagery. In the early 1970s, he began documenting the graffiti on New York subway cars, anticipating the acceptance of graffiti art several years before the emergence of artists like Keith Haring and Jean-Michel Basquiat.

In the spring of 1978, while Matta was living in London, I received a call from him. Gordon was gravely ill, and he wanted to travel to the United States to see him. Matta had worked in Cuba in the early 1960s, so unfortunately his political leanings, public statements, and support of the Cuban regime produced some very negative feelings in the US Department of State. He was having a great deal of difficulty obtaining a visa and had called to ask if I could help him. At the time, Kingman Brewster, the former president of Yale, was the US ambassador to the United Kingdom. I called him, and following the ambassador's compassionate intervention, Matta received his visa two days later. He and his wife, Germana, asked if they could stay in my home for a few days. My son, David, generously gave up his room. Matta and his wife ended up staying a month. When they left, they gave a beautiful drawing to David and a painting to his mother to say thank-you for their use of David's room and for allowing them to feel so much at home.

Their visit also revealed the other side of the hunt—where sometimes the artist is left completely unaware of what has become of his work. When Matta arrived at my residence, he saw a large painting of his from 1947, entitled *The Pilgrim of Doubt*, which I had acquired from Pierre Matisse in the early 1970s. He stopped in front of the work and said, "You have *my painting*." Something about the way he emphasized his statement made me curious enough to ask him about it. "Matta, what do you mean by 'my painting'?" He quickly clarified that Pierre Matisse had been his art dealer during the war, adding, "Pierre never paid me for that painting and several others, which he still has."

Matta wasn't arguing with me over my current ownership, but seeing the work sparked some deep issues. I listened as Matta explained, "When I was away from New York, near the end of the war and into the late 1940s, I lost to Matisse my wife Patricia, as well as some very important paintings. My ex-wife he can keep, etcetera, etcetera, etcetera." Pierre did eventually return all of Matta's artistic possessions, but not his wife.

Like many of the artists I have known, Matta's energy was not solely dedicated to art and contemplative thought. He had a sharp wit and was quick to convert an innocent comment into a clever innuendo. He was nearly ninety-two years old the last time I visited him. I arrived at his residence on rue de Lille, rang the bell, and waited. After a while, Liliane, who took care of his house and assisted Matta, answered the door and ushered me in. At the end of the long hallway, the ever-kinetic Matta was walking briskly toward me. As he came closer, I could see that his fly was open. I diplomatically pointed it out to him. He looked at me, turned and looked at Liliane, who was walking away, looked back at me, and without missing a beat, smiled and said, "It saves time."

I followed Matta to the garden. Looking at the sky, he began explaining the view almost as if it were one of his paintings. He was speaking about connections. I do not need to look at my notes from that time to still remember, nearly verbatim, the things that he said as we sat there. "Everything is connected to the earth: our feelings, the creatures we can't see…. We build these cities from the countryside where we go to vacation. They are like the trees' roots, reaching for the sky upside down, like the first time I traveled to Paris." He recalled his early days in Paris. "I was working with Le Corbusier. I studied to be an architect, you know. I didn't do paintings yet. I only had drawings. When I left his *atelier*, I went to Spain."

He then went on to explain how in Spain he became friendly with the famous poet and playwright Federico García Lorca. "It was Lorca who wrote me a letter of introduction to Salvador Dalí. I took my drawings to Dalí to see. He looked at them carefully and gave me his blessing." Matta puffed up his chest, and with a slow exhale and a visible sense of pride, he repeated Dalí's words, "*Ahora si*, perhaps you are an apparition of Saint Anthony."

Matta turned his gaze from the sky, looked at me, and said, "Can you imagine? An apparition of Saint Anthony! But then he told me that now I had to go and perform miracles. Ford gave me my first set of brushes, the first temptation of Saint Anthony, etcetera, etcetera, etcetera." Matta turned his head, and looking at the sky he said, "Did you know that the celebrated nineteenth-century French novelist Stendhal lived and wrote in this very same building?" We sat there a few more moments and then Matta exclaimed, "I can't believe I'm looking at the same sky as did Stendhal! Everything is connected to the earth…*aux ames citoyens!*"

CHAPTER FIFTEEN

NIKI DE SAINT PHALLE

NIKI'S COLORIST WORLD

"Life shrinks or expands in

proportion to one's courage."

– ANAÏS NIN

The power of art can be embedded in the element of surprise, by challenging us to reexamine the ways in which we previously imagined or looked at images in our environment. The range of possibilities for how art can surprise us is immeasurably vast. Perhaps the art is produced on a grand scale and is coated with ceramic colors and shapes, making it so inviting that you want to "go inside" the art. If you can in fact go inside, well, then not only have your senses been challenged but your physical world and your experience of the art object has been forever altered. That ability was the special genius of the French sculptor Niki de Saint Phalle. Niki's work clearly demanded attention and aimed to burrow its message of purpose into our lives.

Among the many remarkable things Niki did in her life, one of the most fascinating was to challenge the meaning of color by first embodying it in the form of ghostly white relief sculptures, designed to be shot with real ammunition from a real gun, which could be fired by anyone who wished to try. As it "bled out," the wounded ghostly relief would ironically take on a new, vibrant life, becoming coated in a rainbow of colors that splattered and dripped from paint sacs embedded within the art. That's where Niki's art adventure began.

My own adventure into Niki's life and art began in the late 1980s and early 1990s. By this time, Niki was focused on creating her monumental Tarot Garden masterpiece in the Tuscan hills of Italy. I was very fortunate within a few years to curate one of Niki's exhibitions and come to call her a friend, but at the start, nothing could have prepared me for our meeting in the Tarot Garden.

Driving north from Rome toward Tuscany through Italy's breathtaking countryside is one of the great pleasures of travel. I clearly remember my heart skipping a few beats one morning in the early 1990s as I neared the small hamlet of Garavicchio, set into the green hills west of the highway. Silver and gold tiles, glittering from the sun, announced that I was approaching the famous Tarot Garden. Niki had dedicated a quarter century of her working life to realizing her vision of creating a monumental sculpture garden. Here, she could embody the unity of art and nature in an outdoor environment to inspire fantasy and dreams.

On a hillside above fourteen acres of Etruscan ruins, Niki married her artistic gifts, skills, and creative imagination to redefine the symbolism found in the twenty-two tarot cards, which had fascinated her for years. In this magnificent architectural environment, she fulfilled her own monumental vision. It was an astonishing and rare achievement for any artist, but particularly for a woman in the male-dominated world of sculpture.

"Come in, Jeffrey. We'll have lunch inside the Empress." That was my welcome and my invitation! The entire experience was as surreal as the setting. The Empress is a goddess, which immediately conjures up images of beauty and power. But there was a sort of spiritual primitiveness to the idea of lunching in the belly of the Empress, as if we had been symbolically devoured. The dining area shimmered, and the entire surface of the room was covered in fragmented mirrored mosaics. It was almost as if a disco ball factory had exploded, and all the fragments had been lodged into every visible surface. There is a very visceral irony to using broken mirrors to reflect internal beauty, and the message was not lost on me. Coughing, and always sounding a little bit out of breath, but nonetheless perpetually enthusiastic, Niki ushered me over to the mirrored dining table. "Come, Jeffrey, sit down. Try this chair." It was one of her animal chairs, a mostly black snake. I remember her eyes widened as she leaned over and asked, "How do you feel in the chair?" For any of us looking for conversation starters and ways to break the ice, Niki is a perfect study. Everything was a potential conversation starter. She wanted to know if I felt proud, intimidated, or modest. I said, "Okay. Let's see." I was sitting on an inanimate reptile. I felt a little awkward, but then again, I was about to dine inside an empress. I remember thinking that perhaps I had died and been reincarnated as one of the smaller interior figures of a Russian matryoshka doll. Then reality set in. I was in the world of Niki de Saint Phalle. She so much wanted to breathe life into her art that she created livable pathways into it. I suspended my disbelief and considered the immeasurable value of friendships that promise the extraordinary in life.

The Empress had also doubled as Niki's home for several years, with a bedroom located in one of the breasts and a kitchen in the other. The dining area was on the ground level, and Niki would sometimes join her artisans and assistants there before setting out to work or would use it to welcome special visitors.

When Niki spoke to me about the Tarot Garden, she said, "To a great extent I have been influenced by the past, I have been influenced by all kinds of civilizations. Every time I have gone to a new civilization, be it Mexico or India, I've come back totally enriched. Very often there are references in my work which are an homage to things that I have seen and experienced. In the Tarot Garden, there is a woman holding a dragon by a leash, which is an homage to Uccello's dragon in the British Museum in London. The steps in the Tarot Garden are a reference to the Mayan steps in the city of Palenque in the Yucatan." (After we first met, Niki agreed to let me interview her, and I have placed some of her own words from our many conversations throughout this remembrance.)

I first became keenly aware of Niki's art in the mid-1980s when I saw examples of her colorful sculptures displayed in the windows of several Paris galleries. There were her female *Nana* images, as well as monsters, scorpions, snakes, and birds of every size. Her palette was alive with brilliant colors, mostly primary hues, revealing her whimsical imagination. Her work was both naive and sophisticated, familiar and fresh. When I stared at a group of her works in one window, I remember feeling that her imagery was like a hazy, distant memory.

Niki threaded a variety of elements through her imagination, such as fairy tales, biblical narratives, and mythology, and with her vision, she was able to distill all of it into entirely new creations. The power of Niki's work creeps up on you, because often you are first seduced by her brilliant use of color. Her bright hues seemed to be torn from a distant rainbow. Other colors, like cobalt blues, sometimes accentuated with gold and wrapped around a Nana or a snake, appeared to display the influence of Yves Klein's palette. Her colors were all magnificent and inviting, which is what initially led me to visit Galerie Mitterrand, then on rue Jacques Callot, a small street just off the rue de Seine. I was absolutely captivated. When I left the gallery, I had purchased her work *Nana in Love*. I have kept the sculpture ever since.

———

My route to meeting Niki was through another dear artist friend. While visiting Larry Rivers, I told him about Niki's sculptures and mentioned that I wanted to meet her. He looked at me and said, "Niki is a friend of mine. I'll call her right now." I didn't realize it, but Larry and Niki had a long friendship that dated back to the early 1960s. In late 1961, Larry and his soon-to-be wife, Clarice, had left New York to live in France. For Larry, it was probably not a good professional move, as the Pop Art movement was heating up in New York. But he rented a studio in Paris on Impasse Ronsin, which had once been the address of Brancusi's studio. As luck would have it,

Niki and her sculptor-husband, Jean Tinguely, soon moved to the same floor, on the other side of a plaster wall. As Niki explained to me, it was the aromas from Clarice's cooking that initially attracted her attention. Working in studios separated only by a thin wall enabled Jean, Niki, Larry, and Clarice to become fast friends.

Niki had only just "burst" onto the art scene in Paris with her "shooting paintings," which became part of her interactive, participatory, paint-filled relief sculptures. Various venues would hold events where people were encouraged to shoot a gun at Niki's work. Even other artists would take their shots. She said that both Robert Rauschenberg and Jasper Johns participated. Niki told me that Rauschenberg was even the first to buy one of those works. "It was one of my shooting paintings. I had a collaboration with Bob. I did something in homage to him, and he shot it. There's another one I did for Jasper. This was very rewarding for me, as they were both enthusiasts and supported me. The support of my fellow artists was important for me, because at the time I was considered a real crazy." People asked, 'Who is that crazy girl with the gun, shooting?'"

During Niki's "shoot outs," her white plaster reliefs bled blues, greens, yellows, and reds. For Niki, it was an early example of her "rebirth" iconography, which stayed with her forever. She became part of a movement that challenged the veneration of the art object. Niki, along with Jean Tinguely, Arman, Yves Klein, and others, formed a close group called the "New Realists," who were infatuated with postwar consumerism, in much the same way as Pop Art, then taking off in America and England.

One very bizarre incident, which Niki confided to me had tested her friendship with Larry and Clarisse, was the day of an explosion in her husband, Jean's, studio. Niki thought that it sounded like "the Algerian war had reached Paris." Instead, it was Jean testing an even more forceful weapon to make Niki's sculptures bleed with greater drama. Niki said, "It was a precarious moment in my relationship with Larry and Clarice, because the impact of the explosion was so frightening. But Jean and I apologized profusely and saved the friendship. Jean was particularly skilled at salvaging. It is what he

did as a sculptor." In fact, their friendship ultimately led to Niki creating her *Nanas*, which she immortalized in countless sculptures, drawings, and prints. At first, the life-affirming *Nana* series seemed to be a 180-degree turn away from the violent action and imagery of the "Shooting Works." Perhaps on the surface they are, but the shooting paintings also foreshadow the ideas of rebirth in Niki's new imagery.

The Shooting Works, covered with white plaster, begin as virginal and white but are then impregnated with bullets that release the color of life within them. They remain forever scarred and stained by the ironic beauty and impurity of the experience. "Nana," which is a French slang term used to describe a woman, has its equivalent in the English slang words "chick," "broad," or "dame." For Niki, the work became a celebration and symbolized the empowerment of the female. The monumental weight of Niki's *Nana* sculptures liberated these voluptuous forms to express their grace, balance, spirit, power of seduction, and fertility.

Yet while the *Nana* became a trademark image for Niki, its birth was also the result of a serendipitous collaboration between Larry and Niki in 1964. She explained, "Larry was making a portrait of Clarice during pregnancy, and I liked it a lot. So, I said to Larry, 'Would you do another outline and then I will fill it all in?'" In the collaboration, Niki used the outline to guide her as she covered the figure with her inspired array of images and symbols so completely that there is hardly any breathable space. In fact, the figure is so manic with Niki's symbolism that it almost intentionally exhausts the eye. The entire work reads as if it were a portrait of a tattooed pregnancy.

The only place untouched by Niki's imagery is the face, where she had Rivers execute a portrait of Clarice. When you take a closer look, you can make out the details of images symbolizing seduction, fertility, and rebirth. Butterflies and flowers, birds and kittens, a tiny ballerina, and letters from the alphabet further clarify Niki's symbols, which specifically refer to aquatic creatures, mostly mollusks and crustaceans. There is so much to read in those drawn symbols that one could spend days analyzing them. But nearly all exist in water, which clearly represents the origins of life. Some of her aquatic creatures symbolized rebirth. Some feed off each other. Many of these creatures reappear later in her work as subjects for individual sculptures.

The initial drawing eventually morphed into larger and more voluminous sculptural figures, culminating in large female forms of color, volume, and beauty. As Niki often said, "I wanted to fill the whole body up with life." She also began her efforts to populate the landscape of her art with her signature *Nana* sculptures. "The early collaboration with Larry was the spark for the first Nana, because later, they just appeared in my life, these creatures, full of joy."

In 1988, on one of my trips to Paris, Larry arranged for me to meet Niki. She was living in a wooded area of Soisy, not far from Paris. She was as bright and imaginative as she was physically beautiful. In fact, as a nineteen-year-old model, she had appeared on the cover of *Life* magazine. When I arrived at the door, her first words to me were, "Welcome to Auberge au Cheval Blanc. What do you think?" What I thought was that she had the most striking eyes, and it would take me a minute to get past that blue. After I told her that it was beautiful, she replied, "Yes, at one time this was a brothel. It was once a den of iniquity; now it's a place for my flights of fancy. Is there really any difference?" Only an artist like Niki could make that comparison.

Everything in Niki's world, especially in her adjoining studio, was fodder for creative play. Like Dalí, she was drawn to poetry and mythology. Niki played as much with language as she did with her imaginative sculptures. Even her writings have a certain quality of fantasy to them. Her invented calligraphy was artful, often mixing images with letters. She applied her colors first, before joining them with her black overlaps, altogether different from the traditional way of drawing first and filling in the colors afterward. Her work exhibited a veritable cycle of life and death. Even her delicate, thin, feminine frame seemed to stand in stark contrast to her enormous energy and monumental accomplishments. She often dressed in flamboyant garb and could at first seem virtually unapproachable.

OPPOSITE PAGE: *Larry Rivers and Niki de Saint Phalle's collaborative work, the origin of her* Nana *sculptures.*

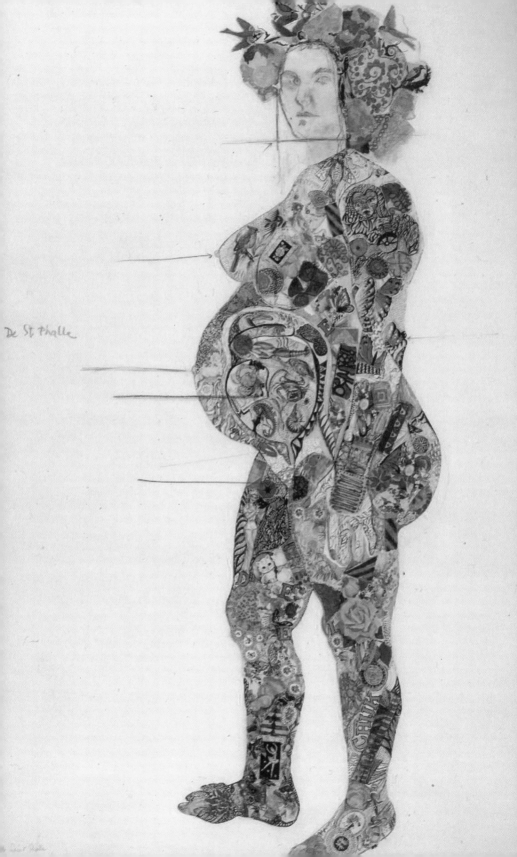

De St Phalle

But in conversation she was funny and imaginative, inviting and determined. Niki immediately set the agenda. "Come in. We'll have lunch. We should then go to Le Bois des Pauvres [the woods of the poor] to see *Le Cyclop*. Jean started working on it at least twenty years ago, and we continue to contribute to it to this day. Then I will take you with me to Noah's Art."

Le Cyclop, also called *The Monster in the Woods*, was Jean's fantasy sculpture, a monumental mechanical construction. It was born out of an undisciplined wreck of industrial debris and reconstituted by the artist into something akin to a metallic one-eyed god in the woods. I must say that entering the rather perilous interior of *Le Cyclop*, with all the gears creaking and clanking while enormous spheres rolled precariously around a clumsy track, was a little unnerving. I remember that Niki kept looking at my face for my reaction. Mostly it was contained in my eyes, wide open with curiosity as well as fear—I felt some relief when I left unscathed and thought this must be a little bit what it was like for Jonah when he exited the whale.

We drove away from Le Bois des Pauvres to Niki's play on words and imagery, her outdoor sculpture repository, which she called Noah's Art. It was a remarkable landscape of colorful forms and figures, including large *Nana* works, monsters, birds, and snakes, among many other imaginary creations. Niki, whose voice was perpetually raspy, said, "They are all my creatures, waiting for the fertile soil. It's like the story of Noah, the way he saved all the animals and waited for the flood to dry so the world could begin again. But of course, I am not Noah. I have many more assistants helping me than he had."

Yes, she liked humor too. I was thrilled by the consistent thread that ran not just through her art but through her life, a life that relied on the consistent belief in renewal. Even in this repository for her outdoor sculptures, separate from any public view, she had designed a storage area, a kind of safehouse for the sculptures to reside, until the time when each work would reenter the world in a new environment, awaiting new experiences.

OPPOSITE PAGE: *Niki in her studio with* Red Nana, *1994.*

Many years later, when I was working with the Jerusalem Foundation, gifting the large Roy Liechtenstein sculpture, *Modern Head*, to the city, I remember seeing Niki's project in Israel, a park featured on the grounds of a zoo. She had translated her interest in the story of Noah's ark into a tangible world where children of all ages could interact with her animal sculptures. She worked with the architect Mario Botta, who designed the ark while Niki created the animals. In a way, the many sculptural creations that filled this Noah's ark were a precursor to her Tarot Garden.

In 1972 in Jerusalem, Niki had completed an enormous sculpture based on the image of the golem, a mythological figure from Jewish folklore. (The structure also partially foreshadowed Jean's *Le Cyclop*.) Niki brilliantly created a monumental monster that could be climbed on as well as entered. Once inside the belly of the beast, one could be spit out by riding to the ground on one of three red-tongued slides protruding from the beast's mouth. Niki's idea of being consumed by the golem but liberated by your own will brilliantly captures the conflicted nature of the golem myth in folklore. It was the perfect vehicle for her continuing interest in the perpetual and transformative nature of renewal.

That same theme of perpetual renewal is embodied in Niki's *Stravinsky Fountain*, created with Jean Tinguely, adjacent to the Centre Pompidou in Paris. It is probably my favorite public sculpture in Europe. Niki and I visited it often; she always wanted to be sure it was working and functioning in the intended way. At one point during a visit, she explained her relationship with Jean, saying, "Jean was considered like somebody who was dangerous, he was going to overthrow the establishment. We knew each other quite a few years before we started living together, and actually love grew out of friendship because we were really working together. We liked each other's work. He helped me do certain things, and he was a great enthusiast for my work from the beginning, as I was of his work. We continued being a working team until the end. It was very exciting because we were so different. We had totally different points of view. It was really a merging of two entirely different worlds. I think you can see this very well in the *Stravinsky Fountain*, where you see Jean's machines and my colorful and figurative creatures dancing together. We used this complete opposition and joined it together. You can call it masculine and feminine. You can call it whatever you want, but it is two different worlds meeting and joining to make one thing. I think it was an extremely proactive, creative relationship for both of us."

In the fountain, her colorful figures are combined with Tinguely's dark, foreboding machines, which mix the water and the sky and somehow turn and move in a manner that conjures aspects of Stravinsky's music, such as *The Rite of Spring*. It is as if the bright, beautiful, colorful, lively turning figures and symbols of Niki's iconography represent the first part of the *Rite*, the dance and embrace of spring, while Jean's dark, foreboding machines suggest the sacrificial dance of death in the *Rite's* second part. Because they exist together, the images move back and forth between life and death in a perpetual water ballet that seems to churn, spew, and recycle the water of life.

Everything about Niki's art always seemed vividly alive. Being around her, you couldn't help but feel drawn in and want to be connected. Niki's imagination also wasn't limited to the imagery of her art. She was very imaginative, clever, and savvy about generating support for funding the arts. Participation in some of her fundraising events made supporters feel as if they were involved in the creative process. For example, part of the funding for the Noah's Art project in Jerusalem came from donations that afforded donors the opportunity to "adopt" one of the animals. If you contributed a certain amount to finance a particular animal, a plaque would be mounted on the animal and named according to the donor's wishes. It was a brilliant fundraising concept to link the donor to Noah's journey to save the animals.

In another example of clever financing for her Tarot Garden, Niki created consumer items such as perfume. She received some criticism, but she was pursuing something more durable than temporary commercialism. For many people in the United States,

Niki's sculpted perfume bottles were their first introduction to her unique iconography. While she was undoubtedly promoting sales with colorful and eye-catching snakes intertwined on top of her perfume bottles, the proceeds nevertheless helped build the timeless Tarot Garden.

Every idea emanates from something. Niki told me that it was during her first visit to Gaudí's Park Güell in Barcelona in 1955 when she began to envision her future sculpture garden. She explained, "I will influence somebody someday, just as I have been influenced by others. For example, I was very much influenced by Gaudí, when I was making my huge Tarot Garden. And I am sure someday, somebody will come and have the same feeling in looking at my sculpture garden that I had when I saw Gaudí and said, 'Hey, one day I'm going to do that,' because in every century there is some huge garden. Since Gaudí, I have done the biggest garden, and in the future, there will be someone else who will do one too. And I am very proud that it is a woman who did the garden this time, and it was the big adventure of my life." Clearly the mosaics and flowing sculptural forms that appear in Antoni Gaudí's work helped inspire her Tarot Garden. Her imagination, however, led her more toward blurring the borders between the mysteries of humans, art, and nature.

With the tarot cards as symbols for managing the many mysteries of life, Niki set out to reimagine their iconography. Each figure, representing one of the cards, was set into the landscape of her Tuscany garden, and many of the sculptures were interactive destinations that could be entered and experienced internally, such as the Empress. As Niki explained it, she designed the Empress to appear as a sphinx, the third card of the tarot.

But her joyous art took a physical toll on her own life. Niki's side of any conversation was continually interrupted by a persistent cough. I had noticed it many times but never felt comfortable enough to discuss it with her. Something about the Tuscan surroundings, and the empathy I felt, gave me the confidence to broach the subject. "Niki, I have noticed your cough now for a while. Isn't it time to do something about it?"

OPPOSITE PAGE: *Niki's brilliant and colorful creations, juxtaposed with Jean Tinguely's brooding work, at their* Stravinsky Fountain *at the Centre Pompidou in Paris.*

"It is from those earlier experiments with materials," she told me. "I used a lot of urethanes, and it turns out they did some damage to my lungs. It has gotten worse over time."

"Is there anything that doctors can do to help?" I asked.

"Well, not really. I use an oxygen tank more these days. That helps a little. But no, there isn't much they can do."

This is where I pressed her. "What about your environment? This is all fantastic, here in the tarot, but have you thought about moving to a drier climate?"

The conversation was interrupted by several of her workers, and we didn't pick it up again that day. Instead, we spent the rest of the day walking through the garden while Niki explained all of her imagery. She had poured an astonishing amount of physical work, imagination, financial planning, strategy, and pure, inspired genius into every aspect. As I left the garden, I turned around one more time to look back at it all.

The mosaic monuments were still shimmering against the landscape, as if they were alive and breathing, shifting the reflected light with every gust of wind that blew through the trees. The colorful forms themselves seemed to be rising through the hills, reaching above the landscape, as if they were painting an independent prism of colors back into the sky. It seemed like an impossible fantasy come to life. I remember thinking for a moment about all the wonders of the world. Before the Tarot Garden of Tuscany, there were the seven man-made wonders of the world. As I walked away that day, I felt as though I was leaving the crucible where those earthly monuments came to meet inside Niki's garden. I even imagined I had seen the eighth, and woman-made, wonder of the world.

Something about the surreal nature of the day made me feel the need to return to a more familiar reality. I had heard that not too far from Garavicchio there was an Italian baseball stadium, so I took a slight detour on my way back to Rome. When I arrived at the stadium, it was empty. I got out of my car and began to walk around. In the distance, I heard familiar noises, so I walked toward them. As I got closer, I could hear the distinct sound of a baseball landing in

OPPOSITE PAGE: *In Niki's* Tarot Garden, *Garavicchio, Italy, circa 1992.*

a glove. It's an unmistakable sound. From where I was, I couldn't see who was throwing the ball. I could only hear it. So, I followed the sound into the stadium.

There on the field, I saw an astonishingly familiar sight. It was one of my former players, Rich Thompson, a pitcher from when I owned a Minor League baseball team in Oklahoma City. (Today, he is a gifted attorney and baseball agent in Long Island.) Only a year before he had been playing for me; now he was pitching for an Italian summer league team. After the Tarot Garden, the scene was the perfect transition back into reality. Seeing one of my players on an obscure baseball field in Tuscany extended the surrealism of the day and yet assured me that one can never escape the reality of life.

———

The same year as that trip, I lost my sister and only sibling in a tragic aviation accident. It was a stunning shock and an unfathomable loss. I wanted to do something, anything, of significance in her honor. I decided to commission an artwork to be donated to Yale in her memory. I thought of Niki as the perfect artist to create something for the Joseph Slifka Center for Jewish Life. Niki very graciously agreed to do it. Honoring the center's namesake as well, she created a mosaic interpretation of Joseph and his coat of many colors. Before the completion of the final mosaic, I visited Soisy, where Niki showed me a richly colored work on paper that she had made for the proposed installation. It was beautiful. She gave me the gouache so that I could review it in my own time. We rolled it up, and I left with the working image that will forever represent a vivid memory.

I returned to Paris in a taxi. When I entered my hotel room, something felt wrong. I realized that I had left the rolled-up artwork inside a tube in the well of the cab's rear window. It was gone, and I instantly knew that I would never see it again. I was sickened by what felt like pure negligence. But the feeling of my own failing was compounded by what it all seemed to be saying to me. My goal was to create a precious memory of my sister and somehow in that process, my inattentiveness only accentuated the symbolic nature of loss. I knew I needed to explain it to Niki.

Niki may have been the only person and artist to understand the situation and not show a moment of judgment. She, better than most, understood the notion of rebirth. Niki created a second work for me. I did not lose that one, and today, in memory of my sister, the finished mosaic of Joseph and his coat of many colors is permanently installed against the west wall of the entrance hall of the Joseph Slifka Center for Jewish Life at Yale.

A few years before I lost my sister, Niki had lost Jean Tinguely, her long-time partner and husband. With his passing, the art world also lost one of its most innovative artists. After Jean's death, Niki spent more time in New York, where I was fortunately able to see her. Beyond enduring her grief, she was suffering more severely from her breathing problems. In nearly a decade of friendship, I saw a person whose efforts to deal with adversity seemed more rooted in the art of judo than of chess. She wasn't one to concede. She was more likely to try to disable a challenge and turn a disadvantage to her favor.

Yet for the first time, I had the sense that she was torn between finding solutions and watching the clock wind down on her life. But even in that dark uncertainty, Niki's imagination never flagged. The frailty and vulnerability of her physical state seemed to have freed her mind to visualize pictures of more violent rebirth. She imagined exploding paintings, where an image could be broken apart but then come back together in a perpetual cycle of destruction and renewal. It was a similar concept to the *Stravinsky Fountain*. But without Jean and without her own physical vigor, it would be difficult to make this imagined vision come to life. Ultimately, she found assistants and an engineer who understood how to configure the electronics to simulate the idea of a painted iconography breaking apart and coming back together.

She called the works *Tableaux Eclatés*. Niki explained, "We looked it up in a dictionary and tried to find a meaning. It really means exploding painting. But they're not exactly exploding, because they are

ABOVE: *Niki de Saint Phalle*, #19 Baseball Player *(Tony Gwynn), San Diego, CA, 1999.*

214

actually about order and chaos. Order is what they are when they are all together. If you just look at them, you don't see any of the difficult technology, because I don't like to show the technology. I like to hide it. Some people like to show it. I prefer making magic boxes, so that people don't know what is going on inside. People walk in front of one of these, and it starts moving by itself. You don't have to plug it in, nothing. Only in front of a human being will it work. Otherwise, it doesn't exist. It's just there as a painting. But when a human being moves in front of it, it bursts forth and responds, so it is in communication with another."

The first few three-dimensional paintings consisted of representations of new beginnings as well as images of overcoming adversity. But while Niki's mind was ready to move ahead, her body was not. We spoke more openly about her health. She now needed an oxygen tank by her side, and it weighed on her normally uplifted spirit. I suggested that she consider moving to the American West Coast. "Niki, San Diego and La Jolla have among the best climates in the world." She listened but was not convinced. However, her doctor also suggested a move to Southern California. Ultimately, finding conditions where breathing didn't require her to drag an oxygen tank helped propel Niki to embrace a healthier climate. She ultimately described it as "Resurrection in La Jolla! It has not only been revitalizing but stimulating, and has brought me all new subject matter. All kinds of new things have crept into my work, whether it's whales or the sea or the feeling of infinity."

Everything about the landscape, light, climate, and nature gave her renewed energy. She even became a San Diego Padres baseball fan. Fascinated by the superstar player Tony Gwynn, she executed a large, spectacular sculpture of him swinging a bat for the San Diego community.

With her newfound inspiration, she developed new painting techniques to represent the space and light that saturated her California views. Niki's life and art were reborn once again. Using the Tableaux Eclatés format, she revived imagery from nature, now turning to the ocean, the desert, the sunlight, and air, and discovered new iconography to address her timeless subjects.

In 1994, I worked with Niki to cull a collection from her recent work for an exhibition in New York. Everything about the work was vibrantly alive. For Niki, I think the concept of paintings that break apart and then rejoin in a perpetual cycle of change and renewal was directly connected to her own history. This included her relationship with Jean and his kinetic machine art, her use of vibrant color, and her unspoken need for reinvention. But I also believe that for Niki, the concept of changing forms was at the very core of her being. It was an inherent part of her sense of survival. It's who she had to be.

To navigate a male-dominated landscape and be recognized as an equal, Niki had to create an image more powerful than the first impression of her naturally striking beauty. At the start of her career, she literally had to pick up a gun and shoot her way past preconceived notions of femininity. Like Annie Oakley, who had to be the best shot because simply being a good shot would not have swayed an ingrained sexist bias, Niki had to make the gun perform tricks that defied the purpose of its invention. Seen in this light, she didn't embrace collaboration with dominant male artists out of any sense of self-doubt. Instead, it was quite the opposite: she wanted to be completely in command, and what better way to do that than to first appropriate a gun (something traditionally identified with men and male pursuits) for her work. She had men and women lining up to shoot.

In her own words, she once told me, "I am an enthusiast for life, for the good and for the bad, but it's mainly for the good. So, whatever I see, whatever touches me, whatever moves me in some way, whether it's a color or emotion, something that I have to deal with, I'll find a form and a way to translate this into paint or a drawing or a new color or a combination of colors so it's an actual translation of how I feel as a human being."

I saw this outlook become diminished with the loss of Jean and the slow constriction of her breathing, but then I saw everything be renewed, resurrected in La Jolla, where she was able to extend her life for nearly another decade. Her extraordinary talents were exhibited in her *Tableaux Eclatés*. I consider my friendship with Niki to be one of the most profound experiences of my life. I still miss her intellect, charm, and imagination. But I will forever cherish the lesson her energy and art taught me: life is boundless when you embrace the vibrant and natural cycle of change.

CHAPTER SIXTEEN

COLLECTORS AND A MENTOR

MAKING A DIFFERENCE

"If a picture speaks to me, if it tells me something

about myself, then I want it. Then I have to have it."

— NORTON SIMON

We create worlds out of thin air that support our efforts to prove we exist. We leave our footprints in the ever-shifting sands of time. Our marks are almost randomly and irrationally etched to endure or, sadly, to be washed away. Through it all, we categorize between the temporary and the permanent and value them accordingly. Collectors of art, invariably, aim to reside on the permanent side of the ledger. Of those art collectors who amass great collections, there are also a select few who embrace the "field of dreams" spirit and convert their collections into public institutions, with the unwavering belief that "if I build it, they will come." The "they" are those among us who may not otherwise have the opportunity to experience such great art in person, to empathize with or be inspired by it, absent the existence of an institution designed to showcase humanity's endeavors.

The concept of collecting significant works of art goes back many hundreds of years, but the second half of the twentieth century, after World War II, saw great attention and energy focused on assembling collections that would be destined to become public

OPPOSITE PAGE: *Norton Simon's Henry Moore sculpture,* Draped Reclining Woman, *1958, which arrived in New York on the* Queen Elizabeth II.

institutions. This magical and fast-paced era produced some of the most astonishing art collectors of any century. For me, much like the thrill of becoming acquainted with extremely talented artists, knowing some of the leading American business magnates, whose art collecting matched their meteoric successes in amassing extraordinary wealth, was inspiring. Quite often, their collections were reflections of their personalities. Serious art collecting naturally involves long-term commitment allied to dedication, energy, and expertise. I admired the "true" collectors, who spurned speculation and were motivated by their love of art rather than any eventual financial gain. Many, in fact, became my clients.

For a collector to embrace that feeling of deep commitment and also want to share it with the world is rare and in many ways every bit as creative and inspired as the artists whose works fill their collections. Of the many collectors I have known and helped to acquire works, three stand out for their respective drive to turn their collections into public institutions and to share their individual, curated vision. Each of these men was a titan of industry, and each sought in his own way to give back as a means of acknowledging personal success. Their personal drive also led them to amass great art with fervor and unparalleled dedication.

Dedicated collectors like Joe Hirshhorn, Walter Chrysler Jr., and Norton Simon, each of whom was a client and friend, were not motivated by status but rather were guided by a keen competitive spirit. They created collections as if they were harmonizing an orchestra and sought information about their remarkable treasures from dealers, artists, critics, scholars, and auction houses. They were often excited by their quests as a tangible expression of their personal visions—and their art collections became an integral part of who they were.

Hirshhorn, Chrysler, and Simon had one trait in common: they left their treasures to the public to be enjoyed in perpetuity in important American museums. But while these men ultimately shared a common interest in creating public art museums, their motivations and reasons varied. Still, fulfilling that ambition, regardless of the reasons, has proven the importance of altruism above all endeavors as the most lasting gift we have to give.

We have all benefited from the cultural contributions of these collectors, who looked beyond their great wealth and business acumen to leave a legacy that affirms our purposeful existence. Without a doubt, they were compulsive in their search to acquire art objects. Yet all maintained a discerning eye, even if the pursuit of masterpieces could mean sometimes throwing caution to the wind.

I was also fortunate to work with many other collectors whose collections did not become public museums. They were more private in their pursuits and acquired their masterpieces for their own enjoyment. Saul Steinberg and Edgar Bronfman Sr. embodied the American success story. And their experiences of intensive, focused art acquisition produced personal collections of extraordinary quality. In 1965, I met Paul Haim, a man with a remarkable style and vision, and also unusual courage. I came to consider him one of my foremost friends and a mentor.

Time has helped me gain a perspective on how truly remarkable each of these men and their visions and contributions were.

JOE HIRSHHORN

Joe Hirshhorn was an exceptionally shrewd Wall Street investor, a business prodigy, who parlayed his career into the prospecting and mining of minerals in Canada. He was fond of taking risks in business. He had emigrated from Latvia to America as one of twelve children of a widowed mother. He would buy works of art from artists in droves when possible, often leaving an artist's studio having acquired everything in sight. If one work was great, five were better.

While Joe collected American art produced between the end of the nineteenth century through the second half of the twentieth century, what interested him most was pursuing paintings and sculptures that could keep his collection current, fresh, and alive. His sculpture holdings became a "who's who" of twentieth-century sculptors, including Henry Moore, Pablo Picasso, Alberto Giacometti,

Alexander Calder, David Smith, Joan Miró, Marino Marini, Barbara Hepworth, Giacomo Manzù, Jean Arp, Henri Matisse, Jacques Lipchitz, and others. He pursued important, interesting objects with a great intensity for several decades.

What I learned from Joe was that art is really about love. In the end, he would say it is about something you want to live with, look at, and "share with others." For him, the concept of sharing was the catalyst for what eventually became the Hirshhorn Museum and Sculpture Garden in Washington, DC.

Occasionally, Joe would attempt to pay for works of art by trading securities from his mining ventures. My friend and mentor Paul Haim, who had a gallery on rue du Faubourg Saint-Honoré on the Right Bank in Paris, called me one day to say that he had sold two sculptures to Hirshhorn and was being paid in securities in a Hirshhorn venture called Snow Drift, a Canadian mining company. He asked me if I had heard of Snow Drift, to which I replied dryly that it sounded like something one didn't want to step in. Paul did, and eventually he paid the price for that exchange. When I did business with Hirshhorn, I always insisted upon conventional transactions, which meant a check rather than involvement in his mining investments. I had no desire to follow mining securities on the Canadian stock market. Even to this day, I believe one should try to pursue the familiar. As my mother often said to me, "Shoemaker, stick to your last." Art is what I know well.

In the years that I knew him, Joe always felt that he had a special responsibility to preserve his collection and keep it intact. He rarely sold a work unless he was occasionally upgrading a particular example for a better object by the same artist. Unlike Walter Chrysler, who enjoyed making trades, Joe preferred buying and felt his collection should be left to the public in some form. As a private dealer, I occasionally approached Joe as a possible source for acquiring works, but his ultimate vision was to create a permanent home for his massive collection intact. He stuck to that vision, and his art eventually became part of the cultural life of the nation.

224

In a sort of ironic way, Hirshhorn the mining magnate converted his art collection into a museum by "mining" the interest of the United States government. While the US Congress had intended to establish a national museum of contemporary art as far back as the 1930s, the combination of the Great Depression and World War II made those plans unsupportable. It wasn't until the 1960s that Sidney Dillon Ripley, the secretary of the Smithsonian Institution, had a vision and a plan to expand the many museums under the Smithsonian's auspices. By this time Hirshhorn's extensive art collection was well known, and Ripley saw the opportunity to revisit Congress's initial desire for a national museum of contemporary art. For his part, Hirshhorn saw the opportunity to make his collection public and have it be protected in an institution that would bear his name, in a partnership with the United States government. In an agreement that served everyone's interests, Congress established the Hirshhorn Museum and Sculpture Garden in 1966, and Joe donated his enormous collection to the Smithsonian. The Hirshhorn collection opened in 1974 on the National Mall in Washington, and it remains a widely acclaimed art museum.

From the early 1960s to the mid-1970s, Joe lived with his wife, Olga, in a three-story Norman-style chateau on a twenty-two-acre estate in the Round Hill section of Greenwich, Connecticut. Their mammoth stone mansion had a view of the distant Manhattan skyline. I often brought sculptures and paintings to his residence. I never wasted his time with works that were less important than those already in his collection. I remember the day in 1974 when he acquired Picasso's 1906–1907 sculpture, *Kneeling Woman Combing Her Hair*. He made his decision quickly, after ten minutes of negotiation and discussion. Saturdays in New York were usually Joe's days for visiting galleries, and he often stopped by my office to see what might be new. He always relied on his own sensibilities and always sought to acquire important examples of work by artists ranging from Thomas Eakins in the nineteenth century to the most recent work of Henry Moore in the twentieth century.

Joe had an exacting eye and a high standard for excellence. A large outdoor Marino Marini *Horse and Rider* sculpture (which I referenced earlier) dominated his courtyard in Greenwich. Like many of Marini's sculptures, this masterpiece exhibited a sense of tension, as did the complicated man who owned it. No less impressive was Joe's New York Park Avenue apartment, where he kept countless works of art. Many sculptures sat on windowsills above the radiators. For lack of wall space, paintings were stacked on the floors, in the hallways, and even in spare bedrooms. Later, when I collected a few Henry Moore maquettes, I debated putting them on the windowsill in the manner of Joe Hirshhorn. I just didn't have enough of them, however, to duplicate Joe's décor.

Joe often competed with Walter Chrysler. They had some epic battles to see who could collect the most important works from an artist's studio. When Hirshhorn learned that Chrysler had acquired the one remaining painting that the artist Raphael Soyer had kept for himself from his *Homage to Eakins* series, he was not at all happy. To those who loved him, Joe was always "a little man in a hurry." I can attest to that. Nothing ever deterred him from his energetic pursuit of excellence and the remarkable vision he had for what eventually became one of America's premier museums.

WALTER CHRYSLER

Walter P. Chrysler Jr. was born into the world of business and industry. His father had founded the Chrysler Corporation, and while Walter did in fact work in the automobile industry for a short time, his passion seemed always to be centered around art collecting. It became the main focus of his life.

There is a well-documented story about Walter's early interest in collecting. While in boarding school when he was fourteen, his father had given him $350 as a birthday gift, which he used to purchase his first work of art, a small watercolor. As the story goes, his dormitory master determined that the rendering of a nude woman was inappropriate for a teenage boy, so he confiscated the watercolor and destroyed it. As it turns out, Walter had a keen eye from an early age—the watercolor was an original work by Renoir. I can't imagine how insanely frustrated and angry something like that would have made me, but I can imagine that it could have served as a lesson or perhaps an early seed to inspire Walter to create an institution that would protect his art from such ignorance.

I met Walter Chrysler in the mid-1960s, when I began my career as a private dealer, and we formed a special relationship. He was already an incomparable collector, who visited Europe often in the late 1940s through the 1960s. For Walter, it was always about the adventure. Despite having been raised in the automotive business, he preferred to travel by private train car in order to more easily cross Europe. With an insatiable appetite for art of all centuries, including antiquities, Walter approached his purchases with a discriminating eye. He was a truly original thinker with vision, extraordinary knowledge, an unparalleled memory, and highly refined taste. Today, collectors often follow the current rage, but Walter possessed a profound understanding of both the past and the present. He eventually filled an enormous warehouse on Charles Street on the Lower West Side in Manhattan with the treasures he had acquired in Europe and the United States.

I visited often and was always overwhelmed by the quality, quantity, and range of his interests. When he opened the doors with the keys that he kept in his pocket, one quickly realized that there were no alarms in the building, and it was so poorly illuminated that it was almost a miracle he could find what he was seeking in the disarray and the dark. Somehow, the works survived the chaos. It was like rummaging through an old antique store, except all the objects were treasures, and even masterpieces, by artists from the seventeenth to the twentieth century. The warehouse housed works from such luminaries as Picasso, Léger, Degas, Matisse, and Toulouse-Lautrec, as well as Old Master paintings. It was magic.

Walter also introduced me to his sister Bernice, who lived in the Carlyle Hotel on Madison Avenue. She was primarily interested in Impressionist paintings. Often, when I showed him an Impressionist work, Walter would say, "My sister might like that." And more often than not, much to my delight, she did!

Like Joe Hirshhorn, Walter continually upgraded his purchases and collections. As with most great collectors, he was obsessed with "the chase and the capture." He collected artists in-depth and was able to eventually use these works to trade for other artists he felt were lacking in his assemblage and might be crucial for his vision. At one time he owned several major Picasso works, including the 1902 *Deux femmes au bar*, a pivotal Blue Period work, and *The Charnel House* of 1944–1945, a black, white, and gray painting depicting genocide and the Holocaust. I remember seeing them both in his warehouse, propped next to each other, leaning against a bare concrete wall. He willingly traded these works and others.

In Walter's warehouse, it was always hard to single out any individual work without considering the rest of the collection. His interests were never about what was fashionable at the moment but more about where the works he acquired would fit within his view of the history of art. His eventual focus was on the creation of an institution that could house his acquisitions. He once explained to me that he had a plan for a museum that would be a comprehensive undertaking, with him making all the decisions. There was nothing that artists or artisans created that did not interest him. He had an equal passion for American and European furniture, glass, silver, Tiffany lamps, rare books, stamps, paintings, sculptures, and works on paper. He crossed the artistic thresholds of most of the world's cultures.

Walter also never collected his art from a corporate office. No one would have realized that he had assembled a large part of his vast art collection while operating out of a small antique storefront on the southwest corner at Eightieth Street and Madison Avenue in New York. It was a nondescript "shop" that attracted traders and sellers seven days a week, attempting to do business with him.

During the summer, in order to see Walter, I would drive up to his residence in Provincetown, Massachusetts. He displayed much of his vast collection in an old church in the center of town. I would arrive with works that often resulted in complicated trades. I remember on one occasion flying up to Provincetown on a small plane with a Marino Marini sculpture, which I had acquired from the artist at Walter's request. Walter simply said, "Leave it here. We'll find a solution." We always did. Sometimes it could take as long as six months, but we always found a way to devise a mutually beneficial trade.

In my first trade with Walter, I exchanged a Raphael Soyer painting entitled *Homage to Eakins* depicting the history of American art for a Matisse bronze and a Degas bronze dancer (much to Joe Hishhorn's consternation as I would later learn). I also recall acquiring from him some special Blue Period Picasso watercolors, which were absolute masterworks, and which Walter kept in the Charles Street warehouse on the stone floor with their faces to the wall, where he had left them last. It was a miracle that they were in such great condition when I acquired them. I couldn't afford to keep them and sold them in Paris and privately in America. Of course, I would love to have them all back today. *C'est la vie!*

I recall selling one of the Blue Period watercolors to a dealer on the Right Bank in Paris. I later discovered that he had simply walked with it across the Seine to another dealer on the Left Bank, who paid more than double what I had received.

Walter eventually fulfilled his vision in establishing the Chrysler Museum of Art in Norfolk, Virginia. It is filled with treasures from many disciplines: American and European glass; paintings and sculptures from all over the world, from 1440 to 1980; and extensive collections of furniture, ceramics, and antiquities. He died in 1988 and left the museum 75 percent of his Chrysler trust. Collectors like Walter are rare to find in the twenty-first century. He was not consumed with acquiring for personal status or to best another person in the auction room. His sole focus was on rare and beautiful objects. Walter holds a special place in my mind, because of his vision, energy, and wide-ranging curiosity about all forms of art.

NORTON SIMON

During the late 1960s, I received a call that began, "I hear you know a lot about paintings and sculptures. My name is Norton Simon." It was the famed California billionaire industrialist, whose vast holdings included steel, household goods, and businesses in the food industry, including Hunt Foods, Canada Dry, and even *McCall's* magazine in the print media. More importantly, he was also a prominent Californian and American art collector. He said he'd like to meet me so that I might offer him some paintings and sculptures of interest. It was an intriguing introduction to say the least.

Shortly afterward, I returned from England on the *Queen Elizabeth* ocean liner with a 1957 outdoor sculpture by Henry Moore entitled *Large Reclining Woman*. Even though the sculpture weighed almost two tons, it traveled with me as baggage on the ship. Watching it be hoisted onto the pier on New York's West Side after the ship docked was a new experience. Shortly thereafter, I called Norton to inquire about his interest. I sent him photographs and waited for a response.

Norton's timing was always subject to his crowded schedule, so it took several months before I heard back from him. He called on a Friday afternoon to ask if he could see the sculpture the following morning. I exclaimed, "Norton! You've been interested in this bronze for six months, and you give me a few hours' notice to have a storage facility opened on a Saturday, when the building is closed and the alarms are on?" He said simply, "I want to see the sculpture. Saturday. Figure it out." And I did. He acquired the work. *Large Reclining Woman* still resides at the Norton Simon Museum in Pasadena.

Norton often invited me to the Pierre Hotel, where he kept an apartment when he was in New York, usually with his wife, the well-known actress Jennifer Jones. On one occasion, he asked if I could bring a Henry Moore midsized indoor working-model sculpture to him at seven in the morning. I wheeled it through the lobby of the elegant hotel on a dolly and rode the service elevator to his suite, where he greeted the sculpture enthusiastically. He eventually purchased it. I had described it to him the previous day while he was on the phone with his stockbroker, maneuvering with his daily investments. Norton was the consummate multitasker.

I once asked him why he wanted to see artworks so early in the morning. He explained it was because he wanted a clear mind. By 8:00 a.m., his mind was on the stock market. But he never looked at his vast art collection as anything resembling stocks and bonds because, as he once explained, that would mean relating those treasures to a marketplace, and he felt that if he did that, he might as well own a gallery. For him, it was about collecting intellectually important and visually interesting objects.

I spent what seemed like a lifetime helping him collect a host of treasures. He was always remarkably discreet about his acquisitions and displayed little interest in the spotlight or in publicity, with one glaring exception: his unsuccessful 1970 run for the United States Senate. He would often ask me to visit auction houses as his agent to evaluate jewelry and art purchases. The jewelry was for his wife. He wanted the utmost secrecy. No one ever learned about all the jewelry I bought for her or the art I helped him acquire.

Norton had a perceptive eye, yet he always sought many opinions before his purchases. This kept me alert, as did his frequent calls at six in the evening, usually at the start of my family dinner hour, which often resulted in canceled meals. I never minded, however, because it inevitably led to a fascinating conversation about art, markets, business, and life. Norton occasionally resold or traded objects. Like Walter Chrysler, he was forever hoping to upgrade his holdings. This vision, of course, is the hallmark of a devoted collector.

Norton always demonstrated great wisdom about the definition of value. On one occasion, while I was visiting him at his home, we had a lengthy discussion about a tenth-century bronze from India, a dancing Shiva he had acquired for $900,000. His concern was that because of a lack of recent public or private sales, there was no way to establish its comparative value. Was it worth $1 million or $10 million? There was no way to know, so he relied on intuition and his passion for the work. He delighted in endless discussions about relative values.

Toward the end of his life, Simon was struck by a devastating disease, Guillain-Barré syndrome, which affects the central nervous system and eventually leads to paralysis. Of all the people who could have been afflicted with this debilitating ailment, Norton was the last person imaginable. He was endlessly energetic and vital. It was tragic to see his mind unaffected but his muscles and body unable to respond. He was essentially a prisoner of his body.

One of the unusual traits I always noticed about Norton throughout our long relationship was that he rarely said thank you. Near the end of his life, in 1993, he called and said he'd like to see me. Would I consider flying out to California to spend some time with him? I happily obliged. When I arrived at his bungalow at the Beverly Hills Hotel, I saw him smile gently, with a look I never forgot. "Sit down," he directed. "I asked you to come to California for one reason. I wanted to thank you for everything you did for me." His words resonated deeply. I sat down on a chair, stunned. I remember becoming quietly emotional, surprised by his graciousness. Seeing him in such a frail state, I thought this might be our last visit together, and indeed, it was.

SAUL STEINBERG

Saul Steinberg was a uniquely American success story. A businessman and financier, he was best known for founding Leasco, a computer time-share leasing company, soon after he graduated from the Wharton School at the University of Pennsylvania. He parlayed that success into an audacious acquisition of the much larger Reliance Insurance Company. His unsuccessful attempts to take over Chemical Bank and Walt Disney Productions didn't cloud his impeccable record as a visionary of American industry. He was a brilliant man and probably more well read than anyone I have ever met.

Soon after I launched my own business in 1965, Saul called me at the recommendation of a mutual friend. He knew that I was buying important works of art for private clients, and he asked if I would help him build a collection of modern art. He lived with his young family in a new home in Hewlett, Long Island. I introduced him to works by Henry Moore, Matisse, Picasso, Léger, and Giacometti, among others. He derived great joy from his acquisitions, which he valued as much as the stocks, bonds, and companies that he dealt with daily.

Saul was always interested in doing things in novel and exciting ways. And he was certainly not very subtle. One afternoon, he arrived at my office in a Mercedes stretch limousine. I had never seen one before—this was one of the first in America. He eventually moved to New York and purchased a seventeen-thousand-square-foot duplex apartment formerly owned by John D. Rockefeller Jr. at 740 Park Avenue. His first assemblage of modern European Masters was amassed over the course of more than a decade. He even surrounded himself with some of his treasures in his offices. This initial collection was soon supplanted by an astonishing number of German Expressionist works. Important examples by Kirchner, Nolde, Schiele, Pechstein, and others became an all-consuming interest. He had great curiosity in wide-ranging fields. He devoured books—in his apartment he would stack hundreds of them vertically, some even in his bedroom because he had no library shelf space left. The books were not meant for ostentatious display. He had read them all.

New York City often presents interesting architectural and logistical challenges when trying to move large works of art into residences. I remember when Saul first moved into his Park Avenue apartment, I arranged for a crane to hoist a nine-foot, almost two-ton marble carving of a standing cardinal by Giacomo Manzù onto an outdoor sculpture terrace facing east, outside the dining room. The mammoth effort started at six in the morning, and Saul accompanied me to watch the whole exercise from the street below. It was one of many such sculptures that we hoisted onto that terrace early in the morning.

One summer after Saul had acquired a vacation house in Quogue, Long Island, he asked if I would spend my free time that summer filling his home with model ships to be purchased from the greatest model ship makers in America. I visited craftsmen all over the country, many of them in New England. By the end of the summer, we had purchased more than fifty models, many of them in bottles. If I live for a thousand years, I shall never understand how to put a ship model into a bottle.

One day in the early 1980s, Saul called me to say that he now wanted to collect Old Masters. That was Saul. He asked if I might take some time to immerse myself in that world. I did, and over the course of the next two years, I helped him transition from his modern German Expressionist works to this new passion. Although I happily obliged, this was not without risk for both of us. Within the art world, Old Master paintings and drawings are frequently regarded as a treacherous commodity, since genuine works and attributions are often difficult to assess. One needs the advice of experts and scholars. Some scholars devote themselves exclusively to one artist and focus on authentication. It's no easy task.

Many of the works Saul acquired dated to the sixteenth and seventeenth centuries. They posed a major challenge. But I was glad to be able to help him acquire masterpieces by Peter Paul Rubens, Frans Hals, and other Dutch, Flemish, and Spanish Old Masters. Today, the Rubens resides in the collection of the Israel Museum.

Saul lived an extraordinary life and was undeniably the most intelligent person that I have ever known. He was truly a genius. Sadly, he suffered a series of strokes and died on December 7, 2012, at the age of seventy-three. Remarkably, his mother had died the very same day.

EDGAR BRONFMAN SR.

During the late-1960s, I received another phone call that would dramatically alter the course of my art career. Edgar Bronfman was the chief executive of Seagram's, a multinational corporation with its headquarters in the eponymous Seagram Building on Park Avenue and Fifty-Second Street in midtown Manhattan. In 1958, his family had commissioned famed architects Ludwig Mies van der Rohe and

Philip Johnson to design the special edifice. Vincent Scully frequently lectured on the landmark masterpiece in his courses at Yale.

Edgar called me to say he had heard my name as a promising young dealer with a knowledge of modern art. He asked if I might help him acquire some sculptures for the open plaza in front of the Seagram Building. It was an enormous honor, since he was a collector with a keen interest in Picasso, Henry Moore, Hans Hofmann, and Marino Marini, among others. I was continuously amazed by his knowledge and unsurpassed energy. He was an early proponent of art in public places.

In his office, we discussed his vision to adorn the headquarters' outdoor Park Avenue plaza with monumental sculptures, and we agreed on a plan. I would visit Europe during the following months to explore or commission works that would be appropriate for Edgar's unique building. He suggested an advisory fee of $25,000 to encourage me to embark on this journey and to acquire works for the company. The fee was an unusually large commission at the time, and I accepted the challenge without hesitation.

I made several trips to Europe and met directly with a number of great sculptors and painters. In my experience, the best approach is always to go directly to the source. This ensures building a rapport and long-term relationships. When I returned from my last trip, Edgar and I met again in his office. I suggested ideas for four or five major sculptures and presented renderings, photographs, and concepts. They included works by Moore, Picasso, Marini, and Calder.

A week or two later, we met again. He had disappointment written all over his face. He explained that his sister Phyllis, the family architectural guru who had suggested Mies and Johnson as the architects, had vetoed the concept of a sculpture court on Park Avenue. She believed that the plaza in front of the building could not support the weight of the sculptures because New York Central Railroad tunnels ran underneath. To this day, I still believe that she didn't want to see three-dimensional art objects compete with the building's architecture. In subsequent decades, many sculptures, some of them massive, have populated the plaza without any problems.

Edgar, a consummate gentleman, whom I still recall with the highest esteem, paid me the full fee anyway. I argued that I hadn't finished the project, but he insisted. It was a generous gesture from a special human being. This was an early lesson that I carry with me to this day: the importance of follow-through. I followed through with the project he wished to accomplish, and he in turn held up his end of the agreement. Edgar became a friend, and I worked with him on many personal acquisitions of sculptures and paintings in the ensuing years, including a Marino Marini horse, purchased from the artist, which remains one of the most stunning sculptures I have ever seen.

PAUL HAIM

During one of my early trips to Paris in the mid-1960s, I met Paul Haim when I walked into his gallery at 50 rue du Faubourg Saint-Honoré. I eventually came to consider him one of my foremost friends and mentors. Upstairs, in his second-floor office, his unique design sense and style were immediately apparent. The walls were covered in a burgundy velvet, much like the decor in my own office today. Many of the sculptures, such as those by Jean Arp, were highly polished, and his way of presenting them was magnificent.

In his private inner office, Paul had a small Picasso sculpture, *Femme debout*, sitting on his desk, the largest of a series of sculptures with the same title. I loved it immediately. We conversed for at least an hour about my future plans and my desire to become a private art dealer. He could see that I liked the Picasso sculpture but unfortunately could only pay for half of it at that time. Without hesitation, he suggested that I take it with me, send him a deposit, and pay the balance in time. As I was leaving with the sculpture in hand, I complimented him on the very sporty belt he was wearing. He explained that it was a New York City Police Department belt purchased on a trip to New York. He proceeded to take it off and hand it to me. He was a generous man, and that first day was the beginning of a special friendship that lasted four decades.

I clearly remember selling him a Matisse paper cutout, *Mimosa*, which he soon placed in a Japanese museum collection. A month later, an unexpected check arrived in the mail, with a note from him saying, "I made a successful sale and wanted to share some of my good luck with you." The message was clear: he was more than generous, which was an anomaly in the art world. There was no code that required him to share any of the resale proceeds with me. I wondered why he had so much trust in me, to which he once replied, "I sized you up the second you walked into my office. I knew who you were immediately."

Paul's family had escaped Nazi-occupied France early in the 1940s and fled to Brazil. He had to abandon his medical school studies and worked odd jobs, including as a dancer on the Copacabana Beach in Rio de Janeiro. In Rio, he met Alexandre Iolas, who would become a well-known Surrealist dealer when he returned to France after the war. I admired Paul's mobility and all his global activities. My father had encouraged me to do the same.

Paul also returned to Europe after the war and became a leading force in selling important modern art from an office in Belgium. Eventually, he would place leading works around the world. At first, he focused on wealthy Egyptian collectors who were determined to acquire works by French masters like Utrillo and Vlaminck. Shortly thereafter, he was instrumental in exploring the burgeoning modern art market in Japan and was highly respected there for the rest of his life. After he had his initials, PH, elegantly stitched onto the outside of the awning of his gallery on rue du Faubourg Saint-Honoré, the letters became an amusing reference point for Japanese dealers and collectors, who would visit his gallery and refer to it as the "Picasso House."

Paul and I shared a common affinity for many of the twentieth century's great artists, like Fernand Léger and the sculptor Auguste Rodin. My personal, lifelong passion for Léger came from Paul. With Paul's introduction, I soon met Paul Petrides, the expert on the works of the popular painter Maurice Utrillo. Petrides had compiled all the catalogs of Utrillo's work. When I asked him if he had any sculptures he would consider selling, he replied that he had one on his outdoor terrace. I wanted to wait until we arrived at the apartment to find out which sculpture it was. When we met, we discovered the elevator was broken (of course), so we walked up eight flights of stairs. There on his outdoor terrace was a Rodin *Thinker*, covered with leaves and Paris pollution. Petrides was willing to sell it to me, if I met his price and if I agreed to take it out of his apartment that very day. I agreed.

Every opportunity presents a challenge. I picked up this heavy bronze sculpture and carried it down the eight flights of steps. Somehow, I managed to avoid an injury. The next challenge was transporting it to New York. I asked the hotel concierge to help, and I purchased two tickets for my return flight: one for me and one for my Rodin seatmate, which I attempted to clean with a damp rag. At the airport, I carried it up the ramp, wrapped in a blanket, and the captain helped me put it in the seat. I had to remove the blanket to fasten the plane's seat belt. When the flight attendant came by, I told her, "He doesn't eat or drink, he just thinks." I'm not sure she found it funny, but I did. He also didn't have a passport. Now, however, when you buy a work of art in France, you have to get a passport for the work, or it will not be allowed to leave the country.

The lessons I learned from Paul Haim helped me navigate the burgeoning and expanding art market. He instilled in me a desire to always maintain high standards, and he encouraged the continued development of my critical eye. Those high standards meant a career-long focus on quality and on maintaining as impeccable a reputation as he had. I also learned to challenge myself constantly in the worlds of both painting and sculpture. Our initial meeting created a friendship that flourished for years. We spoke on the telephone several times a week, saw each other often, and did countless art deals around the world. When he died in 2006, he left me with wonderful memories of business, laughter, love, friendship, and an incomparable generosity of spirit.

Great art comes from dedicated dealers. For decades, I have been fortunate to know and work with several other colleagues and friends with international reputations. As dealers, each of them has made major contributions and has helped set the standards of excellence for innovative art, particularly Arne Glimcher and his son Marc of the Pace Gallery; Bill Acquavella and his daughter Eleanor and sons, Nicholas and Alexander, of the three-generation Acquavella Gallery; and Larry Gagosian, who now overseas sixteen gallery spaces worldwide. Giving art and artists space to flourish are essential to the creation of historic works with enduring meaning.

Over the years, I absorbed another lesson from many of the remarkable collectors whom I had the pleasure of helping: the ability to pursue two passions at once. For them, it was primarily business ventures and art. For me, art was my primary business, and fortunately it was also a passion. But one of my earliest and most enduring loves was baseball. By the late 1980s, my successes with art allowed me to become more than a spectator and devoted fan.

Baseball team ownership is a very different undertaking. Relative anonymity and discretion defined my art business; indeed, some of my more significant major art museum donations do not even have my name attached, and I prefer it that way. Professional sports team ownership is very much the opposite: the spotlight is constant and often strong. Almost everyone has an opinion, and sensational stories sell papers or are enticing online clickbait. But there is a reason why one of our greatest sports movies is called *Field of Dreams*. Baseball is for dreamers, and for nearly two decades, it indulged my dreams.

CHAPTER SEVENTEEN

LEADING OFF

"Love is the most important thing in

the world, but baseball is pretty good too."

– YOGI BERRA

When I was eight years old, I attended my first baseball game in the old Yankee Stadium with my father. It was the Yankees versus the Boston Red Sox. The sounds, smells, and sights have been etched in my brain and my heart ever since. It was love at first sight. My father and I sat high behind third base, but I thought we had the best seats in the ballpark. (One of the reasons why I so enjoyed sitting in the front row as a team owner is that I could never do that as a child; it is a special treat that never became tiresome.) Dom DiMaggio, Joe DiMaggio's brother, led off for Boston, and I recall he was wearing *glasses*! I could not imagine trying to hit a baseball coming toward you at ninety miles per hour and depending on glasses to see it well enough to hit it.

The old Yankee Stadium was a splendid ballpark, enhanced by its dazzling surface of bright green grass, an oasis in the South Bronx. Even though that first game enthralled me, I left distraught. I think it was Al Zarilla who caught what looked like a home run destined for the right field seats and secured the game for the Red Sox. The whole way home, I was inconsolable. My father, however, taught me a very important lesson. He said, "Don't worry. There's always another game." I've carried that saying with me for the rest of my life.

When I eventually owned my own Major League team, I noticed that when you lose, there is a dead silence in the clubhouse, eerily reminiscent of a morgue. When you win, the magnificent loud sounds of celebratory music pump through the clubhouse. But that's life; not surprisingly, I've always preferred the loud music.

In the world of baseball, however, having perspective is important. A season is a long haul of 162 games, making it unlike any other sport. You need a special commitment to attend 81 home games if you work for a Major League baseball team. If you don't have that commitment, a love for the game, and a willingness to make sacrifices, you should not sign on to a life in baseball. Baseball is all-encompassing, so I tried to avoid getting too exuberant with the peaks or too low with the valleys. Read a bad article about yourself or your team? Get some bad news? Miss out on an opportunity for a great trade? You can't let it get you down. There will always be another moment.

———

My modicum of success in the art world was what enabled me to pursue my passion for baseball, although throughout my almost two decades in Major League Baseball, I continued my work as a private art dealer. I formally entered professional sports in 1989 due to my friendship with the late Bobby Murcer. Bobby was the star outfield successor to the iconic Yankee star Mickey Mantle, and like Mickey, he was a fellow Oklahoman living in Oklahoma City. In the mid-1980s, Bobby was working with the Yankees, and he knew that I was considering buying a Triple-A Minor League franchise. I wanted to learn about professional baseball, and the Minor Leagues seemed to be a good place to start. When Bobby called me one day to say that Oklahoma City had a AAA team, the 89ers, and its owners, Bing and Patty Hampton (from the Cox Cable family), were considering retiring, it piqued my curiosity. I was ready for the challenge to see if my business skills from the art world would translate to baseball.

The first time I walked into the Oklahoma City offices to meet the organization, I saw a large square-shaped machine inside the main entrance. It was a fax machine. Surprisingly, sports teams were among the first to use this "advanced technology" because they had to communicate frequently and quickly with each other.

Three months later, I purchased my first professional baseball team and my first fax machine. I acquired the team with two partners, friends who wanted to join me. Although owning a professional baseball team was exciting, it certainly was not without risks, to my finances and my reputation. But I have long believed that one should never be afraid to take risks. This lesson has served me well on many occasions, but never more so than in my initial leap into professional baseball.

The team's general manager, Jim Weigel, had been one of the competing bidders and had fought aggressively to acquire the 89ers, driving the price up considerably. Normally one would be livid toward someone who bid the price up, but I soon realized he was talented, knew the Oklahoma City market, and was exactly the continuity this franchise needed. I kept him on as the general manager, which turned out to be a wise decision. We remain friends to this day. I made Bobby Murcer the team's president. I knew he was a wonderful man, and I felt that he was well respected in the community and could be an important asset.

At the same time the sale was being completed in Oklahoma City, Braniff Airways ceased operations, essentially shutting down the only direct flight from New York City to Oklahoma City. For me, this meant the beginning of an endless series of cross-country flights, with only one connection through Dallas. Several times per month, I endured a seven-hour journey to the middle of the country in pursuit of my newfound passion. It makes me laugh when I think that I was able to travel to Paris and back more quickly than it took me to fly one-way to see my Oklahoma City 89ers. But it was worth it.

At that point, I was traveling to Europe for my art business and traveling all over America for baseball as well. I got to know the people working in the concession stands, the grounds crew, the clubhouse kids, and especially the young, talented players hoping to "make it" to the Major Leagues. I also met George W. Bush, then the general partner of the Texas Rangers—the 89ers were the AAA team for the Rangers—and later the US president. And while the Major League parent club controlled the signing of players, by working with their talented farm director Marty Scott and general manager Tom Grieve, I was able to encourage several signings, including Steve Balboni, who played a crucial role in our championship victory in 1992. (Steve, who had been a slugger for both the Yankees and Kansas City before spending three years with the 89ers, is one of the nicest men I ever met in the game.)

At the formal closing, Patty Hampton was joined by some of her partners. When I walked into the boardroom, I immediately recognized Allie Reynolds. Allie was a Native American who had pitched for the Yankees in the late 1940s and early 1950s, and he was one of my father's heroes. After the sale, he remained with us as a fan. His health was deteriorating, and when he could no longer negotiate the steps to the skybox, we bought a large, comfortable chair and had four people carry him up and down the flight of steps for every game he wanted to attend. I was grateful to be able to extend this bit of comfort to him, recalling my wonderful memories of watching Allie play, with my father seated beside me.

Early on, I wanted to put in place people I knew and could trust to help me run the organization. My wonderful daughter, Nancy, had a job in New York working with the Roundabout Theatre, but we needed someone in Oklahoma City to help with marketing and events for the team. As George Steinbrenner once told me, the most important thing was putting "fannies in the seats." Nancy's skills were perfect for building a successful baseball organization, so she moved to Oklahoma City, where she also became my eyes and ears for nearly everything about the team.

Shortly after her move, Nancy and I had a lively conversation about baseball. Never much of a baseball fan in the past, she started off saying, "Have you been following what Steve Balboni is doing? He's been on a tear." Nonfans or even casual observers don't usually speak baseball jargon, and right then, I knew she was committed to the game. Nancy was excellent in her marketing role and in her dedication. She was a Beach Boys fan, and for one of our promotional events, they played a concert at the ballpark. Nancy organized it all. It was a huge success, but she barely got to enjoy the show.

———

Oklahoma City presented a unique set of challenges. The All-Sports Stadium, an old 1930s ballpark, was in dire need of renovation. We commissioned a study to find out why fans were not attending the games. Much to my dismay, I discovered that very few women came. When I inspected the stadium, the problem was clear. The women's bathrooms were outdated, filthy, and outfitted with some kind of contraption from the 1930s that was apparently meant to serve as a toilet. I immediately had the two big bathrooms on both sides of the stadium on every level replaced and modernized, at my own expense. Details matter. That winter, rather than talking about prospects for the team, I talked about the new bathrooms, and guess what? Women started coming to our games.

One of the treats of Minor League Baseball is that it offers a somewhat relaxed atmosphere compared to Major League Baseball. Early that first year, Bobby Murcer approached me and suggested, "Why don't you go out and shag some flies during afternoon batting practice? You still look like you can go out there and mix it up." So, I made the misguided decision to go to the clubhouse, put on a uniform, and try to blend into the scenery in right field. How wrong I was. Juan González, who was later called up from our team with great fanfare by the Texas Rangers, hit a towering fly ball that started to descend in my direction. It was almost as if I were seeing three baseballs, and I focused my attention on the one in the middle.

The actual ball landed two feet from me with a loud thud, which thoroughly entertained players and onlookers from the team. As you pass your prime as an athlete, you lose your three-dimensional perspective and your sense of timing. That was the beginning and the end of my short and uncelebrated Minor League playing experience. Father Time is about the only one who never misses a ball.

On another occasion, I learned something about the customs of baseball etiquette. Stump Merrill, who had managed the Yankees from 1990 to 1991, was now managing their AAA team, the Columbus Clippers. One weekend, the Clippers came to play in Oklahoma City, and I witnessed first hand chewing tobacco's unique role in the sport. (This was at a time when little was known about the deleterious effects of smokeless tobacco.) Stump and I, along with Bobby Murcer and our general manager, walked into the clubhouse to discuss the latest league gossip. The four of us sat, facing each other. As we talked, Stump proceeded to chew and then spit out his tobacco juice, aiming at a receptacle that he had placed in the center of the room. His first ten shots made it into the spittoon, but his last one most certainly did not. It sprayed all over the brand-new white rug that I had just installed, and all eyes turned to me. I laughed it off, much to their relief.

The 89ers had a talented infielder, Ray Sánchez, who later played for the Yankees. He sometimes preferred taking additional batting practice *in* the clubhouse rather than in the batting cage on the field. Smashing baseballs against the painted plaster walls didn't improve the décor, and the clubhouse eventually looked like a disaster zone. Between the spittoon and indoor batting practice, I faced a few interior design challenges, which were quite different from the world of art, although my passion for beautiful things also inspired me to get involved in many of the club details, including the team brand, logo, and uniforms.

In late August of 1992, Hurricane Andrew devastated South Florida, where many of us had personal ties from baseball's preseason. I decided to mobilize our franchise to help. We made the playoffs that year, and I proposed that fans bring canned goods for the hurricane victims in exchange for complimentary playoff tickets. Right from the outset, I was told Oklahoma City was a sleepy town and that once the September football season began, nobody cared much about baseball. The ballpark held fourteen thousand people, and, at our first playoff game, we had seventeen thousand fans in attendance, with cars lined along Interstate 44. The fire chief was somewhat agitated, telling me we were in violation of the fire codes. I explained that all these people had brought canned goods for the hurricane victims in Florida, and I asked him to help us out for a couple of hours. With a full ballpark on that beautiful day, and for the two other playoff games, we collected and donated almost forty thousand cans of food for the Florida relief effort.

———

One of the singular pleasures of a life in baseball is meeting unique characters along the way. Tommy Thompson was such a man. A baseball lifer, he began his career as an infielder with the St. Louis Cardinals farm system in 1967. For several decades, he managed, coached, and scouted in the Minor Leagues for various organizations, including managing our team when it won the American Association Championship in 1992. Tommy was very fond of telling his players, "Boys, we only have one more mountain to climb." In our final playoff series against the heavily favored Buffalo Bisons, we unexpectedly won the first three games in Oklahoma City and then our fourth in Buffalo and with it the AAA American Association Championship.

Many years later, when I owned the Marlins, I brought Tommy to Florida after he was diagnosed with multiple sclerosis, because of his expertise in teaching young players the intricacies and subtleties of baseball and how to have genuine respect for the game. His player development skills were unsurpassed, and from his wheelchair, he imparted great wisdom in our Major League clubhouse. Early on, I promised him that he would have a job as long as I owned the team. Sadly, when the new owners took over, he was terminated, but I will always remain grateful for what he did for my teams in Oklahoma and Florida.

Because the Texas Rangers were Oklahoma City's Major League affiliation, I was fortunate to develop a close relationship with George W. Bush, who was then an owner and general partner of the Rangers. Shortly after our championship victory, I called to offer him a championship ring, but he said he hadn't done anything to deserve it. I will always remember his sense of humor and gracious humility, which displayed themselves on more than one occasion and which were so characteristic of his entire family.

In the summer of 1993, soon after winning that AAA championship, I decided to participate in a bankruptcy court-ordered auction to buy the Baltimore Orioles. The Orioles had both a storied history and a new state-of-the-art stadium, Camden Yards, which showcased new ways to reinvent ballpark architecture and the fan experience. For me, it was an appealing entrance into the Major Leagues.

There were three serious bidders, including Bill DeWitt (the extraordinary future principal owner of the St. Louis Cardinals), Peter Angelos (the eventual victor in the auction), and me and my group, which included several New York businessmen and friends. We were prepared to pay $150 million and no more, but by the time the bidding got to that amount I received some unexpected motivation to make additional bids. As the auction reached $145 million, I overheard Peter saying, "Who the hell is that guy on the other end of the table?" That fueled my competitive spirit. He also kept telling everybody prior to the auction that I would move the team out of Baltimore, which was simply not true. At that point I made the strategic decision that even though I hadn't planned to go higher, I would continue bidding. I got the price up to $172 million and then stopped. By then, Peter had his answer to who the guy on the other end of the table was. It was an inauspicious start to our relationship, but over the arc of time I came to admire Peter greatly. Today, he and his extremely bright sons, who still own the Orioles, are a very positive presence in the game.

It's astonishing how things have changed since that surreal day. Then, we were three groups in a very public courthouse venue, and the process was entirely controlled by the bankruptcy court. In baseball today, the league exerts much more influence on anything relating to a franchise control transfer or outright sale. The disparity between that Baltimore experience in 1993 and what happened in 2012, when Frank McCourt sold the Dodgers to Guggenheim Partners led by Mark Walter, is the latest step in changing the process to where both the commissioner's office and the league owners are the final decision makers.

———

In 1994, tragedy struck my family. My sister and her husband died in a private plane crash in Alabama. I put my dream of owning a Major League baseball team on hold. I avoided the limelight and devoted several years to trying to care for her family. But in 1998, I learned that the general partner of the Montreal Expos, Claude Brochu, was selling his controlling interest in the team. As a rule, general partners control the team's destiny, and each Major League team has one designated general partner. If Major League Baseball or the limited partners in Canada had found anyone else to buy out his shares, I would have never been attached to Montreal. Even though the owners' group was composed of ten of the wealthiest and most prominent men and corporations in Canada, including Bell Canada, Loblaws, and the Desjardins Group (Canada's largest federation of credit unions), none of the existing owners wanted to acquire Brochu's $18 million portion. So, I purchased his minority controlling interest and percentage in the team. I spoke French, had some new ideas, and planned on bringing plenty of energy to this endeavor. Even prior to my arrival, the Montreal market was challenging because revenues and fan support were limited; however, I was focused solely on the opportunity to do something positive for baseball.

I have always appreciated challenges, whether they be pursuing a work of art, a baseball player, or, in this case, a franchise. From day one, I approached this involvement with the intent of improving the situation and embracing my new partners. I started with the philosophy that we were all in this together, and all of us would collectively invest in the team and take the long view to achieve success. I believed we could give fans a special experience and improve the team's performance by raising the payroll and eliminating the practice of constantly trading players. Unfortunately, my partners didn't share my view, and we got off on the wrong foot right at the start.

Just as I had enjoyed working with my daughter in Oklahoma City, I was keen to have a member of my family involved with the Major League franchise. My son David was thirty-two years old and a rising star at Morgan Stanley in New York. But he enthusiastically agreed to join me in this adventure. My father had identified him as a special talent very early on when he was about six years old, saying, "That boy should go to law school," which he eventually did. David was young, but also highly knowledgeable, energetic, and articulate, which didn't sit well with the Canadian partners. The first thing they objected to was his title, so I changed it from president to senior vice president. But the title didn't matter. David was still responsible for the day-to-day operations of the team and reported directly to me.

I was concerned with a myriad of issues from day one. It soon became clear that the environment in Montreal had additional challenges that made it not particularly hospitable to baseball. Anticipation is a critical skill for any leader—being able to see around corners to predict what is coming next is paramount. One of the first major issues involved television rights: instead of the broadcast media paying the ball club for the rights to televise its games, the stations were asking for the team to pay for the right to use their airwaves. It was backward, but they wouldn't budge. So, we made the difficult decision to take the team off broadcast television.

Prior to the purchase, the Canadian limited partners and Brochu also told me they had secured financing for a new stadium, and they promised that they had excellent architectural plans. But when I showed their plans and model to my friend, the world-renowned architect Richard Meier, he was immediately concerned. The broad conception seemed very unstable, and there were no accompanying structural drawings or engineering calculations. They also lacked a serious site plan for the new stadium. I was learning that business was approached differently up north.

Although I was a minority owner, as the controlling general partner, I took the lead in running the franchise, but there was constant conflict with the other partners. Before agreeing to purchase Brochu's share, I had explained my plans to raise the Expos' payroll from $17 million to $31 million to retain the players we needed. I thought Montreal fans were weary of their team being treated more like a Minor League team to supply US-based Major League teams with their great players. The partners initially had agreed to raise the payroll. But when the time came to provide the money to pay the players, not only did they fail to meet their obligations, they repeatedly ignored requests and phone calls for nearly a year. I had made a commitment to the players, so I paid the entire sum of money myself. That, however, only inflamed the situation. Coming from the United States, I was already viewed suspiciously. Now, because I was shouldering the full cost, I was also by default amassing a larger share of the team, as was clearly specified in the partnership agreement that we had all agreed to and signed.

The math behind this agreement was both basic and clear. If the team needed to raise additional funds, and one or more of the partners refused to contribute, their overall financial stake in the team would shrink after the extra money was raised. By refusing to contribute to the costs of operating the team and forcing me to shoulder the entire load, the financial math meant that by 2002, I owned almost 95 percent of the franchise. Investing in the Expos would bring life to the franchise and increase the value of the team for all the partners, but to use the old expression, my partners didn't want to "play ball."

Why they would not honor their earlier commitment, made as part of our original partnership agreement, is anyone's guess. They may have concluded that it was pouring good money after bad, given their prior experiences and their fear that Major League Baseball would dissolve the team. But I had a different philosophy: I have always felt that one should do it right or don't do it at all.

Months later, one of the limited partners, Pierre Michaud, an executive from the Loblaws food chain, approached me in the team suite prior to an evening game and asked me if the partners could buy back their shares at their initial percentage, after I had invested my own money and the shares had been diluted. When I politely declined, he furiously wedged himself in front of my face and said, "You know you really have to do this. We don't like Americans up here, and by the way, we don't like Jews." I was dumbfounded but not entirely surprised. I turned around, walked out, and never spoke to him again. To this day, I am still amazed by the gall and hubris of my Montreal "partners."

CHAPTER EIGHTEEN

MIAMI

> "Miami is the gateway to Latin America
>
> and is the perfect venue for a global game."
>
> – ROB MANFRED

In January 2000, I attended my first owners' meeting in Phoenix, Arizona. In retrospect, it was one of the most historic gatherings in Major League Baseball's history. As luck would have it, this was the meeting at which the owners collectively agreed to create and fund Baseball Advanced Media (BAM), which would become MLB Advanced Media, a limited partnership of all club owners. As the internet and interactive arm of baseball, it manages the league's official website, MLB.com. It offers statistics, news, and standings to the more than four million hits it receives each day. Subscriptions to MLB.com provide viewers with access to live video and access to most games, as well as to everything baseball, from statistics, schedules, and news. The platform became a multibillion-dollar enterprise, the single most successful league-owned digital company, and the envy of sports leagues everywhere.

Five months later in May 2000, as part of the collective bargaining negotiations with the Major League players union, Major League Baseball began discussing "contraction," which was a polite way of saying that four teams were being considered for elimination, largely due to their precarious financial positions. The four teams

OPPOSITE PAGE: *The makings of a winning team: Star catcher Pudge Rodríguez tags out J. T. Snow in the first round of the playoffs in the 2003 National League Divsion Series.*

259

were Montreal, Tampa Bay, Minnesota, and Florida. Fewer teams meant less national revenue to share. At that meeting with all thirty owners present, I read a statement declaring that, as an owner of the Expos, I had no wish to exit baseball, and I didn't find the proposed solution equitable, but I was more than willing to collaborate to find a mutually beneficial solution. Potentially the easiest one, moving the Expos to another geographic market, was not feasible, since that would result in too great a financial windfall for me as a new owner. I very much understood that, and we all tried to think of another potential solution for the industry.

Commissioner Bud Selig, to his credit, had vision. Even though his good friend Charles Bronfman, who used to own the Montreal franchise, often said that Montreal was a great Major League market, Bud recognized that baseball needed a change. In Montreal, only minimal sponsorship revenue was available, the free ticket requests were substantial, and both the current and long-term situation were not sustainable.

It became clear to me that contraction was partly a negotiating ploy by the league. I wasn't sure how this very complex and intricate process would resolve, but during my life, I had learned to thrive with uncertainty and to occasionally expect the unexpected. A group of us met often with Bob DuPuy, then president and chief operating officer of Major League Baseball. Bob was, and remains, a brilliant, well-organized executive and a special human being. We discussed the creative potential of an unusual and novel three-way franchise trade, which to my knowledge had never been done before in baseball or any other major sport. I would agree to sell the Expos back to Major League Baseball, and it would control the team's destiny and do with the team as it saw fit. Major League Baseball would then also sell one of its other franchises to the current Florida Marlins owner John Henry, and as he exited Florida, I would assume control of the Marlins franchise.

The first sale candidate was the California Angels, owned by singer Gene Autry's estate. John Henry had originally entertained the idea of purchasing the Angels, but after much negotiation, the deal never materialized. Henry felt this California club didn't have a good enough team or a strong enough Minor League system to win in the foreseeable future, so he rejected that option. In fact, the Angels went on to win the World Series in 2002, the very next year. So much for accurate predictions in baseball.

Then, the Yawkey Foundation in Boston announced that it was planning to sell the Red Sox. As in any franchise decision, the power and approval for a sale rests exclusively with all the owners of MLB teams and the commissioner's office. A sale can be negotiated, but if twenty-three of the thirty team owners and the commissioner don't approve it, then it simply does not happen. Even when a franchise is passed from one generation to another, this same process is followed.

The third team in play was the Florida Marlins. It was well known that the Marlins had lackluster fan support and minimal local television revenue. The team played in Broward County, in a football stadium that it shared with the Miami Dolphins. Frankly, the situation sounded quite similar to the Expos imbroglio. But baseball was in my blood. Since college, I had dreamed of creating a successful Major League team and one day winning a World Series, and I refused to abandon my dream.

In the fall of 2001, I agreed to sell the Expos to Major League Baseball for $120 million, but at the last minute, John Henry would not agree to a $120 million sale price for the Marlins, an even swap. Instead, he demanded $158.5 million. We would not budge and neither would he. This stalemate led to some creative thinking on the part of everyone involved, including Bob DuPuy.

The result was a transaction unprecedented in Major League Baseball or in any other professional sport. Our arrangement involved the implementation of a note (Major League Baseball had never loaned a team money). I was able to take the $120 million from selling the Expos back to the league, transfer it to John Henry, add a $38.5 million note, and acquire the Marlins. Henry would then take his $158.5 million and be "allowed" to win the auction for the Red Sox. The $38.5 million note was tied to a few triggers, such as whether we could build and move into a new ballpark in Miami in the next five years. If we didn't, we would pay the note back over ten years, interest-free, starting ten years afterward. It was a risk I was willing to take.

All through the off-season, the parties negotiated this complicated three-way franchise swap. The contract with the Marlins and the Red Sox finally closed on February 15, 2002, the exact day that spring training began. It came down to one final detail: the Florida Marlins would keep the team bus! Our clubhouse manager was driving north on the Florida turnpike and didn't know whether he should report for spring training duty in Jupiter, where the Expos played, or in Viera to the north. It turned out to be the Marlins in Viera for 2002.

Part of this complicated understanding allowed me to keep a mix of both Expos and Marlins employees. We replaced a few of the Marlins executives with our own very competent group from Montreal, including Claude Delorme, P. J. Loyello, and some of the baseball operations executives. Michel Bussiere, a former Expos executive, became the Marlins' chief financial officer. Bussiere and Delorme, among others, later helped deliver a Miami stadium that was on time and under budget, a rarity in baseball stadium construction. That new stadium won numerous LEED (green) awards for environmental responsibility, which I had insisted upon during the planning of the new facility.

In sum, the unprecedented historic swap was a win for all parties. But the transaction was not without controversy. Some people in Boston didn't think Henry had won the bid fairly. However, he subsequently won the hearts of Boston fans by bringing them their first World Series Championship in eighty-six years. Then, on September 29, 2004, MLB announced that the Montreal franchise would relocate to Washington, DC, for the 2005 season, a transfer that has proven to be very successful for the industry and for the owners. The fees paid by the new Washington owners were shared by all thirty Major League teams. Ted Lerner and his extremely capable family took their mission to return baseball to the nation's capital very seriously and operated the Nationals in a highly professional manner. The Washington Nationals have flourished in their new stadium and even won a World Series in 2019.

When I arrived in Miami in February 2002, I confronted a difficult situation. John Henry had evidently had one foot out the door for two years. In addition, the highly competent and respected Dave Dombrowski, who had been general manager of the Marlins franchise since its inception, had left for Detroit. Without him, the organization was not functioning well, and the team headquarters looked like a ghost town. From time to time, the tense situation was enough to make me wonder, *What is it all for?* But my love of the game kept me there.

Meanwhile, our penurious former Canadian partners were clearly embarrassed and sought to take out their frustrations through the courts. They filed a Racketeer Influenced and Corrupt Organizations Act lawsuit (RICO) against me that had no basis in legal precedent, but it triggered a two-year arbitration process. David handled this lawsuit, moving from Miami to New York for six months to prepare for the case.

We proved that the Canadian owners had not contributed the previously agreed-upon funds for their pro rata shares, as specified in the partnership agreement, which they had all signed. Their money was needed to run the ball club, and without it, I personally had to make up the difference. During the arbitration, the Canadians never provided a satisfactory answer to the arbitrators about their abdication of their contractual duties.

Jeffrey Kessler, a well-known sports attorney, was counsel for the Canadians. But he was no match for our Proskauer attorneys, Brad Ruskin and Wayne Katz. Kessler failed to win a single argument, score an important counterpoint, or garner a sustained objection. The Canadians thought that by suing us they would save face, but they ended up embarrassing themselves further. The narrative in the Canadian media was that the most sophisticated people in the province of Quebec got hoodwinked by a New York art dealer and his thirty-seven-year-old son. But I knew that the real narrative was that they didn't honor our written partnership agreement, and the

Canadians ultimately lost the case on every single count. Although our intentions were always good in Montreal, I must confess my satisfaction with the final legal result.

In Miami, I wanted someone I could trust to oversee the day-to-day business, so I asked David to assume the role of president of the Marlins. Jeff Torborg came to Florida from Montreal as our first manager. We were also joined by some of our Montreal coaches and training staff, including bullpen catcher Pierre Arsenault, now a gifted scout. The highly respected John Silverman continued in Miami as our very capable and professional equipment manager.

I spent 2002 getting to know the players, coaches, and operations and conducting an overall talent assessment. I saw something special in my new team. We made marginal improvements and viewed the year as a time to prepare for 2003. But when the 2003 season started off poorly (16 wins vs. 22 losses), even with the players we had added, I grew concerned. After much thought and discussion, I spoke to Jeff Torborg, and he agreed that a new manager would doubtless be better for all of us. Changing managers is never an easy decision, and I was fond of Torborg. But we both knew we needed new blood.

So, in May I embarked on a listening tour within the organization and sought advice and thoughts from many of our executives. I walked into the office of Bill Beck, our much-respected traveling secretary, who had been in baseball for a long time. I asked him, "What are we doing wrong here, and what do we need to do?" He offered one name, a "real fixer-upper," as he put it: Jack McKeon. In 2000, Jack had turned around the Cincinnati Reds, almost getting the team to the playoffs that year. Perhaps he could have even more success with our extremely talented but thus far underachieving group of players. Jack had recently been let go by the Reds and was spending most of his time smoking cigars and mowing his lawn at his home in Elon, North Carolina.

I arranged an incognito lunch meeting with Jack at the Rascal House, then in North Miami, which was away from the stadium, in the hope that we would be inconspicuous and not elicit rumors. I arrived to see what appeared to be an elderly man, sitting on a bench outside the restaurant on Collins Avenue, wearing a plaid jacket, a plaid shirt, and plaid tie, none of them in harmony with the other. I said "Jack?" He looked me squarely in the face and replied loudly, "Jerry?" Admittedly not a great first impression, but it didn't bother me. We still laugh about it to this day.

"Trader Jack," as he was affectionately called, proved to be remarkable. Our general manager, Larry Beinfest, and David joined me, and we had a magical afternoon of baseball conversation tucked away in a rear booth at the Rascal House. Jack had been around the game for a long time, having worked for a number of owners, including the renegade Charlie Finley in Oakland and the eccentric Marge Schott in Cincinnati. He had his own views and was never shy about sharing them.

Jack, seventy-three years *young*, won me over, and I hired him a few hours later. We signed him on a Friday, and he came to the ballpark on Sunday morning. He sat in the clubhouse at the old Joe Robbie Stadium, and players kept coming over to me thinking the "old man" in the corner might be my father. I just kept telling everyone, "You will find out who he is." As I began speaking to the assembled group, I talked about Jack's background and how respected he was. I encouraged them not to be misled by his "full head of gray hair." Jack came to the microphone next, looked every-body over, smiled, and then said, "This train is heading north. If you're gonna play for me, you're gonna have to leave your fucking egos at the door." There was a startled, dead silence for at least thirty seconds. Jack had made an indelible impression on these young players, and on me as well.

He proceeded to talk about his philosophy of running a ball club, and immediately the entire team wanted to play for him. We got some credit in one or two places for hiring a man who was in his seventies. By the time he won the World Series later in the season, he was the oldest manager in the history of the game to accomplish that feat. Jack would arrive at the ballpark early and do his "exercises" by briskly walking around the warning track that ran along the perimeter of the field a couple of times in his running shorts, holding a cigar. His definition of a workout was well suited to him.

———

At midseason, we brought in some special players. Our first trade was for the pitcher Ugueth Urbina, who was playing for the Texas Rangers. We needed a closer with real experience. He had been my closer in Montreal and had a unique approach to game-day preparation. During games, he would go to the clubhouse and sleep until the sixth inning; then he'd wake up refreshed and head to the bullpen. Nobody was allowed to disturb Uggi. It was unconventional behavior, but he performed and delivered. He had the guts of a bullfighter and the guile of a chess master.

In order to get Urbina from Texas, the Rangers wanted our first-round pick from the prior year and a Minor League hopeful. We reluctantly gave up our draft pick Adrián González to have a shot at winning the pennant, and maybe more. Adrián is a special individual, athlete, and human being, but we had to take that chance. It's always difficult to give up good players. To win at the negotiating table, you need to take risks, and you have to give to get. Often, that involves making hard decisions. Jack's mantra was, "Do you wanna win a World Series, or do you wanna protect Minor League hopeful prospects?" He was right. I instructed our general manager, Larry Beinfest, to make the trade.

Even before Jack had signed on, and just before spring training began, I told Larry that we had some great young pitching arms, but we had no stability behind home plate. We badly needed a first-rate catcher. The Rangers hadn't re-signed Iván "Pudge" Rodríguez (a future Hall of Famer), whose stock had faded in the minds of many scouts. He was a free agent. Larry speculated that Rodríguez's career might be over because of possible back injuries. I disagreed. I felt the only thing wrong was our inability to take a risk and make a decision; I had learned years before that hesitation can be a detriment.

I called Rodríguez's agent, Scott Boras, and negotiated a one-year contract. The $10 million price tag may have seemed exorbitant, but having great young pitchers meant we needed a commanding defensive presence behind home plate.

When Pudge struggled with his offense, he went AWOL from the team for two days to go see his old hitting coach Rudy Jaramillo in Texas. Jack McKeon didn't like that, and after Pudge returned to the team Jack benched him. But Jack was nothing if not fair. He was never afraid to take a pitcher off the mound, even in the middle of a pitch count. If you weren't making the effort, he would remove you from the game. When Hanley Ramirez once made a half-hearted effort to retrieve a ball in the outfield, Jack stormed onto the field and theatrically escorted him to the dugout. It didn't matter who you were. That's who Jack is. He has exceptionally high baseball standards. He demanded that individual players not ruin anything for the team, nor for themselves. You had to show up and be willing to give your best. If you did that, Jack could inspire and motivate you like no one else.

One of the special players we brought up on that 2003 team was Dontrelle Willis. He was a young rookie in spring training in the Minor Leagues, but he was different from anyone I had seen before in baseball. He made his presence felt at once. He was a unique personality, with energy and character, unorthodox pitching mechanics, and a great understanding of the game. To witness him repeatedly fool batters with his windup was astonishing. For me, he was probably the Fernando Valenzuela of his generation. I remember meeting his remarkable mother, whose strong work ethic as a welder on the San Francisco–Oakland Bay Bridge was equally impressive. It was obvious that she had instilled good values in this young man and passed her work ethic on to him, and I respected that. He was a real student of the sport and had a joy for playing the game and for simply being around the ballpark.

Dontrelle once came to me in the parking lot, adjacent to the stadium, and showed me his new car, a 1956 Chevy. I recall he turned on his music, blasting the speakers from his trunk, as the car vibrated, creating the effect of a moving circus. When he opened the trunk, I must admit to never having seen so many electronic gadgets and so much high-powered machinery in such a small space. As he showed me every element, what I saw was the delight of a young man who had finally made it. Music was his outlet, apart from making batters look foolish. He has gone on to have a very successful broadcasting career, which should come as no surprise to anyone who knew him on the field and off.

Miguel Cabrera, a third baseman in our AA Minor League affiliate, was another talented and prized player we brought up at midseason during our championship run. I always watched and studied our Minor League players on the back fields during spring training in order to make a note of developing players with future promise. When one of our outfielders was injured during the season, we scoured our Minor League system for a replacement. I asked about Cabrera, who was playing for the Carolina Mudcats, our Double-A affiliate. Larry Beinfest told me that he had done well offensively, but he wasn't an outfielder. I reasoned that in baseball, until you get pigeonholed as a position player, you grow up playing positions all over the field. I asked Larry to arrange to put Cabrera in the outfield to see how well he would perform.

Three days later I went to Larry and asked what Cabrera had done. "He caught three fly balls without a problem," he said. That was good enough for me, and I made the decision to encourage bringing him up. In his first Major League game as a pinch hitter, his very first hit was a ball that sailed over the centerfield wall for a walk-off home run and won the game for us. After that, he played left field and became an integral part of our championship team. I can't wait to see him in the Hall of Fame.

Prior to 2003 I recall saying to our team executives, "The guy who tortures us the most in baseball is Juan Pierre in Colorado. Why don't we try to trade for him?" Nobody wanted to do that because we already had Luis Castillo as our leadoff hitter. I said, "So what?" As I have maintained, people and situations are too often put into boxes and constrained by the past. Changes to the norm can be helpful. (It was a similar situation to Miguel Cabrera.) It is often easy for baseball executives to hinder themselves by following a formula, sometimes to the detriment of the team. I was trying to reevaluate our needs. For me, Juan Pierre represented speed. Speed makes pitchers uncomfortable by putting pressure on them at the top of the lineup with good hitters behind the leadoff batter. So, it made sense to try something new, and I encouraged our executives to do that and make the trade with the Rockies. We would now have two leadoff hitters at the top of the lineup to "set the table."

The last piece of the World Series Championship puzzle fell into place at midnight on July 31, at the trading deadline. We brought Jeff "Mr. Marlin" Conine back from Baltimore to Miami, where he had started his career. We all knew of his reputation for being a true professional and had often seen him play. The trade was completed with one minute to spare. The fact that he had helped win a World Series for the Florida Marlins in 1997 only made it sweeter when we won the World Series with him in 2003.

There we had it: the ingredients for a potentially magical team—and a magical run to October.

CHAPTER NINETEEN

DECISION-MAKING UNDER PRESSURE

PURSUING THE CHAMPIONSHIP

> "The ballplayer who loses his head, who can't
>
> keep his cool, is worse than no ballplayer at all."
>
> – LOU GEHRIG

For the entire second half of 2003, the Marlins were the hottest team in baseball. But the baseball season is a long and constant grind, and players are subject to fatigue. At the end of a lengthy road trip to the West Coast, I could see that team morale was low. We had lost some nail-biting games, including one to a Todd Helton walk-off home run in Colorado in the bottom of the ninth inning. We then went to San Francisco and continued to struggle. Our next stop was Pittsburgh, but we had a day off prior to starting that three-game series. I asked our traveling secretary, Bill Beck, to call the pilot to see if we could land the plane in Las Vegas for a few hours. Word came back that the pilot had agreed. I'm not sure why I chose Las Vegas, but I knew I wanted to regain our momentum in a spontaneous and fun way.

When everyone had boarded, I asked for the team's attention. Over the plane's loudspeaker I inquired, "Is there anybody here who would object if we stop in Las Vegas for some fun for a few hours?" Not a peep of objection. When we arrived in Las Vegas, Juan Pierre, our most conservative, mature, and responsible player, later remarked

OPPOSITE PAGE: *Official Florida Marlins 2003 World Series Championship ring.* 273

that he worked too hard for his money and was not going to gamble it away. So, I joined him in a coffee shop while his teammates and coaches tried their luck at the gaming tables. Jack McKeon was a big winner that night, and I think Mike Lowell and Pudge were successful as well. Miguel Cabrera did not participate, as he was not old enough to gamble legally, even in Las Vegas. In my eyes, though, he was always a big winner.

After several entertaining hours, we returned to the team bus; we needed to leave by midnight to make our airport departure slot for Pittsburgh. Everyone was accounted for, except one player. We were going to leave in five minutes without him, but he showed up huffing and puffing and with a huge smile on his face. Apparently, he had elected not to join his teammates at the gaming tables but had found success elsewhere. Our stop in Las Vegas helped us regain our momentum.

We won the Wild Card spot by two and a half games. The three division leaders in the National and American Leagues made the playoffs for the first round. The fourth Wild Card spot was for the team with the best record in three divisions, after these three leaders. That team was the Marlins.

The Marlins won the first round of the playoffs against the San Francisco Giants, winning the third of five games at home in Miami when Jeff Conine made a memorable throw from left field to Pudge Rodríguez at home plate to prevent J. T. Snow from scoring. Even before the ball hit Pudge's glove, Urbina came running in from the mound completely elated and jumped on Pudge. I was thankful the umpire had already called the play, since I feared Urbina would knock the ball right out of Pudge's glove in his excitement. I rushed down to the field to see the players and had my shirt partially torn off my back by the jubilant fans as we exited the stadium. It was a moment to savor! All three men—Rodríguez, Urbina, and Conine, plus Miguel Cabrera, Dontrelle Willis, and manager Jack McKeon—had joined us during the season. Some of the executives had been reluctant to add these talented players during the year, but I wanted to create new chemistry. I got lucky.

We didn't play very well at the start of the National League playoffs' second round against the Chicago Cubs, and we were down three games to one. But when Josh Beckett pitched the fifth game in Miami, our prospects improved. He was his usual superstar self. We emerged victorious and flew to Chicago to continue the series. The feeling of being at Wrigley Field under those circumstances was as if I had stepped into a creation by one of my Surrealist painters. It seemed like pure imagination. Things happened that made no sense. One could never write a script to match it.

The sixth game on October 14 featured an infamous foul ball. Mike Mordecai hit a ball just behind third base toward the outfield stands, where Steve Bartman, a Cubs fan, was sitting in his front-row seat facing left field. Bartman was blamed for reaching to catch the ball and thus preventing Cubs outfielder Moises Alou from making the catch. But the replays told a different story. Watching the tape, it was clear that Alou would not have been able to catch the ball because of the angle in which it landed in the stands. It was impossible to jump that high vertically and then move horizontally, as he would have had to do, to make the catch. For years, Bartman was chastised for his enthusiasm. A ground-ball error on the next play by the Cubs shortstop Alex Gonzalez (not to be confused with the Marlins shortstop of the same name) opened the floodgates. We continued to score and won the ball game.

The Marlins won the final game of the National League Championship Series, 9 runs to 6, securing the pennant. Our center fielder, Juan Pierre, who exhibited quiet leadership by example and was always the consummate professional, made the most joyous noise I'd ever heard from him, exclaiming, "We shocked the world, we shocked the world," as he ran toward the infield. That image has been replayed over and over as one of Major League Baseball's iconic moments. I will never forget the tiny, crowded visitors' clubhouse after the game. As I was climbing its steps, I saw the Cubs general manager, Andy MacPhail, who had come to congratulate me. Even while distraught from the loss and the weight of a nearly century-old Cubs championship drought, he could not have been more gracious. That's who he is.

Our clubhouse celebration was led by Pudge, who had his arm around Jack and was showering champagne on anyone he could reach, enthusiastically yelling, "We're gonna win a World Series for you, Jack. I've never won anything, but we are going to do this for you!" Pudge was wildly excited and felt we could do no wrong. He was completely convinced that we would win the World Series. He was in a unique "zone" that postseason, focused and determined. This was the same player whom many had written off as not healthy enough to keep playing. Instead, he would go on to play for Detroit, New York, Washington, and Texas. He became a first-round ballot Hall of Famer. I am happy knowing that I had a role in contributing to his lengthy career and to his only World Series ring.

At the beginning of this truly magical season, no one could have predicted that we would be taking the field in Yankee Stadium for the first game of the World Series. After all, just a few days earlier our entire team and coaching staff were elated simply to have beaten the Chicago Cubs to win the National League pennant and earn a trip to the World Series. The next day, we were stuck in Chicago, awaiting the winner of the American League Championship, which pitted the age-old rivals, the Boston Red Sox and the New York Yankees, against each other. We couldn't board our plane, since we didn't know who would win and where we would be headed. So, we rented a ballroom in our hotel and watched on multiple television screens as the Yankees and Red Sox battled for the historic championship.

We sat patiently through what seemed like an interminable game, until McKeon finally got so fed up that he refused to wait any longer and declared, "We're heading to gas up the plane and fly somewhere come hell or high water! If we have to circle over New Jersey, who gives a damn?" As we prepared to depart, Aaron Boone hit his memorable home run in extra innings to send the Yankees to the World Series. To this day, he is known in Red Sox Nation as Aaron "Bleepin'" Boone; I guess that's how the Red Sox honor royalty. We realized we would be playing the Bronx Bombers and flew directly to New York.

What a tremendous feeling this was, especially given my past affection for the Yankees. Now as we prepared to compete for the game's highest honor, I was beside myself and trying not to show it. At the Chicago airport, I was so enthused that I sprinted up the steps to the plane, slammed my head on the overhead entranceway, and fainted, to the amusement of some and the consternation of most. But better to put the owner on the injured list than anyone on the winning team.

———

After the Marlins won Game One of the World Series on October 18, Game Two was scheduled to be played at Yankee Stadium again the following night. The Yankee powerhouse bounced back, winning 6–1. Hideki Matsui became the first Japanese player to homer during a World Series. It also turned out to be the last World Series game that the Yankees ever won at the old Yankee Stadium.

The series moved to Miami for Game Three. It was a pitchers' duel between Josh Beckett of the Marlins and the Yankees' Mike Mussina for the first seven innings, before and after a rain delay. The Yankees exploded in the last two innings to win 6–1.

Game Four was one of the most memorable games I've ever witnessed. We jumped out to an early lead against the iconic Roger Clemens, and after trading leads through nine innings and watching the Marlins' Carl Pavano's stellar pitching performance, we won with an Álex González leadoff home run in the bottom of the tenth, just inside the foul pole and barely clearing the fence. In Game Five, before a sold-out crowd of nearly sixty-six thousand people, the Marlins took back the series lead with a 6–4 win. The action then moved back to New York, where we won Game Six and the championship.

On Sunday, October 26, after our Saturday night win, we flew home to Miami with our families. We were tired, but it was a euphoric and celebratory flight. When we landed in Miami, thousands of fans were waiting at the airport and lining the roads outside. I turned my phone on and had dozens of voice messages. In the middle of listening to them, I heard a woman's voice say, "This is the White House calling. The president would like to speak with you." Another message from the same woman reiterated that the president was calling. In the third message from the White House, the tone had changed slightly. "*The president of the UNITED STATES is back from the Far East. He would like to speak with you but thinks you're avoiding him.*" From the car, I frantically dialed the number the operator had left and promptly had President George W. Bush on the line. "Mr. President," I said, "we've been on a plane flying back from New York. Hence my delay in getting back to you. I'm most definitely *not* avoiding you."

He responded in a very interesting way. "You know, Jeffrey, I watched the series from start to finish. That guy Castillo can really play second base." He had watched the entire final game on Air Force One, en route from an official visit to the Far East. It was especially thrilling since he was a former Texas Rangers owner. He may have been the president of the United States, but more importantly in my eyes, he was a baseball guy, and he showed me that he was still very much connected to the game. We talked about Josh Beckett's great pitching performance and the Marlins as significant underdogs. We spoke for thirty minutes, at which point I said, "Mr. President, don't you have something better to do than talk to me?" To which he replied, "Jeffrey, sometimes they don't give me a damn thing to do around here on Sundays." I knew he was kidding, but I was truly honored by his congratulatory call.

After the magical World Series, we received a formal invitation to visit the White House. In contrast to our current polarized climate, everyone on the team was excited to meet the president. Trader Jack was in great spirits, truly "over the moon." At the White House, he made President Bush laugh repeatedly. The president's brother Jeb, then the governor of Florida, was also at the White House that day and thrilled to be part of the celebration. The two Bush brothers were very much in their element and completely relaxed and delighted to be talking baseball for a few hours.

ABOVE: *President George W. Bush congratulates Jack McKeon in the East Room of the White House, January 2004.*

An amazing and utterly memorable parade followed in Miami, in front of an absolutely jubilant crowd. It took an hour to travel approximately one block in Little Havana on the main avenue, Calle Ocho. There was so much pure joy everywhere, and I can still see the faces today: women playfully flirting with the players as we passed by one block, men with tears in their eyes on the next. What a wonderful, unimaginable moment.

Mayor Manny Diaz was an ardent Marlins supporter and a genuinely wonderful person who cared deeply about his community and had a unique and impressive vision. With a potential stadium deal in mind in the near future, he stood in front of the huge celebratory crowd and said, "If we build it, will you come?" His question was met with enormous positive applause. Little did we imagine the political resistance and other obstacles that would stand between that moment in 2003 and opening the new ballpark in 2012.

I wasn't sure what to do for Jack to thank him for helping us win the World Series, so I bought him a Mercedes. He was surprised and very pleased, but after he drove it a few miles, he gave it to his son.

One thrilling element of a World Series victory is the championship ring. I wanted something very special for the players, so I invited two well-known designers, as well as the legendary jeweler Tiffany's, to participate, but for the most part their proposals too closely resembled one another. I researched other designs, and the most impressive ring I saw was the California Angels' World Series ring from 2002. A Canadian company from Calgary, Intergold, had been the creative force behind the design.

I approached the company's head jeweler, Miran Armutlu, and he came to New York, where we discussed my idea for the ring. The art dealer in me wanted it to be special. He executed all my wishes with great precision and startling craftsmanship. I had promised the players during the playoff run that if they took care of their job, I would do mine, and they would have a ring they would never forget. Urbina said to me weeks earlier, "Can we have white gold instead of yellow gold?" I replied, "You can have pink gold, green gold, or blue gold, as long as you win!" I wanted them to know that their ring would also be a grand slam! Eventually we took the measurements of everyone's ring finger for sizing, but Urbina, always a maverick who marched to his own drummer, had us measure his thumb. That's where he planned to wear his new white-gold World Series jewel.

My own priceless moment, where I truly knew our win was real, came when I flew to Mount Holyoke, Massachusetts, to have an expert in the work of Georges Seurat examine a drawing. I was able to have my plane land at Westover Air Reserve Base in western Massachusetts. As I was walking down the steps with the drawing tucked under my arm, I saw seven or eight guys rolling out a red carpet. I was sure they had mistaken me for someone else, but they shook their heads and said, "No, sir, we are all Red Sox fans up here, and you deserve the red carpet for beating the Yankees!"

CHAPTER TWENTY

JOSÉ'S BRIGHT LIGHT IS EXTINGUISHED

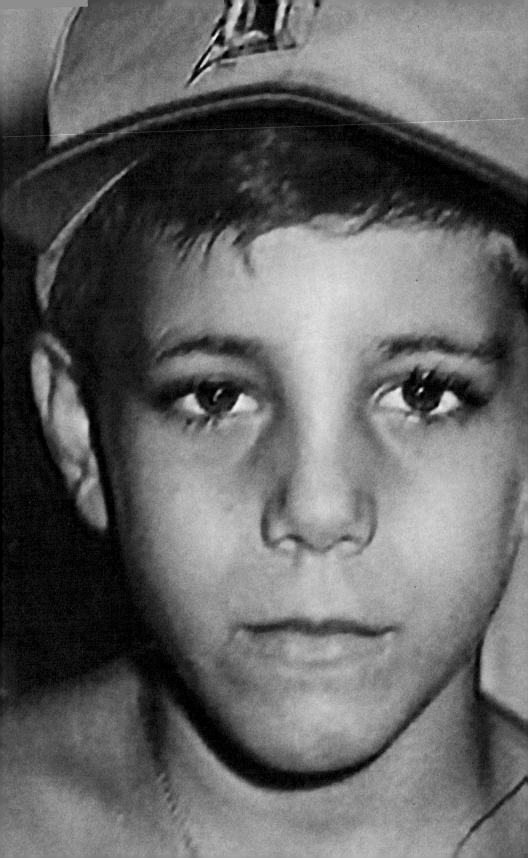

"If a man can bridge the gap
between life and death, if he can live on
after he's dead, then maybe he was a great man."

– JAMES DEAN

Simply put, José Fernández was one of the most special and unique people I have ever known in baseball, the art world, and in my entire life. When I first met him in 2010, he was just a kid, but one who knew he was blessed with immeasurable talent. He was undeniably authentic, and he believed with a strong conviction in everything he said and did.

His story is extraordinary. He played on the national youth team in Cuba and was a breakout star even as a twelve-year-old, as much for his outspokenness about the Castro regime as for his megawatt smile and million-dollar arm. In his early teens, his unconventional nature and criticism of the hard-line communist government got him tossed into jail several times and led to his eventual escape from the island. Jail is no place for a kid. His fellow inmates were tough customers. But astonishingly, they left José alone. Baseball in Cuba is such a revered sport that they respected him and his rare talent.

On the night he escaped from his home in Santa Clara, a small motorboat was readied on the southern part of the island. The rendezvous spot was a beach near the city of Trinidad. It was his fourth attempt; José had been arrested on a third attempt. This time, the motorboat was equipped to carry ten to twelve people across the Gulf of Mexico to the Yucatán, taking the shortest route from Cuba. José, knowing that the police often watched him, went to a friend's house through the front door, changed his clothes, exited through the back door to a second home for another wardrobe change, then took a roundabout route to arrive at the cove in the pitch blackness to find the small vessel that would be his salvation.

The authorities eventually realized what he had done to elude them, but it was too late to stop the boat. The best they could muster was a hail of bullets aimed at the small group on board as a sendoff. During the harrowing journey in the darkness, the water was choppy, and a woman fell overboard. Without a second thought, José jumped into the sea to save her. Only after they were safely back on the boat did he realize that he had rescued his mother. That was José: impulsive, caring, and, ultimately, heroic. Everyone reached Mexico safely.

From Mexico, José and his mother eventually arrived in Tampa in 2008, where they had friends. José enrolled at Braulio Alonso High School. He was fifteen when he arrived and was taken under the wing of a generous and spirited attorney, affectionately known as Uncle Ralph, also with the last name of Fernandez but not a relative. Ralph gave José excellent guidance and care throughout his short life.

José taught himself English by reading and watching television and movies. He was genuinely devoted to his new language and eventually spoke better English than some of my Yale classmates. He captured the subtleties of the language. His American accent was almost impeccable, which was a testament to his perseverance and desire to fit into American society as quickly as possible. He also became an American citizen in record time.

Successfully challenging other local hopefuls, he made the high school baseball team. He was a star pitcher, with a fastball nearing 100 mph. In Tampa, droves of scouts often swarmed around his

286   OPPOSITE PAGE: *José pitching for his Little League team in Santa Clara, Cuba.*

games. The Marlins showed an early interest in his talent. When I saw him on film, I asked enough questions of our scouts and evaluators that they took note, and they ultimately also decided that José might well be not just excellent but truly remarkable. I supported their valuations and encouraged them to select him right out of high school, in the 2011 draft. When our turn came, we drafted him in the first round.

——

From the beginning, José showed flashes of brilliance both on and off the field. The year after he was drafted and was playing for our Single-A team in Jupiter, he visited the Miami stadium on an off day with a few teammates. As I was watching the game with them, José turned to me and asked, "Can I pitch the ninth inning?" I replied, "No, I don't think so, kid. Anyway, I'm not the manager." He had a great sense of humor and was always ready to compete. Had I agreed, no doubt he would have found a uniform and a glove and walked out to the mound.

José wasn't perfect. Due to his youth and naiveté, he made some questionable decisions, one of which ultimately led to his untimely loss. In his constant effort to improve himself, one year he decided that in the off-season, he was going to push cars around a racetrack to build up his leg strength. I called his mentor Uncle Ralph to say our executives were concerned that José's plan might not be a great idea. Could he intervene? So, what did José do? He bought a bicycle and began an obsession with yet another physically demanding activity, peddling hundreds of miles each week. He had an energy that was impossible to contain.

Professional sports is a business. As an owner, you invest lots of money in athletes who are often unpredictable. You are taking a chance because you have little to no control over the choices that each player makes. But ultimately José was a chance worth taking. Against all the advice of my baseball executives, I encouraged bringing him directly from Single A to the Major Leagues in April of 2013. Our pitching rotation had suffered unexpected injuries during spring training, and we were in need of two starters. I knew what I had seen in Single A in Jupiter, where I often went to watch him pitch during their season. To me, it wasn't a risk. If you are not willing to take a chance, you are just mirroring what everyone else does. Once again, our strategic decision resembled the decision we'd made with Miguel Cabrera in 2003. Success never follows if you don't occasionally depart from your customary mindset.

Soon after José became a Major Leaguer, the team flew north to play the Mets. It was early April. We landed at Newark Airport, and as I watched the players deplane, I saw José coming down the steps carrying two plastic shopping bags. I walked over to him and said in a benevolent manner, "What are you doing with these? Professional baseball players don't travel with shopping bags." Like his team-mates, José had the usual paraphernalia—clothes, a new laptop, and electronic gadgets—but he did not own luggage. I offered to meet him the next day to help him buy suitcases. I took him to a Tumi luggage store where, to his credit, he selected the least expensive bag. I told him he needed a better-quality travel case, that he had earned it as a Major Leaguer about to start his first-ever game in New York. With his new bag, he now looked like a Major Leaguer on the road.

And he certainly played like one. He was the dominant figure in his first game on the big stage in New York against the Mets on Sunday, April 7, 2013. I still have my ticket stub from that game, one of the few that I have saved.

Following his Major League debut, José's pitching arsenal began drawing attention to the team. The energy level and joy in the ball-park was something to behold. José arrived soon after we were in our new stadium, and the community wanted to see this sensational young player whose charisma and talent had captivated everyone. Fans were looking for something to celebrate, and they found it in José. Miami's Cuban community was especially proud and enthusi-astic. The feeling was mutual, as José was drawn to all our fans. At the end of many games, young fans and adults alike would line up waiting to greet him. He autographed every piece of paper they put before him. He was absolutely special. He *was* Miami.

I remember he called me after he joined the team and said he wanted to buy a new car, "I want something fast." Thinking of this great talent who was also a large investment for the Marlins, I said, "How about something fast but with some protection around it?" We ended up going to a Bentley dealership during an off day. It was the typical story of a kid starting with very little and wanting to have something tangible to represent his rapid rise to success in America. Ultimately, he chose not to purchase a super fast car but a practical sedan, and we all breathed a little easier.

About a year later, I asked him what he wanted for his twenty-first birthday. He replied, "I'd love to see my grandmother who is still back in Cuba, but that's impossible." I knew from José that his grandmother not only loved baseball but had played a major role in teaching her grandson how to play. His wish became my next challenge. I made a few calls. I spoke to a friend of mine who had previously been the US ambassador to Jamaica during the Bush administration. In order to follow the right protocol, she steered me to people in the Department of State and others in our diplomatic channels to Cuba. The US was beginning to reopen relations with Cuba, and the process was extremely complicated, but eventually we made some progress.

One day, a US diplomat called me to say that José's grandmother had been quoted by Dan Le Batard in the *Miami Herald* as saying that if she made it to the United States, she would never go back. They were concerned. They didn't want a defection on their hands. As a result, I made it clear that she would merely come to visit occasionally, usually when José pitched. Then she would return to Cuba. Not long afterward, I received a call informing me that she would be granted the necessary visa to visit her family in Miami, as she wished. People who know me are aware that I often love surprising people whenever I can, and I thought it would be fun to surprise José.

José's mother, Maritza, and Alfie Mesa, a talented Marlins executive, met José's grandmother Olga at the Miami airport on November 9, 2013, and took her to lunch on the way to her hotel. Later, we had arranged for the MLB television network to do an interview with José in the clubhouse. It was, of course, a setup. José knew nothing. After a long interview, the reporter ended by asking one final question: "If your grandmother were here, what would she say to you?" He replied, "Well, that's impossible. She can never get out of Cuba." I was standing behind a door with his grandmother watching the interview on a monitor. At that moment I opened the door and had her walk toward her grandson. He had a look of utter shock. For the first time, our loquacious ace pitcher was speechless. Eventually he mouthed the words, "Oh my God, oh my God, oh my God"—the same words I had uttered when we won the World Series! José gathered himself and hugged his grandmother while crying joyfully for several minutes.

The rest of us watched in complete silence, even wiping away tears of our own. Then José, bursting with pride, proceeded to give his grandmother a tour of the entire ballpark, holding her hand tightly the entire time. He had enormous respect for his family. As promised, his grandmother abided by the rules and returned to Cuba when José was not pitching.

I needed no validation of my insistence on bringing José to the Major Leagues. In his first full season, he became the National League Rookie of the Year. Together, we went to Orlando to collect the award. As we arrived at the ceremony, I noticed José wasn't wearing a jacket. I told him he needed to look more presentable for this momentous occasion, so I gave him the jacket off my back. Amazingly, it fit! If he hadn't had a proper shirt, I would have given him that too.

That same season, after one game, our current manager Don Mattingly was sitting in his office with his coaches when José walked in, went directly to the mini-refrigerator, and took a beer out of the manager's stash. No one spoke—we had never seen anything so brazen—and everyone looked around at each other. I felt I had to say something, so I remarked, "Hey José, who do you think you are? You've got some nerve!" After an awkward second, we all started laughing. He had a completely disarming manner. He had had the unmitigated gall to walk into the office as if it were his own, but his charm and charisma helped him get away with it.

OPPOSITE PAGE: *José with his grandmother, Olga, who surprised him in Miami on his twenty-first birthday.*

Such behavior was no different from Josh Beckett watching cartoons rather than paying attention to the manager during a pregame World Series speech, or Ugueth Urbina taking a five-inning nap in the clubhouse before heading to the bullpen. The rules of the game on the field are obviously different from those in the clubhouse. It's a baseball team, not a staid corporate office, and individual idiosyncrasies are part of the tradition. José had a rare combination of talent, charisma, and energy. When he was told in 2014 that he needed Tommy John surgery and he couldn't pitch for at least a year, it was a moment akin to taking a paintbrush out of Picasso's hand.

He lived by three principles that drove him each day: preparation, winning, and having fun. During his short life, he may have aggravated a few people. Some thought he was being given special treatment. But corralling that energy would have been a mistake. Instead, I urged his manager to channel it. His brash charm and touch of hubris were qualities to work with, not repress.

———

In 2015, José called me to say that he had hired the prominent Scott Boras as his new agent. As an owner, you often act as a mentor and encourage your young players. But eventually you're at the opposite ends of the negotiating table. The players all have agents, and you just tell yourself to be fair, to understand the system and the other side, while also taking care of your own team's interest. I've had many meetings and phone calls with Scott and found him a highly capable negotiator. Nobody represented his players better and with more passion. I got along with him just fine, but I also knew that in the end, our team made its own decisions.

The Marlins wanted to sign José to a long-term contract if he would give the team one year of free agency. When a player arrives at the Major Leagues, under the agreement with the Major League Baseball Players Association, he remains with his team for six years. The team agrees to pay the player's salary for the first three years, and there is a minimum salary during this period. During the second three years of a player's service, he remains with the team but his financial position changes. The process goes to arbitration if the team and the player can't reach an agreement, and at this point, the player is represented by an agent. After the sixth year, the player can enter free agency, which means he is free to negotiate with any team he chooses. In José's fourth year, we offered him a contract which included that first year of free agency. Scott was opposed to that plan. He told José, "Believe in yourself. Go through arbitration, and you will get what you deserve in free agency starting a year earlier."

Free agent years are important, especially at a young age, but ultimately that advice ended up being tragic, given the events that followed. After José's death, his family did not have the benefit of the long-term contract; he also had minimal life insurance, so there was very little money for them. Several months later, the team received a life insurance payment for its policy on José. Without hesitation, I redirected the full payment to José's family instead of accepting it for the team.

José always thought he was not only a superb pitcher but also a great offensive threat. During that 2013 season, he often boasted to me that he would hit a home run, a rarity for a pitcher in any season. I filed that away in my memory. In one of the last games of that season, he was in the on-deck circle and looked in my direction as I sat nearby. I remember teasing him, saying, "So, José, I guess you're not hitting your home run?" Thirty seconds later he walked up to the plate, turned around to grin at me, and proceeded to hit the ball out of the ballpark. I couldn't believe what I had just seen. First, he annoyed the Atlanta Braves by standing and admiring his home run for a few seconds, and then as he crossed home plate, he smiled at me with that mischievous grin, displaying what looked like at least 150 pearly-white teeth. He never broke eye contact. I quickly realized the value of teasing José in order to motivate him.

When Barry Bonds arrived in Miami as the Marlins' hitting coach for spring training in 2016, a friendship blossomed as Barry helped José develop his understanding of the game and refine his hitting skills. José once asked me to ask the manager if he could hit in the middle of the lineup when he pitched. He felt that certain of his hitting prowess, had incredible self-confidence, and was eager to test his limits. In the end, I explained that the decision belonged to the manager, who told him he would bat ninth, the pitcher's normal hitting position.

But those years of joy suddenly turned to unbearable sadness. Early one Sunday morning, September 25, 2016, I received a call from David, who told me to sit down. He said that José had been killed in a boating accident. I was immediately reminded of the call I'd received from an Alabama police officer in 1994, telling me my sister's plane had crashed into the side of a mountain. Hearing the news, there is first a wave of indescribable pain. Nobody can really know how you feel. The pain centers in your brain as you try to comprehend the devastating and catastrophic words. Then your heart breaks, and the pain settles there and never leaves. José was twenty-four years old. I wasn't prepared for his life to end so abruptly, nor were his family, teammates, friends, or the community.

The next few days felt like a blur. I immediately left for Miami, and the first thing I did was to go see his mother and grandmother, south of the ballpark, in a home that José had bought for them. They had turned the house into a shrine of photos and memories of José. It was eerily silent as everyone grieved in his or her own way. Many young people had gathered in a state of utter shock, barely speaking. When I arrived, his mother came over to me and cried in my arms. It was one of the saddest days of my life.

José had a profound influence on me and on all his teammates. I don't think I've ever known a soul in either baseball or the art world with such a dominating presence. He was the definition of a super-star. In retrospect, I think people didn't recognize and appreciate his unique gifts enough while he was still with us. His death was tragic on many levels, not just for the human suffering and personal loss but also the loss for baseball. If you're a fan of this sport, you wanted to see an incredible young man like José, brimming with charisma and talent, have a long career in the game he cherished.

ABOVE: *With José at Marlins Park, pregame.*

A few days later, I gave a eulogy at José's funeral. It was a standing-room-only gathering of thousands, which spilled out into the streets. Somehow, I managed to hold back my emotions and deliver the following remarks.

We weren't supposed to be here today.

As you all know, we tragically lost a giant who was one of the bright lights of our Marlins organization, the City of Miami, and of Cuban people everywhere. His story represented and inspired millions across the world. He worked hard to experience the American Dream and ended up being its very embodiment.

I was fortunate enough to play a significant role in José's life, as he did in mine. I was there when he got called up. I was there when he pitched his first big league strike. I was proud to be there when he was reunited with his grandmother, and there when he won the Rookie of the Year award. No doubt it would have been the first of many such accolades.

I was blessed to have gotten to know not only the player with a golden arm, but also the man.

While some saw him as provocative, I saw him as humble, mature, and never wanting to abuse his personal or professional relationships. He respected generosity, and in turn, gave it back in spades with his magnetic smile that could light up a ballpark.

I think we also know about his famously competitive spirit. For evidence of this, one need look no further than his last at bat of the season two years ago. For weeks, he had been playfully telling anyone who would listen that he dreamt of hitting a home run.

Not having done it as the season drew to a close, this ace who was normally better known for his fastball crushed a pitch into the outfield seats, smiling broadly as he rounded the bases. This was the magic of José. He set the standard for making baseball FUN.

You know, José's impact on people was global. This summer, my wife and I were in Chicago for the Cubs series. As we walked down Michigan Avenue in advance of a night game, we saw someone walking towards us wearing a Marlins jersey. As he got closer, we noticed it said Fernández on the back, so we stopped him to inquire if he'd be attending the ball game. He explained in a thick Dutch accent that he'd saved up his money and flown in from Holland specifically to see his favorite player, José.

How far and wide the admiration went for this young man! Jackie Robinson once said a life is not important, except through the impact it has on OTHER lives. By any measure, José achieved that goal.

Athletically, he was clearly a superstar who would have continued to reach incredible heights in this game. He passed away far too young, like other greats such as Thurman Munson and Roberto Clemente. But more importantly, he was a superstar as a human being.

About a year ago, José tweeted, "If you were given a book with the story of your life, would you want to read the end?" Well, I prefer not to think of this tragedy as the end of his life, but rather as the beginning of his LEGEND. His memory and his love will endure forever.

To José's family, friends, teammates, and our community, I share in the deep pain we're all feeling right now. Some words that often comfort me in times like this are that grief is merely a healing process from the pain of loss. In other words, this pain is overwhelming, but it is also a sign that we are coping, and together we will move on. He will never be replaced, nor forgotten, but he will endure, shining brightly over us all.

José's fame was sudden and intense but not long enough. I will never forget the tears pouring down Barry Bonds's face as he stood next to me and we both watched the hearse pull away.

OPPOSITE PAGE: *The pin worn by close friends and family at José's funeral, signifying his uniform number.*

CHAPTER TWENTY-ONE

UPS AND DOWNS

> "Yesterday's home runs
>
> don't win today's games."
>
> – BABE RUTH

rtists and professional athletes have many similarities in how they approach their craft. At the highest levels of performance, both are constantly experimenting. Artists explore new techniques, materials, and imagery. Baseball players test a new stance at bat, a new pitch, and a new way to grip the ball. Pitchers in particular search for new ways to deceive the batters and conceal what pitch they are sending to the plate. Both rely on repetition to perfect their techniques, but as soon as they get something right, the pressure immediately renews to improve. And each area of expertise operates on instinct: Where do I put this line, or do I move to the right or the left?

Both artists and high-level athletes can suffer from the same stressors: loneliness, self-doubt, and constant second-guessing. But artists have the luxury to create outside of public view. No one is watching them at work; when they exhibit and the critics are unkind, they do not have to face them in the same room. Baseball players are on a public stage, and the reaction is immediate: cheers and applause or loud boos. Even before the crowd noise subsides, sports commentators have started dissecting every nuance of a play.

OPPOSITE PAGE: *Miguel Cabrera, a star from his first "at bat."*

But there are differences too. Baseball is a game of variables—hitting, fielding, running, throwing, often referred to as a player's "tools." If you have a four- or five-tool player, you have a good player, but he is still inherently unpredictable. No one knows how any player will perform when they step onto the field. It is a game of one-on-one confrontations. By contrast, there's no such thing as a five-tool artist—you either have the tool of creativity or you don't. And you have more than a single nine-inning stretch to prove your talent. Baseball players have relatively short-lived careers; artists have far longer to develop and enhance their talents and messages.

Nevertheless, there are other striking similarities between the two worlds. Artists and athletes frequently have a belief in their own invincibility, and taken to the extreme, that belief can lead to tragic consequences. What would Jackson Pollock have done if he had not believed that he could drive while drunk? Even with José Fernández, there were early signs of hovering too close to the self-destruct button. I remember seeing José laughing with another player from Cuba, Yasiel Puig, before a game against the Los Angeles Dodgers. Afterward, I asked José, "Why are you laughing with him when you are about to play him?" José's response was classic bravado. "I'm not laughing," he said, "I'm just setting him up. I'm going to strike out that asshole four times tonight." During the game, José tried to raise his pitching speed from 100 miles per hour to 104. He ended up hurting his arm and needing Tommy John surgery. It was a reminder to not let your ego get in the way of your abilities. In many ways, that is a lesson for everyone at all levels of baseball, or even life.

━━━

Once the euphoria of the World Series victory had passed, the Marlins entered a period of new challenges. We lost some key players to free agency, and even though we were World Series champions, the win did not translate into an increase in revenue. Corporations did not flock to sponsor us; ticket sales increased only minimally. Unlike other teams, the Marlins had been saddled with a long-term local television contract that did not generate much income, all of which limited our ability to compete for free agents. Baseball is a game of money and finances, where players are often understandably drawn to the highest bidder. Over the next few years, we lost key members of our lineup, including Derrek Lee, Pudge Rodríguez, and even Miguel Cabrera and Dontrelle Willis when they became free agents.

But it wasn't just free agency. From early 2002 through the ensuing decade, as an organization, we did have a few luminaries, including outfielders Giancarlo Stanton and Christian Yelich, and José Fernández. But three important contributors in fifteen years simply isn't a good enough record. Even the 2007 decision to wait until the second round to draft Stanton meant we could have easily lost him. Our baseball executives also missed an opportunity to draft Jason Heyward in the first round. Instead, we drafted Matt Dominguez, who did not perform as our scouts had predicted.

Teams that succeed in the draft generally follow a basic guiding principle: select the best athlete available. Jason Heyward went on to be a star for Atlanta. Beyond the draft, successful teams are built through trades, free agents, and waiver claims. Indeed, our trades in 2003 had been integral to our World Series win. In addition, success often comes from having a deep and talented Minor League system. Unfortunately, our drafts at that level mostly evolved to become "solid" Major Leaguers rather than standouts.

Analyzing players in any amateur draft means they usually fall into one of four categories: some are clearly destined to be superstars, others will make significant contributions at the Major League level, some will be journeymen players, while most will ride off into the sunset with fading baseball dreams. Assessing the nuances in these last three categories is an extremely difficult process. An organization needs first-rate amateur-level scouts who can find, evaluate, and recommend talented high school and college players participating in the June draft, as well as professional scouts who scour the Major and Minor Leagues. In defense of any baseball operations team, success is often a matter of luck.

Nothing illustrates this dilemma better than the stories of four key players, initially brought in to supercharge our lineup prior to the opening of the new Marlins ballpark in 2012. Signing high-profile free agents does not always guarantee that a transformation will materialize. I personally wanted us to acquire ace closing pitcher Heath Bell. The previous year with the San Diego Padres, he had led the National League in saves and seemed a good fit for us, but he struggled from the moment he arrived in Miami. At one point, early in the season, I found him sitting alone on a couch in the laundry room. He was in tears and motionless, transfixed by a washing machine spinning around and around. I learned that his father was dying of cancer. This family tragedy, of course, affected his play on the field. I completely empathize with how a personal struggle can impact a professional performance. Baseball requires relentless intensity and focus, and, at that time, his mind and heart were elsewhere.

José Reyes was another player whom we acquired and then had to trade. The dynamic shortstop with the gifted rifle right arm was one of the most high-profile players that we signed in 2012, when he became a free agent. I fondly recall that he and I met with two of our team executives in the lounge of New York's Carlyle Hotel and talked into the wee hours of the morning. Sadly, his trade became surrounded with unnecessary intrigue and media accusations that I had advised José to buy a house in Miami shortly before the Marlins traded him to Toronto. This was never the case. In fact, I did not want him to buy a house in Miami, knowing a trade could be imminent. When we were both at a New York ALS (Lou Gehrig's disease) chapter dinner together, I casually asked him if he was still considering buying a home. He replied that he was leaving the country for ten days and answered, "Not yet," so we turned to a different topic. A week later, the Marlins traded him. Somehow our conversation leaked to the press and was misrepresented. For wanting to know his situation and protect him, I paid a price.

After stints in Toronto and Colorado, José signed with the Mets. I don't like having unresolved matters, especially with people

I respect. After he joined the Mets, our team was in New York to play a three-game series. Before the start of the first game, I went to see him in the Mets clubhouse. I spotted his smile from across the room. We embraced and chatted. He was very gracious, and I'm glad we were able to put the unfortunate episode behind us.

In contrast, another player who was acquired and traded in 2012 was not as gracious. In the wake of his trade, Mark Buehrle sent me several texts that were full of vitriolic and filthy language, due in part to the fact that he couldn't take his pit bull dogs to Toronto, which had banned the species. Baseball commissioner Bud Selig was aghast at what Mark had written but added that he was not surprised.

———

Baseball executives and managers know intellectually that it is not a good idea to develop strong emotional attachments to players, who can be traded at any time, but that did not prevent some from leaving an indelible mark on my heart. Rondell White in Montreal was one such player; I remember tearing up after going with our general manager to inform him that he was being traded.

Another player who I will always remember is Luis Castillo. Luis grew up in the Dominican Republic in a level of poverty few of us can imagine. He made his first baseball glove out of bent cardboard and lived in a house with dirt floors. He didn't have a full pair of shoes and instead wore mismatched castoffs. To get to practice, he rode a bike with no seat. His mother delivered sandwiches to try to scrape together a bit of money to pay his baseball league fees. He reached the Majors out of talent, grit, and deep faith. He even built a crèche in his clubhouse locker. Once, I gave him a Saint Christopher's medal from the Vatican that had been blessed by the pope. I will never forget his smile or how he immediately placed it in his crèche.

Another player did not become a marquee name, but I never forgot Jeff Allison. He was the Baseball America High School Player of the Year when the Marlins drafted him as a pitcher in

2003. Unfortunately, our scouts did not realize that Jeff was also struggling with some substance abuse issues, and injuries propelled him into serious addictions to heroin and OxyContin. But I would not give up on Jeff. We helped him during stays in rehab outside of Boston, and I made sure to visit him and encourage him. It was a long road, but I had faith that he would embrace his future and turn his life around. Today, he is married, has a family, and works as a teacher and a coach. No Hollywood screenwriter could have penned a better ending. Jeff makes me proud.

Perhaps the best definition of baseball insanity is doing the same thing over and over and expecting different results. By 2014, I began to make some overdue changes to the Marlins organization. I elevated Dan Jennings, one of our scouts, to become the general manager, while Mike Hill became president of Baseball Operations. I first met Mike in an elevator in Anaheim, CA, at the 1999 MLB Winter Meetings.

Inside that elevator was another Mike, Mike Berger, who would later become one of our most heralded, professional, highly regarded, and respected scouts. Berger had been a catcher and had played for me on our Minor League team in Oklahoma City. When the elevator stopped at the next floor, Mike Hill walked in. Berger introduced us and commented that we ought to get to know each other, since we had both gone to Ivy League universities. I asked Hill what college he had attended, to which he replied, "Harvard." Being a proud Yale alumnus, I looked him squarely in the eye and said, "Where is that?" It didn't take him long to realize that I was joking. That teasing would last for the next fifteen years. From the start, though, I had enormous respect for Mike Hill's leadership abilities.

The Marlins also recruited a number of highly prized evaluators, the lifeblood of any successful team. We hired Jeff McAvoy from Tampa to become our senior vice president for player development, and he more than lived up to his reputation for recognizing talent. To help with our pitching at both the Minor and Major League level, Jim Benedict and Marc DelPiano joined us from Pittsburgh, where they had been responsible for drafting and developing many important players, including outfielder Plácido Polanco. In their first season with the Marlins, Jim and Mark turned around the player development system. We vaulted to become among the top three teams in Minor League Baseball during 2017.

One of my favorite hires of all time was Perry Hill, the best infield coach I ever saw. We first met in Oklahoma, when he was a roving infield instructor for the Texas Rangers. I had lost track of where he was working, until I happened to be at a Yankees-Tigers game in New York in the late 1990s, prior to my involvement with the Expos. I saw Perry coaching third base for the Tigers. When I became the general partner of the Expos, I told our general manager that we should hire him and then immediately contacted Perry. The very next day, I got a call from Tom Hicks, then the owner of the Texas Rangers. The Rangers had just tried to hire Perry but had been told that the Expos had already signed him. Hicks offered to trade players for Perry, but I wasn't letting him go. He has a special devotion to the game, a great eye, and is a superb and respected teacher. Players would show up for instruction and Perry had them compete against each other. He taught his players how to "see" the ball and to "funnel it" into the glove. During his first year in Montreal, he guided shortstop Orlando Cabrera to winning a Gold Glove. After he won, Orlando gave Perry his trophy.

Perry was with me for the rest of my Major League run, until I sold the Marlins and the new owners sadly let him go. Those are the relationships that, if you are truly fortunate, and I was, you make in baseball.

CHAPTER TWENTY-TWO

JACK, JOE, FREDI, OZZIE

THOUGHTS ON MANAGERS

"The secret of managing

is to keep the guys who hate you

away from the guys who are undecided."

– CASEY STENGEL

As an owner and a lifelong baseball fan, I had confidence in what I could see. Just as I knew what I was searching for in art, I knew what I was looking for in baseball and what I saw in players. But I also knew my role as an owner. The best relationship I could have with my organization was to have faith in the people I had selected. No matter who the manager was, I never made a lineup, or suggested who to play, or how to play, or how to guide the team. While I was happy to voice my opinion, I also ensured it was done in conjunction with other evaluations. My job was to put the pieces together in an effort to maximize our potential; the manager's job was to orchestrate it.

But during my time in Major League Baseball, perhaps no job changed as much as the manager's. As in many industries, in baseball, technology began to compete directly with human observation and intuition. Today, in most executive offices and clubhouses, science is what governs the majority of decisions.

OPPOSITE PAGE: *Marlins' manager Jack McKeon celebrating our World Series win inside Yankee Stadium. He's always been head and shoulders above the rest.*

From my perspective, the major problem is that baseball is *not* a science. Thirty years ago, managers in the Major Leagues possessed time-tested skill sets. Some managers spent half of their careers working their way up simply to a manager's spot in the Minor Leagues. Only a skilled few made it to the coaching staff on a Major League team before even possibly becoming a manager. It was a step-by-step process, just as it was, for example, in the automobile industry during the 1960s and '70s, where it was possible to start on the assembly line and rise to the level of senior executive management, learning every facet of the business along the way. Today, that level of familiarity is a rarity, in baseball and many other businesses.

At the same time, the selection process for hiring a team manager has also changed. It is often about personalities and even a partnership with the general manager, the executive responsible for all aspects of directing a team. These partnerships rarely existed as recently as the end of the twentieth century. The hiring of Aaron Boone by the Yankees and David Ross by the Cubs, both former players and bright personalities but without managerial experience, attest to this new direction.

Finally, intuition has been largely replaced by analytics. Legendary managers of the past, such as Chuck Tanner, Sparky Anderson, Jim Leyland, and others, focused on their own clubhouses, creating their own lineups and making their own decisions, for better or worse. There was little if any emphasis on analytics coming from the general manager's office. Today, intuition has largely been taken out of the managerial equation, to the point where the likes of Billy Martin, Lou Piniella, Casey Stengel, and Leo Durocher might not even be considered for a manager's job.

Certainly, baseball has always used numbers. In the 1950s, Branch Rickey, who brought Jackie Robinson to the Dodgers, hired a statistician, John Ross, to calculate and study hitters' tendencies by developing spray charts. It was always advantageous to know whether a hitter preferred hitting to the left, right, or center of the field to set up a defense, and spray charts guided that defense. Added to that is the recent concept of "defensive shifts," which encourages

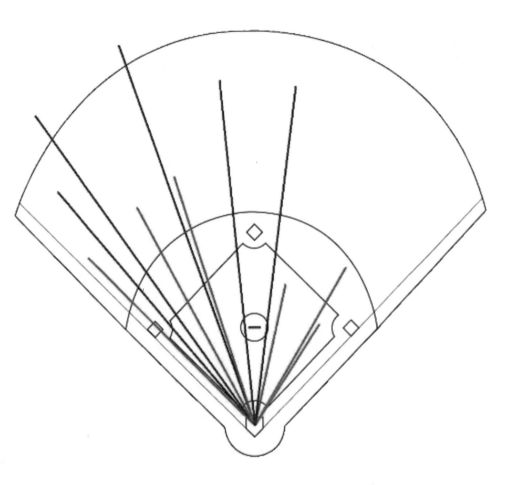

ABOVE: *A typical spray chart showing the ball's varied trajectories after it is hit by a batter.*

multiple members of the infield to alter their positions for a specific hitter, based on analytic evaluations of that player's tendencies.

Today, as opposed to hand-drawn charts, the game is run through simulators to calculate probability-based outcomes, with the expectation that a computer will increase a team's chances to win. The human element has almost evaporated from the game. Managers function more like data analysts; intuition seems to have disappeared. Managers are encouraged to study matchup charts prepared by analytic departments and given to them prior to batting practice. I have a difficult time imagining St. Louis Cardinals and Hall of Fame pitcher Bob Gibson being informed that, because of simulation and analytic matchups, he was going to start in the second inning, after the "opener" pitcher had completed his first inning. The concept of an "opener," now used by a growing number of teams, takes advantage of the statistical matchups against an opposing team's lineup at the beginning of a game.

For some teams, the transition to a decision-making process based on data and away from experience and intuition has yielded a new dugout culture. It used to be that when players returned to the dugout after an at-bat, they would sit down with their coaches and other players and discuss what they had observed. Now, they watch videos of their performance on laptops. Self-discovery and discussion have been replaced by dissecting subtle movements captured by camera angles; it has become an internal process rather than an external process. Technology has also changed who plays and in what order. Many senior officials in organizations produce starting lineups and submit them to their manager early on game day. These lineups even specify the sequence of available relief pitchers, who, because of new rule changes, are required to face a minimum of at least three batters before they can be replaced.

When the incomparable Hall of Fame Atlanta Braves general manager John Schuerholz worked closely with his manager, Bobby Cox, it was Schuerholz's role to find and sign winning pitchers like Greg Maddux, Tom Glavine, and John Smoltz to help make his manager successful. Today, that partnership wouldn't happen, primarily because of analytics.

Baseball seasons are 162 games long, not including pre- and post-season games. On any given day, a player's ability will be determined by many factors, including emotional, mental, and physical variables, such as a player's daily family life and even the meal consumed prior to a game. In other words, this "potpourri" of human traits cannot be measured exclusively with analytics. No computer is sophisticated enough to do that. Nonetheless, managing a team today is less about gut feelings and time-tested experience. There is even a movement away from general managers having extensive backgrounds in scouting and player development and toward recruiting cool, analytical, data-driven savants, often young Ivy League graduates, which has meant that, unfortunately, tablets, smartphones, and analytic trackers have greatly reduced the importance of the natural thought process of smart baseball people.

I know many will suggest that these musings belong to a bygone era. I can appreciate change and innovative evolution, but there is a fine line as to how far one can go down this road without impacting the pure joy of the sport. Individual players often over-think their at-bats, relying too much on advanced reports and what they are told by coaches instead of using their natural abilities and instincts. Great pitchers, like José Fernández, want to process the hitter in front of them instead of relying solely on advanced reports and analysis. The same problem exists in building a team. Overanalyzing a player trade using analytics and being driven by statistics can sometimes result in a missed opportunity. If a desired player is traded elsewhere, clearly analysis helped to cause this paralysis. And when analysis causes paralysis, perhaps the sport has gone too far.

Scouts' opinions used to be the ultimate factor in building a team—deciding when to spend large sums of money on talent is part of the lifeblood of a ball club. An experienced eye in baseball is no different from an eye discerning artistic talent. The similarities between a great baseball player and a great artist have always been about quality. But quality can be an elusive commodity, which is why experience, worldly knowledge, hunches, and gut feelings are as important—if not more so—than algorithms in building a successful franchise, whether in baseball or in art.

I had a front-row seat to witness the pendulum swing toward the analytical measurement of young talent. Twenty or thirty years ago, there was no draft model scored by a computer to determine outcomes and selections. Recent changes now mean that all thirty teams have armies of tech-savvy employees analyzing young players for the amateur draft in June. Mine may be a minority view, but I believe there needs to be a healthier balance between instinct and intuition on the one hand and technology on the other when viewing and assessing talent. As it now stands, the human element is far less significant than the recitation of a young pitcher's "spin rates" and the review of film and photos from multiple camera angles, analyzing every split second of his pitching delivery. Currently, a decision to pursue a pitcher can even include placing electrodes on his torso as part of a high-speed video analysis to precisely interpret his motion, mechanics, and delivery. Yet in the end, all team scouts are fishing in the same pond; only the bait has changed to focus on technology rather than an experienced scout's opinion.

The value of both professional and amateur scouts cannot be underestimated. While scouts gather vital information on the athletic abilities of the players they are observing, the good ones are also able to study and appraise the psychological makeup of a player. That ability allows them to measure something that analytics cannot decipher, specifically the *authenticity* of a player, the human element of the game. Scouts are truly the unheralded men in the trenches. They scour the world for talent, looking for a hidden gem in a pitcher or a position player, something that an analyst sitting in a baseball operations office cannot do and likely cannot see. As such, for me, they are the essential component of a ball club.

Amateur scouts seek out potential prospects in high schools, junior colleges, and colleges and explore the possibility of signing young foreign players outside the United States. They make suggestions to their organizations and prioritize their preferences in preparation for the annual amateur draft. That draft stocks teams with young talent, much the same way as in the NFL and NBA. Professional scouts search for players in both the Minor and Major Leagues. In addition, they also evaluate opposing teams to prepare for upcoming games and series. No computer program can ever understand people as well as another person's well-trained eyes, brain, and heart.

—————

Analytics have also led to changes in philosophy for how teams are managed at all levels. Perhaps the classic example of the divergence in philosophies between general managers of the not too distant past and more contemporary general managers was on display during the 2008 World Series. Pat Gillick of the Philadelphia Phillies was at one end of the spectrum and Andrew Friedman, then guiding the Tampa Bay Rays, was at the other end. The comparisons between generations were dramatic. Gillick, now rightfully in the Hall of Fame, was an experienced general manager, having worked for three other teams over the previous twenty-five years. He had always been viewed as a leader and a thinker, who was only one step away from a PhD in baseball (if such a degree existed).

Even though the Rays did not prevail against the Phillies, Friedman epitomized the new approach and skill set that the young Theo Epstein had initially brought to the game when he was with the Boston Red Sox in 2004. The skills Friedman relied on simply to get the Rays to the World Series, with limited financial resources, were drawn from experience he developed on Wall Street. Friedman, now the brilliant president of baseball operations for the Los Angeles Dodgers, and his new generation of young, computer-savvy front office leaders have had a major impact on baseball by changing what drives decisions, including how general managers are hired and operate within their franchises. But this new style is not necessarily the last word.

Even with all the changes in how teams are run, it remains an important challenge for any baseball organization to identify the right managerial leadership. No matter what an algorithm produces, managers are the on-field leaders for twenty-six players and an inner circle of coaches. Their job is to organize and prepare the players for each game, to guide a disciplined group of talented athletes into forming a cohesive unit, where each player knows his specific role. The clubhouse is the players' domain, but the manager remains the guiding force. He delegates responsibilities to his talented and experienced coaches, who help the players continuously refine their skills, even at the Major League level. The manager meets daily with his superior, the general manager, to discuss team issues and is ultimately responsible for creating a winning environment. What makes a good manager become a great manager is his ability to motivate and have the players believe in themselves.

The sharp-witted and crafty Jack McKeon is one of the all-time great managers. He had also been a general manager and acquired the moniker "Trader Jack" for the many trades and deals he made during his reign at the San Diego Padres in the late 1980s. He bridged the gap between front office and dugout by managing teams well into the twenty-first century when he won a World Series title for my Marlins. His views about the game and its evolution are also noteworthy because he witnessed it all.

McKeon's view was that in the 1980s, players seemed to play harder and were focused on winning for their team. In the '80s, being a .300 hitter over the course of a season made a player an elite athlete, but today, the narrative is very different. From his perspective, players now are more concerned about themselves and their personal statistics and are far less focused on the team's name on the front of their uniform. For example, left-handed hitters, who can easily record a hit by bunting to the vacated left side of the infield, often choose to swing away instead. They are looking for the more sensational extra-base hit, even though an infield single is practically theirs for the taking. This is a small but prime example of how the game has changed.

McKeon's philosophy is that to build the best team, players need to leave their egos at the door when they enter the clubhouse. This was his philosophy when he became the Marlins' manager, and time and again, he implored his players to see the path to victory in a new light. He wanted to see 100 percent effort from every player, every day. His 2003 World Series ring proves that he was right. For him, then and now, it is all about creating a dynamic culture, a team effort focused on winning. I watched as he changed our team's chemistry and camaraderie, working like a master chemist with multiple different elements.

In the current climate, McKeon sees an overemphasis on analytics, to the point where players have almost been turned into robots, with both players' and managers' instincts slowly disappearing. For example, pitchers used to be challenged to pitch eight or nine innings. Today they are challenged to pitch only five innings. Analytics now mean that pitchers are often told how many pitches they can deliver and the number of innings they will be allowed to pitch even before a game begins and they set foot on the mound. The new theory is that pitchers need to be protected from arm injuries. But there are many, like McKeon, who believe that inactivity is more detrimental to a pitcher than too much activity. At the peaks of their careers, the Braves' greats, Maddux, Glavine, and Smoltz, often scheduled two bullpen sessions between their starts. Yet today, the occasional bullpen session is nothing more than eyewash, meant to impress a bullpen coach who will report what he saw to the manager. It's yet another example of analytics driving baseball, and it's a setback for the game and for fans who love watching pitching duels, hoping to see a pitcher throw a no-hitter or that rare perfect game. Yes, there are still no-hitters, but limiting a pitcher's pitch count makes that far more of an elusive and even accidental outcome in a game.

McKeon pushed his players to play hard and perform. He was a manager in the Major Leagues for sixteen seasons, and yet he never managed a pitcher who required Tommy John surgery. Today, with the enormous contracts given by teams to star pitchers, I can well understand trying to protect their assets, but there has to be a middle ground. For McKeon, the only analytic computer he relied on was between his ears—he evaluated his players with his eyes, and he drew upon his deep knowledge of baseball and his time-tested instincts to control the game.

Evaluating pitchers using the eyes may yet return. The heavy reliance on analytics, such as baseball spin rates, has led some players to attempt to game the system. Pitchers—no one knows exactly how many or how widespread—were found to be using foreign substances to enhance their performances. Clear products, such as Spider Tack, allow a pitcher to maintain a better grip on the ball and can raise spin rates by 25 percent, making the pitch more difficult to hit. But such tactics aren't playing the game on a level field. Pitchers have hidden these chemical enhancements in their hats, gloves, even their hair and the sides of a uniform. Now there are penalties.

In an effort to crack down and return more integrity to pitching, Major League Baseball now requires pitchers to show their hands to an umpire at the end of every half-inning as the pitcher leaves the mound for his team dugout. In a move that makes them seem as if they have become baseball's equivalent of airport TSA screening agents, umpires have even inspected pitchers' belts. Additionally, umpires may conduct random spot checks of a pitcher's hand between innings, and the mere act of wiping one's hand before a spot check can subject a pitcher to immediate ejection. Given this heightened scrutiny, I have to wonder if, at some point, team front offices will insist on renegotiating player contracts, because what they bought—and were sold—may not be an accurate representation of true pitching ability.

The changed environment also impacts many more players beyond pitchers. During the almost two decades that I was active in Major League Baseball, I observed a seismic shift in the way players developed their strength in order to be successful on the playing field. Unfortunately, these changes have often been followed by injuries, with position players and pitchers spending inordinate amounts of time languishing on a team's "Injured List" (IL), unable to play and perform, which becomes costly for their teams. Indeed, conditioning the contemporary player is yet another striking example of how the game has changed.

Major League Baseball teams play from spring into fall. Keeping players healthy is a major consideration. Over the past several decades, injuries have continued to rise despite advances in physical training and medical technology. Because of the lucrative contracts now awarded to players, their careers tend to be longer, making them more susceptible to injury from prolonged stress as they age. It is universally accepted in the game that baseball players reach their peak performance years during their late twenties, and long-term contracts are now typically offered around that age. But there also appears to be no way to know which players are more susceptible to injuries that lead them to the IL. Younger, unproven players often continue to pitch through mild injuries, while established players with long, guaranteed contracts are less likely to play through an injury, often presenting a major challenge for an organization trying to manage its pitching staff.

A pitcher throwing overhanded goes through five phases before the ball is delivered to the plate: the windup, early and late cocking of the arm, acceleration, deceleration, and follow-through. During the late cocking and acceleration phase of throwing, the sheer force and stress placed on the UCL (ulnar collateral ligament, a small and sensitive ligament on the inner portion of the elbow that provides stability to resist force or angulation at the elbow joint) is more than the capability of the ligament. Pitching mechanics become vital, and poor mechanics and weak flexor muscles can contribute to a weakening of the ligament, which eventually leads to instability and rupture. Elbow injuries cause the greatest problems for pitchers and pitching staffs.

Studies focusing on elbow injury trends in MLB athletes during a twenty-year span indicate that the annual incidence of elbow injuries requiring reconstructive surgery has increased at an alarming rate. One-third of the procedures performed from 1973 to 2015 were done between 2011 and 2015. And a majority of these were to repair injuries to the UCL, a treatment that is often referred to as Tommy John surgery, named after the well-known and successful pitcher Tommy John, who injured himself while playing for the Dodgers in 1974. In fact, as of 2021, 534 Major League players have had Tommy John surgery since Tommy's inaugural operation in 1974. But pitchers are not the only players who sustain this injury. Catchers, infielders, and even outfielders are often susceptible to it too. Pitchers usually need twelve to fifteen months to recuperate before returning to active play, while position players often require less time. It is no surprise that a staggering 25 percent of all active Major League pitchers have a history of elbow reconstruction.

Young athletes are now throwing with more velocity and with elevated pitch counts. While it's the high-velocity pitch with control that wins the lucrative contract, that same pitch also puts an enormous strain on the elbow. To try to prevent these costly injuries, teams now encourage more sustained rest early in a pitcher's career and guard those pitchers who are at the core of a team's success. Team therapists and trainers focus on developing the strength and control of the core, legs, hips, and shoulders, hoping to improve the flexibility and shoulder range of motion as a way of minimizing injury. The hope is that this effort will result in more consistent and higher velocity pitches with fewer injuries to the elbow. It's also helpful to teach and develop correct throwing mechanics. Together, maybe these can be effective ways to decrease injuries in the future.

Not too many years ago, a player who felt injured went to his manager to let him know he was unavailable. But today there is an intermediary, the trainer, who acts as a buffer and tells the manager that the player "can't go," meaning he is unavailable to play. Reliability and dependability have become far less of a guarantee as the game changes. Even active players with longer careers seem to have more prolific injuries. In this environment, Cal Ripken's continuous performance record of 2,632 consecutive games will likely never be eclipsed. While I initially thought that closing the weight room and training room in the clubhouse would reduce injury, I realized it would only be resented by the players, and they would find alternatives in other locations while at the same time eliminating their coaches' involvement. This is the way the game is played now, but I am not sure it is the optimum way to encourage a safe transit for all concerned into the future.

<hr>

When Jack McKeon retired after the 2005 season, the Marlins had been spoiled. The right blend of experience, personality, chemistry, timing, and luck are requisite elements in the mosaic of a successful manager. Jack had them all, and these attributes are not often found in one person. I knew it was going to be a challenge to fill his shoes.

The highly talented and respected Yankee catcher Joe Girardi also retired as a player in 2005 and had made it clear that he wanted to be a manager. I met him in my New York office, and we talked for several hours. He was eager, bright, and energetic. I thought he would be the right managerial fit. Many in the baseball business believe that catchers often make successful managers—after all, the catcher is the only position player who faces the field and sees the game from the same perspective as the manager. He is also an "in charge" player.

I was ready to hire Girardi soon after our interview, but my baseball operations executives didn't appreciate my almost unilateral decision and were opposed to Joe from day one. From the outset of spring training, some of our executives sought to undercut or obstruct Joe's new ideas and suggestions. I am sure Joe sensed the negative atmosphere, but he most likely hoped it would subside by opening day. Unfortunately, it did not.

Things reached a head one Sunday afternoon during a home game against the Dodgers. Because of the intense midday summer heat, I was in an upstairs suite. Larry Vanover, who has excelled as an umpire and with whom I had many pleasant conversations, made a close call on a pitch that he saw as a ball where others firmly saw a strike. Rather than end the third inning, after that call, the batter ultimately reached first base, which led to a Dodgers scoring rally.

The oppressive heat began to abate, and I decided to move down to my seat near the dugout. As I walked toward my seat, I caught the umpire's eye as he was getting a cold drink between innings. After exchanging a couple of pleasantries, I said something like, "Larry, I think you missed that third strike call. Check the video later." There was no anger, and there were no raised voices between us. He knew I respected him. It was Joe who got upset. He looked at me furiously and, in front of all my players, said, "Jeffrey! Sit down and shut the hell up." Shocked and dismayed, I replied, "Are you talking to me?" He said, "Yes. If you don't like it, find someone else." Joe's remark was entirely out of character, and shortly thereafter, I realized that Joe was very frustrated with the friction he felt from the front office. The brief confrontation was not about the two of us; it was about the overall dynamics of the team.

After the game ended, I left for the airport and called David, the team's president, and also Larry Beinfest, the general manager. I gave them the green light to fire Joe, which they did immediately. Upon hearing the news, the players revolted. They were very loyal to Joe, which I admired. Due to both his demeanor and his knowledge of the game, Joe inspired their trust. David called me at the airport to say that I needed to return to the clubhouse immediately.

Back at the ballpark I went directly to Joe's office. Joe apologized, and I reversed the decision. But at the end of the year, Joe moved on and eventually managed the Yankees for ten seasons, winning the World Series in 2009. Joe may be intense, but no one can deny that he is devoted to his players, is fair-minded, and possesses an uncanny sense and passion for the game. I am glad to say that we remain friends. I continue to admire his baseball intellect. In retrospect, I wish we could have handled those events differently and kept his guidance and talents longer for the Marlins.

Before I brought in Joe Girardi, our executives had initially wanted to hire Fredi González, who was the third-base coach for the Atlanta Braves. Fredi had convinced our organization that he had a lot of baseball savvy and experience. Our executives thought he would be a good fit, so Fredi was hired for the 2007 season and remained with the club for almost four years. Highly respected and fully in control of his clubhouse, he was an appropriate choice. But the team wasn't winning and wasn't making enough progress year to year. Baseball, like most professional sports, is a business that demands results. By midsummer in 2011, it was obvious that we needed to move in a different direction if we were going to improve. So, after three and a half years, we changed managers, even though Fredi had great character and worked diligently at his craft.

Larry suggested we hire an interim manager, Edwin Rodríguez, who had been our Triple-A Minor League manager. I was in Italy that July on art business when I received one of many calls telling me that Rodríguez, angered by the attitude and behavior of some of his players, had suddenly quit. The prior Saturday night, he had removed one of his pitchers after a poor performance. Before the game had even ended, he found the pitcher in the clubhouse, laughing and joking with another player, and it made him furious. Rodríguez came into the clubhouse on Sunday morning, announced he was leaving, and walked out. I asked McKeon if he would finish the 2011 season. He did so in his usual highly professional and energetic manner. Meanwhile, I thought long and hard about who should be our manager for next season, when we would be moving to our brand-new ballpark.

On the last day in the old ballpark, the Marlins announced that Ozzie Guillén would become the manager in 2012. I had first met Ozzie in the late 1980s, when he was playing for the Chicago White Sox and was a brash newcomer. I remember sitting in the front row, next to the dugout in Oklahoma City, while the White Sox played the Philadelphia Phillies in a preseason exhibition game. Ozzie, in the on-deck circle, started what I will euphemistically describe as a "conversation" with a fan in the stands. The umpire actually had to encourage him to come to the plate. His penchant for animated conversations with fans and the media alike was typical of Ozzie, one of the game's great characters, although it eventually contributed to his downfall.

Ozzie had been the Marlins' hitting coach for the 2003 World Series year. Afterward, Jerry Reinsdorf, the White Sox's owner, asked if he could interview Ozzie to manage his team. It is one of baseball's great unwritten rules that a team always allows an employee to interview with another team for a new job at a higher level. Ozzie was hired and won a World Series for Chicago in 2005.

At the end of our 2011 season, I asked Jerry if we could interview Ozzie for our manager's job. Jerry was always one of my favorites in the league. He has been one of the most respected owners in baseball history, not merely because of longevity but also because of his passion, intelligence, and common sense. He has had his pulse on the game for decades. Jerry generously said yes. We thought Ozzie would be a natural in Miami, so we hired him and sent a player to the White Sox as part of the "manager trade." Our announcement that Ozzie would be our manager for the opening of the new ballpark was met with frenzied anticipation and enthusiasm from the media and the public alike. There was enormous excitement heading into the new season.

One of the more interesting experiments in Marlins history began with a call from the league office just prior to the 2012 opening day. The talented and imaginative programming executives at the MLB Network asked us to participate in a Showtime reality television series, to be produced by a consummate professional, David Check. The concept was to focus on one Major League franchise each year, providing a behind-the-scenes look into an organization, and it would include unrestricted access to the clubhouse. We would give them unconditional permission to film the organization, including private arguments, player discussions of sensitive matters, clubhouse banter, and more. In exchange, we calculated that we would be the beneficiaries of a marketing juggernaut to help promote our team and the new ballpark, which would now reach a different national audience.

At that time, there was considerable attention and excitement surrounding the Marlins. We had won the World Series during the previous decade, we had just built a state-of-the-art ballpark, and we had promised many new fan experiences in the stadium. We had signed several marquee players, and we had also signed the perpetually provocative Ozzie Guillén as our new manager. Now we had Showtime. What could possibly go wrong?

The answer was, a lot! The frenzied filming of the show was exciting at first, until one unfortunate and fateful night in April when everything changed.

David and I were at a family dinner and received a call concerning an article that was about to be published in *Time* magazine. Apparently, Ozzie had said something to a reporter during spring training about how he loved Fidel Castro, which was certainly not a wise pronouncement in Miami, nor in fact anywhere. After the article appeared, Ozzie tried to correct his words, saying he was misunderstood, that all he loved was the fact that Castro was a survivor. But his remarks produced a catastrophic explosion. There were boycotts and protests by the fans and daily media attacks. This incident changed the narrative. I'm sure Ozzie wished he could take back his words, but baseball is a very public game. When you enter that arena, you lose your privacy and are subjected to the whims of the public and the press. Needless to say, this made for interesting reality television for Showtime, but it was not exactly the type of coverage we had hoped for. By the end of the year, we were looking to replace Ozzie, as the situation was simply untenable.

In 2013, the team hired a young former Marlin, Mike Redmond, who was a catcher and was well-liked by his peers. "Red" had been Pudge Rodríguez's backup during our World Series success and had studied Jack McKeon's every move, often sitting next to him on the bench. But his work ethic did not match Jack's. By year two, Red was still receiving ongoing criticism from frustrated players in the clubhouse. Clubhouse chemistry and success usually stem from the manager or one of the players assuming the role as a leader, who inspires by example. Without direction from the manager or a player, the team doesn't cohere. It was obvious that our team lacked intensity and consistency. As one key player correctly observed to the New York press, "The fire is not there, and we are not giving ourselves a chance to win." In this atmosphere, Red's confidence waned. He has since returned to the National League as a bench coach, which has proven to be a great fit for him. I shall always wish him well.

I started thinking that "outside of the box" might be what we needed. We named Dan Jennings, then our general manager, as our interim manager, but Jennings's new role led to continuous strife in the clubhouse for two months.

By this point, I wanted an established, respected, and solid manager. I thought that if the Dodgers did not bring back Don Mattingly, he would be my choice, and this time, the front office agreed unanimously. Donny had led the Dodgers to a National League playoff and had been successful there. I had always admired his demeanor and his respect for the game. I saw him as a man with class, focus, and intensity, who was a born leader. "Donny Baseball" signed a four-year contract with the team. He has since signed two contract extensions.

In retrospect, Donny addressed problems with great aplomb, but it wasn't enough to compensate for mediocre prior draft selections and player development weaknesses. Managers can't immediately work miracles with the institutions they inherit, and, despite some superb hitting coaches like Barry Bonds and Frank Menechino, and Perry Hill, the premier infield coach in the game, 2016 remained a frustrating and sad season for the Marlins, culminating in the tragic loss of young José Fernández.

CHAPTER TWENTY-THREE

CHANGING THE SKYLINE FOREVER

MARLINS PARK

"The mother art is

architecture. Without an architecture

of our own we have no soul of our own civilization."

– FRANK LLOYD WRIGHT

B uilding a new baseball stadium in Miami required patience, tenacity, and resolve. The Marlins' two previous owners, the late
Wayne Huizenga and John Henry, had both tried and failed to
build a new stadium. After our team won the World Series in 2003, and
only a year after acquiring the franchise, David and I turned our attention
to building a new ballpark. We kept an optimistic view at all times. Little
did we know it would take nearly a decade. Initial overtures to local officials were rebuffed, but in the end, one of our early critics became one of
our greatest allies.

The Marlins' home stadium, Pro Player Stadium, also home to
the Miami Dolphins football team, was a veritable nightmare as a
venue for baseball. Because the field was shared with the Dolphins,
during the early part of the football season some dates of play over-
lapped, which caused dangerous conditions on the field, as the artifi-
cial turf was often badly gouged by both football and baseball cleats.
Unfortunately, one of our players, Damion Easley, stepped in a hole

in the outfield and twisted his ankle in September 2005, which prevented him from playing the rest of the season.

But other conditions made the stadium a challenge. During the baseball season, Miami experiences a tropical rainstorm almost every afternoon, often resulting in batting practice being canceled. The stadium's location, ten miles north of Miami, in Broward County, also made it difficult for fans to reach it from the heavily populated southern areas.

It was always my premise that if Miami wanted to be considered a Major League baseball city, it needed to have a Major League ballpark. My number-one objective was to do something good for the community, although it soon became clear that we needed to get creative to make our case. In 2005, we had many positive discussions but no concrete results. The county and city were reluctant to participate in a public-private partnership, leaving us with no choice but to play some hardball in order to give the fans the ballpark they deserved. Consequently, we formally applied for and were granted permission by Major League Baseball to explore a possible relocation.

David traveled to meet with officials in Las Vegas, Portland, and San Antonio, where he purposely attended games and intentionally sat in the first row. News soon got back that we were exploring other options for the Marlins, including moving the team. This was all done with the intention of getting local Miami officials to realize that the team was marketable and in demand. If they would not negotiate in earnest and consider a public-private partnership, we had to consider leaving.

In 2006, Miami-Dade County mayor Alex Penelas's term expired, and Carlos Alvarez became the mayor, with George Burgess as county manager and Manny Diaz remaining as the City of Miami mayor. (Miami is governed jointly by the two mayors: Miami-Dade County and the City of Miami.) Through the good graces of a mutual friend, the creative Javier Soto, who ran an excellent charity, the Miami Foundation, Manny and David met socially. They formed a strong friendship that continues to this day. Javier helped close the gap between the Marlins and the mayor on many of the key issues facing the creation of a new ballpark. David also devoted himself to building support among local community organizations, from churches and synagogues to Kiwanis and Boys and Girls Clubs, in an effort to reach out, one constituency at a time.

We never hired a lobbyist, something unprecedented among major sports teams. Previous efforts to go down that path had failed. Instead, David and I decided to take the lobbying campaign upon ourselves. David even registered as a lobbyist and met with every county commissioner. The major professional lobbyists were upset. One, Ron Book, a heavyweight in many circles, fought against us in the state capital, Tallahassee, fought against us locally, and opposed us at every step of the way, possibly because we didn't retain his services. But we wanted to be responsible for our own fate and not rely on backroom deals. We played by the rules at every step. We also made it very clear that we never intended to take any government money designated for public services such as hospitals and schools. For someone like me who, for decades, has supported such institutions philanthropically, that was never an option.

The stadium funding was to be based entirely on a "bed tax," which would be derived solely from tourist dollars spent on entertainment venues and hospitality. However, some business leaders in the community had other ideas, such as a second convention center. They banded together to argue against the stadium. Norman Braman, a local auto dealer, went so far as to challenge the Marlins in court. I'm proud to say he didn't win one motion nor a single objection. David told him in advance of going to trial, "Norman, you talk about your love of community. If you take the legal fees you're spending to sue us, we'll match them with the legal fees we are spending to defend ourselves, and we'll donate everything to a local charity of *your* choice." He declined and lost the case. With Braman's determination not to accept our offer, a local charity lost even more.

The best location for a new ballpark was in Little Havana on the sacred grounds of the Orange Bowl. This hallowed land embodied tremendous history. The old stadium had served as the site for five collegiate national championships and two Super Bowl championships. Building a new stadium on that site didn't initially win us kudos with the local historical societies, but it was the best location for the community. The Orange Bowl was crumbling and increasingly becoming a safety hazard for anyone attending events there. We ultimately proved successful, and at my insistence, we honored the Orange Bowl with a section of the new Marlins ballpark dedicated to its rich history. I wanted future baseball fans, both young and old, to understand what had transpired on these grounds prior to the baseball stadium.

Finally, in March 2009, the stadium agreement was complete. It was a great moment, but the honeymoon didn't last long. Immediately after the deal closed and we broke ground, David spoke to Miami business leaders at the Beacon Council's annual event. Years of pent-up frustration spilled over, and he proceeded to lambast all the politicians in the room who had just helped us. Fortunately, the project stayed on track. In the late spring of 2009, while I was on a business trip to Europe, David called with the good news that we'd received the necessary votes from the county commission. We could start to think about building a facility. The vote margin was 7–2. One of the dissenters was the recent county mayor, Carlos Gimenez.

———

From the start, I had envisioned building something special for the city. Architectural edifices often endure generations beyond their creators; in fact, often nobody remembers the creators, they only know only what you leave behind, as it becomes part of the fabric of the community. So, in 2009, I approached an internationally famous architect of sports venues, Earl Santee from the Kansas City firm Populous. I had met him in 1990 in Oklahoma City during preparations for a possible new site for the 89ers and hoped that one day we could eventually create something special together. We connected again in 2009, when we both happened to be visiting London and met at the hotel bar at Claridge's. He ordered a drink and asked, "I guess you want to do something in the spirit of Miami in Art Deco?" I responded that Art Deco was an important part of Miami's heritage, but I believed an important metropolis like Miami ought to look forward, so I sketched a more contemporary structure with a retractable roof on a Claridge's napkin. I wanted the vision to be sleek and a little bit controversial, different from everything else on the Miami skyline. It was an opportunity for the city to build something in a contemporary vein. Ten days later, Earl got back to me with a real architectural drawing of what the building could be. It was everything that I had envisioned and more. There is no architect more successful and brilliant at creating unique ballpark experiences than Earl Santee. I still have the napkin sketch from our meeting at Claridge's.

We also had to start contemplating what amenities we would include in the stadium and especially how to make it exciting and friendly for the fans. One example of our desire to be innovative was David's suggestion that we put a colorful fish tank behind home plate for the amusement of our youngest fans. My immediate reaction was, first and foremost, to find a way to protect the fish. We would need a protective plexiglass that could absorb a 110-mile-per-hour fastball and even a tossed bat. We had several of our players throw their strongest fastballs at a sample as a test. David even appeared on a National Geographic television program with the glass vendor and players to perform impact testing. It was hilarious, yet convincing and effective. We were able to solve our marine-life problems, and the fish tank was a success. No other ballpark had such an installation so popular with the fans. Just as baseball had left an indelible impression on me from an early age, I wanted to provide an additional wonderful experience for Miami's young fans. Unfortunately, the new owners unceremoniously removed it and replaced it with additional in-ballpark advertising.

From the outset, we also wanted the new Miami ballpark to have a retractable roof. In the old park, rain threatened every single day of the baseball season, and it seemed then as if I spent more time studying weather maps and radar than focusing on issues like player procurement and development. Batting practice was constantly interrupted, and games were often delayed and some-

ABOVE: *From a sketch on a napkin to reality in three dimensions.*

times postponed or canceled. Day games in the summer, moreover, were unbearably hot and humid. Consequently, also from day one, I insisted that the ballpark be air-conditioned. Some members of the county commission felt that would be too expensive, but as it turned out, this feature proved extremely valuable and practical to the team and to the overall fan experience.

In the end, the stadium was miraculously completed ahead of time and under budget—a rare achievement in major construction projects, including ballparks.

———

Soon after the good news of the county commission's approval, I was in Spain and met with a representative from Barcelona's Miró Foundation, a museum dedicated to the artist Joan Miró. Along with Picasso, Miró is one of Spain's most illustrious artists of the twentieth century. His works are in most major museums throughout the world. He designed Spain's colorful corporate logo, which is now inextricably linked to the country of his birth. I thought his customary brightly colored hues mirrored Miami's vibrancy and would be perfect for our ballpark.

To try it out, I carried home some color samples from the souvenir shop in the Miró Museum for our architects to consider. The ballpark ultimately became a harmonious amalgam of reds, blues, yellow, and greens, inspired by Miró's palette and Miami's tropical tradition. Sadly, all the colorful tiles in most of Marlins Park have now been painted over with a monochromatic dark blue paint, eliminating the colorful, joyful visual experience that defines the city of Miami. Later, I also asked the Miró family to give me permission to create a large mosaic based on one of his unique works, also echoing Miami's colorful Latin heritage. This extraordinary mural still enhances the entrance to the building and is now the only artwork that has not been removed or relocated by the new owners.

I was focused on creating other enjoyable experiences for the fans. Years before the ballpark opened, I began amassing a personal collection of contemporary nodding sculptural characters, also known as bobbleheads. Air currents and vibrations make the miniature figures nod and shake. Little did I know my passion would grow into one of the world's largest collections of baseball bobbleheads. I decided to lend them to the ballpark for everyone's pleasure and to design an installation we called the Bobblehead Museum. Eventually other generous Major League teams began sending us their bobbleheads to add to the museum. They were charming and whimsical, and to my delight, the collection proved to be a lasting attraction at Marlins Park.

No two bobbleheads are alike, and some are more intricate than others. One of my important bobbleheads is of Willie Mays making his famous catch of a Vic Wertz fly ball over his shoulder. If you look carefully, the ball is supported on a spring in the glove. Now that's a well-thought-out design! After selling the Marlins, I donated my own portion of the bobblehead collection, more than eight hundred examples, to the Baseball Hall of Fame in Cooperstown, New York. Jane Clark, whose family owns the Hall of Fame, is creating a wonderful space at the museum for the bobbleheads and other authentic memorabilia such as baseball cards, which can be seen throughout the year.

When Marlins Park finally opened in 2012, Michael Kimmelman, architectural critic for the *New York Times*, came to Miami. I walked around the new facility with him, explaining the nuances of what we had built. He wrote a glowing article on the front page of the *Times* describing the stadium as "a modern building with genuine panache" and said that due to my art background, I "cared more than most about aesthetics." He opened his review by stating, "After 20 years of retro-style ballparks since the opening of Oriole Park at Camden Yards in Baltimore, nearly all decked out with brick facades and calculated quirks that came to seem as predictable and interchangeable as the old doughnut-shaped arenas, Major League Baseball has its first unapologetic 21st-century stadium." Describing the overall architectural design, he added, "Angled walls and cantilevered ramps create a few elegant geometries, and multi-colored tiles provide decorative pizzazz. It is more than what you found in the grim concrete corridors of the old Yankee Stadium."

In the end, the city leaders, Manny Diaz and Carlos Alvarez, had the vision, tenacity, and fortitude, which eventually benefitted the entire Miami community. Their proud achievement deserves high praise. Proponents of the stadium never lost sight of what was important: reenergizing the sport and building a ballpark that was not only a great work of architecture but also a great work of art. It defines the Miami skyline with grace and beauty and can be seen as far away as twenty miles. As one drives south on Interstate 95, the building directs your view right into downtown Miami. White and pure, it looms impressively from a distance and is very much a statement of twenty-first-century architecture. Marlins Park looks forward rather than backward. I certainly believe the new stadium also unquestionably saved Major League baseball in Miami.

One of the ancillary benefits of building the new ballpark was the singular honor of hosting a Major League Baseball All-Star Game. Although it represented one of our proudest moments, the pathway to selection for this event was far less auspicious. Miami had never hosted an All-Star Game since the team's inception in 1993. It was a saga twenty-two years in the making for South Florida, replete with the bruised egos and dashed aspirations of two previous Marlins owners.

Major League Baseball originally awarded the 2000 All-Star Game to South Florida in 1995, two years after the expansion franchise entered the league. But in 1997, the team was in turmoil, and baseball decided to move the game to Atlanta's Turner Stadium. The purported rationale was that South Florida needed a new stadium, but it wasn't difficult to read between the lines. The impact that an All-Star Game can have on a local host community has widespread ramifications.

In 2002, when I purchased the team, the fans still felt very angry with all the earlier All-Star machinations. I asked David and the organization to begin to develop a plan to get us back on track to hosting an All-Star Game in Miami. As with other baseball endeavors, my primary goal was to do the right thing for the community and give the fans what they wanted.

But we were missing a key component in any competitive bidding process to win an All-Star Game. With new ballparks opening across the country at that time, it was clear that the Marlins needed a new stadium to attract an All-Star event. By 2012, the Marlins were able to guarantee an All-Star Game to the city within the next five years. Both Major League Baseball commissioners, Bud Selig and then Rob Manfred, kept their word, and the league awarded us the 2017 All-Star Game.

The news that Miami would be the official All-Star host for 2017 was extremely exciting. Three straight National League teams had been awarded the game, breaking with the tradition of alternating leagues. Commissioner Rob Manfred led a delegation of the league's most senior executives to Miami to hold a press conference. In attendance were many local mayors and politicians who did not always support the park but now could bask in the glory of bringing this accomplishment home to our fans.

The 88th edition of the All-Star Game was a resounding success, with flawless logistical execution and an exciting game as well. David and his team planned and masterfully coordinated all the events throughout the city. The American League won 2–1 in ten innings. Robinson Canó hit the thrilling game-winning home run and was named the most valuable player. The game aired nationally on the FOX network. We were delighted that ratings increased significantly from the previous year, with nearly ten million viewers. But for me, infinitely more important than the millions of television viewers were our local fans. They had remained loyal, endured an arduous odyssey to arrive at this moment, and relished, deservedly so, a turn in the spotlight, sitting in a sold-out crowd for one of baseball's crown jewels.

CHAPTER TWENTY-FOUR

THE ONLY CONSTANT IS CHANGE

"I'm not concerned with

your liking or disliking me...All I ask

is that you respect me as a human being."

– JACKIE ROBINSON

Societies—and their games—are constantly evolving. They advance in accordance with the environments we create around them. One of Newton's laws of motion—for every action there is an equal and opposite reaction—outlines our expectations whenever the winds of change blow. In baseball, I'm not sure there is always an equal and opposite reaction to every action, but I do think that for every action there is some form of reaction. Some reactions can be anticipated, but others are unexpected.

For almost as long as men and women have been walking the earth, they have searched for new ways to make their environment more convenient. Change may be inevitable, but it is also directional. It can veer off in many angles, but it never takes us back to where we were before we made that change. Even if a change proves disastrous and we are forced to retreat, we can't retreat without the scarring knowledge gleaned from the experience.

OPPOSITE PAGE: *The legendary Mel Allen made baseball come alive over the airwaves.*

In the effort to innovate and find new ways to make our environment more exciting and more entertaining, baseball is no bystander. If the ultimate paycheck for a great hitter resides in reaching fair territory on the other side of the outfield fence, it's only logical to assume that players are going to look for ways to increase their ability to get the ball to clear that fence, and preferably on a more regular basis. That is the natural ambition of every player in the batter's box, and that is why there is such a focused emphasis on conditioning and strength building. However, in keeping with Newton's law, other players—those playing defense—are going to work equally hard to find ways to make clearing the outfield fence more difficult. Hence, training in baseball, like in most other sports, has changed.

Because pitchers are throwing faster and harder than ever before, batters require more safety equipment to protect them from the occasional out-of-control stray fastball. Helmets with ear guards and elbow guards have now become the new standard safety gear in the industry. Fortunately, there are also new materials and manufacturing processes, which make these new protections stronger and more effective, and that's a good thing.

With new training methods have come new training philosophies, new training facilities, and newer and stronger players who are pushing themselves to the limits. Stadiums are changing to reflect this. First and third baseline safety nets have become standard—powerful players hit the ball harder, and fans need to be protected. Close calls on the field or disputed calls might even necessitate a new level of safety gear for umpires in the future, assuming the humanity of an umpire is not replaced by a robot.

The means for getting a close-up view of the action while in the ballpark have also evolved. Replays occur on giant Jumbotron screens, which also deliver entertainment between innings and closer connections to the athletes, as well as endless stats, in-game contests, and player sound bites. Being in a ballpark a century ago was the only way to witness how the game was played, and fans dressed to reflect the standards of the time. Men wore suits, ties, and hats, and women dressed up as well. Today, ballpark fans are much more casual, while at the same time, stadiums are focused on providing high-level comforts, including top cuisine and additional entertainment experiences. At home, viewers are getting a much better look at the details of the game due to the rapid changes in technology. All of this has fueled a twenty-first-century sport renaissance, including how the game is broadcast and new marketing possibilities.

Yet with all the changes, the game of baseball still strives to retain a similar magic to what it had one hundred years ago. The core principles of the game have remained relatively unchanged. Players are still looking to clear the fence, and fans are still looking for ways to feel closer to the players and the teams they support.

———

Merging the classic elements of the game and the cutting-edge world of technology occurs most often in the broadcast booth. As in much of life, conversation as a form of communication has practically disappeared in baseball. It has been replaced by texting, emails, tweets, and other forms of technological communication. Of course, these may contain information, but they lack the emotion of the spoken word.

The one exception to this trend is the power of the great broadcaster. As the game has evolved, so too have the massive national network and local broadcast deals, serving as each franchise's financial foundation. These broadcast deals are in fact the engines that give teams the ability to attract superstars and offer lucrative long-term contracts.

Broadcasters enliven the game and provide a store of knowledge that also allows us a chance to see the purity of the sport and its connections with the past. Today, they have a huge volume of information within easy reach, not to mention replays and multiple camera angles, and are expected to analyze plays immediately. It's a world where watching a ball clear the outfield fence is dissected by technologies and new cameras that can intimately follow the ball's flight and analyze the intricacies of each movement and the direction of every pitch. Great talent in the booth is what brings high level physics and mechanics back down to earthly reality.

Broadcast talent has always mattered to baseball. Sometimes I wonder if my eye for subtle details and vibrant color in art, or an ability to conjure an artist's imaginative creations, are directly related to the hours I spent in the dark listening to Mel Allen calling games on the radio for the New York Yankees. As a child, I used to put a radio under my pillow at night. I didn't want my mother to know I was listening to a game. My father knew, but to use a baseball term, he "let it slide." In fact, my mother probably knew too.

My early years preceded the transistor radio era, so hiding the electrical cord by covering it with a blanket was no easy trick. I would turn the volume down and try not to betray my reaction to the wondrous universe conjured by the radio. With Mel's every word and lively description, I felt as if I were right there at the game and could even catch a fly ball. For me, the Yankees' Mel Allen will always be the gold standard. With his remarkable voice, he set the stage for the other greats such as Chicago's Harry Caray, the Cardinal's Jack Buck, and the Dodgers' Vin Scully, among others.

—

The intricate language of baseball commentary combines colloquial familiarity with pertinent statistics and historically important facts, often served up with infectious passion. The great radio and television broadcasters of baseball have always been masters of the language, capable of delivering the game with an extraordinary vividness. I can still hear Mel's words as he called a home run: "There it is…. There it is! It's going, going, gone!" and a spectacular play always generated, "How about that!" The brilliant combination of surprise and affirmation emanating from his rising baritone seemed to be aimed directly at me, as was the game-scoring projectile he described. That catchphrase, when repeated, was a marketer's dream.

Mel's emphatic words sold seats and very quickly found their way into commercial taglines. When he wasn't using "going, going, gone" to describe a home run, he was coining a slogan for Ballantine beer, a Yankee sponsor, with the exclamation, "It's a Ballantine

Blast!" All the greats did it. They found phrases that made the fans comfortably bond with their preferred team. Their recurring words recalled the same repetitive certainty that ballpark vendors have as they call out their sales pitches for peanuts, pennants, and hot dogs.

Few exclamations from sportscasters are more immediately recognizable than "Holy cow!" Use of the term in baseball dates as far back as the early 1900s, but it became one of Harry Carey's signature phrases even before Phil Rizzuto, the talented Hall of Fame Yankee shortstop-turned-broadcaster, adopted it as his own. It seemed a natural replacement for less desirable on-air profanity. And while Vin Scully had a more modest approach, fans always knew it was game day when they heard his dulcet tones declare, "And now it's time for Dodger baseball." Of course, what was most compelling about Scully was that he worked alone for more than six decades. His colorful commentary graced the airwaves from Brooklyn to Chavez Ravine in Los Angeles.

For a baseball broadcaster, everything depends on the God-given gift of a special voice. All voices are unique; they are as identifiable and individual as a fingerprint. The broadcaster's accent, diction, inflection, and pronunciation will instantly conjure images of the person speaking. Be it on television or radio, the voice of a broadcaster remains his or her primary instrument for conveying enthusiasm and emotion.

Even with an exceptional voice, a broadcaster must learn to control it to deliver an engaging account of a game. The dedicated greats do their homework. They study history, practice their delivery, hone their observational skills, and combine all the parts to produce the most effective communication. When everything comes together, the masterful baseball broadcaster is able to articulate his unique vision and imagery, while leaving just enough room for the individual imaginations of the listeners. In this sense, the challenge is no different from that of any artist with a paintbrush, a palette, and a canvas. Like an artist with all the right supplies, he or she still has to be able to put it all together. Great baseball broadcasting, like great art, is an amalgamation of disparate parts and has now become an integral part of a team's persona.

The tradition of colorful play-by-play commentary lives on today in the calls and insights of such exceptional talents as Joe Buck, Michael Kay, Gary Cohen, Len Kasper, and the San Francisco duo of Mike Krukow and Duane Kuiper, among others. They all bring their own special brand of insight and charisma to the sport.

There are several formulas that work well in sports broadcasting, but few are better than pairing a great sportscaster with one or two exceptionally talented former players. An able broadcaster, who can call the plays with knowledge, preparation, passion, and conviction, combined with the experience and insight of one or two knowledgeable former players, can create remarkable chemistry in the broadcast booth. The perfect example of a dynamic broadcast team, each bringing his expertise into the booth to form an exciting harmony, is the trio of Yankees broadcasters Michael Kay with David Cone (of perfect game fame) and Paul O'Neill, the seventeen-year veteran right fielder. Kay uses his cadence brilliantly, while balancing it against the well-timed insights of Cone and O'Neill.

Every time the baseball heads over the outfield fence, Kay's rich voice utters the succinct signature, "*See ya.*" His commentary almost gives the ball a personality, as if it was once a friend but after a solid swatting leaves the field like a date gone wrong. "*There it goes, see ya!*" The listening audience is given the space to soar with the ball, while Cone and O'Neill consider the trajectory of the flight. Sometimes they say nothing. Or perhaps they paint the space with color and emotion. When they are at their best, the improvised dialogue is an art, a dance between voices, created from experience and orchestrated in observation. This combination of Kay, Cone, and O'Neill has found a way to interpret the music of baseball with a passion that is thoroughly infectious. And Cone is branching out beyond the Yankees. ESPN, recognizing his talent and ability to keenly observe the subtleties of the game, has hired him to join their Sunday Night Baseball analyst lineup.

The New York Mets have adopted that same combination of talent: a practiced broadcaster together with experienced players. The skillful thirty-year veteran of the New York Mets, broadcaster Gary Cohen, is complemented by former first baseman Keith Hernandez, veteran of two World Series and five All-Star Games, as well as the television comedy *Seinfeld*. Mets broadcasts also feature former starting pitcher Ron Darling, who played in the 1985 All-Star Game and 1986 World Series. On the air, the combined talent of these commentators can animate even the inactivity of a power failure during a night game. Cohen, whose cool baritone rises every time a ball heads toward the stands, has a signature call once the ball crosses the outfield fence. Cohen stamps its passport with his pertinent phrase, *"It's outta here!"*

Typically, in the case of a home run and indeed most plays, the color commentary defers to the play-by-play call. It's almost as if the play develops communally in the broadcast booth through experience and intuition. Hernandez and Darling call on the same instincts they used on the field. They can see in a flash if their participation will assist in creating a visual image or risk interfering with the scene. From my perspective, these two men working in conjunction with Cohen repeatedly add brilliance to the plays. It's not a job for every former player, but this pair has effortlessly made the transition from artistry on the field to colorful broadcasting in the booth.

Radio also maintains a large presence and pull in baseball. In Chicago, Len Kasper, the former television play-by-play caller for the Cubs, and before that the Marlins, made a surprise move in 2021 to the White Sox broadcast booth, where he now primarily calls the team's games on radio due to his love of the purity of AM radio baseball broadcasting. Whether seen and heard or only heard, Kasper maintains his exquisite sense of timing, which keeps listeners very engaged.

The San Francisco Giants duo of Mike Krukow and Duane Kuiper relies on two former players, working without a seasoned play-by-play broadcaster. It was a new combination when they began, and it has worked successfully. Between them, they mix play-by-play with color commentary to create their own unique brand of broadcasting. They met as teammates when they were both playing for the Giants and cemented an unbreakable friendship that has taken them from the playing field to the broadcast booth. Their combined chemistry, experience, knowledge, and humor have made them among the most popular broadcasters in baseball.

Giants baseball also delivers some of the best radio broadcasting talent in the game. If one can't catch the television broadcasting talent of Kruk and Kuip (as they've affectionately come to be known), one can listen to Jon Miller on the radio. As the voice of Giants radio, Miller projects a near-operatic baritone to deliver his own insightful interpretation of play-by-play action. His unique inflections and tones are instantly recognizable to fans anywhere.

The ability to translate observed action into vivid visual imagery through the descriptive use of language is the lifeblood of radio broadcasting. With radio, we require the colorful, insightful, expressive energy emoted through a brilliant voice as a way to invite the stadium, the game, and the action into our minds.

The musicality that I've alluded to in some of the individual sportscasting talent can also be found in the Yankee Stadium radio team of John Sterling and Suzyn Waldman. Rarely missing a game, Sterling brings Mel Allen full circle and provides his play-by-play commentary by stamping Yankee calls with his signature emphasis on the word "the." In doing so, he creates a musical pitch as he mimes (for example) a pitcher's wind up with "Theeee pitch is…" His signature home run phrase, "*It is high, it is far, it is gone,*" possesses a poetic rhythm, perfectly timed to the action on the field.

While Sterling's calls might at times sound musical, Suzyn Waldman brings experienced musicality to the timing of her color commentary. The Massachusetts-born Waldman is a former musical theater actress and singer. A true professional, Waldman has stayed tough and dedicated in an unbalanced, largely male-dominated profession. Her musical experience is evident as she has even confidently sung the national anthem at many Yankees home games. Together, Sterling and Waldman, with their well-informed narratives demonstrating the brilliant harmony of teamwork, have shattered barriers. They continue to exceed expectations with their superb radio broadcasting.

———

Among all the talent in baseball broadcasting on radio or television, Joe Buck is in a league of his own. Simply put, Buck today emits pure gold rarely seen for decades. Everything from his spoken cadence to his insights and extensive knowledge flows with engaging certainty. As the son of a Hall of Fame broadcaster, he has followed in his father, Jack Buck's, footsteps. Clearly, sportscaster DNA is in Joe's blood. It starts with that voice—like a superstar player or a master artist, you either have it or you don't. Joe Buck has the voice, but beyond the inherent tone, there is a technique that enables him to deliver a range of emotions with exceptional clarity. Similar to a trained opera singer, his control seems to begin in the diaphragm. No matter how emotional or exciting the action is on the field, he is able to capture it in his voice and emote it through the various octave shifts of excitement without ever losing his breath or failing to keep a fan fully engaged.

Early in his career, he provided play-by-play for the Louisville Redbirds, a Minor League Triple-A affiliate of the St. Louis Cardinals. Around 1991, Joe started filling in for his dad, covering Cardinals baseball on local television. It soon became apparent that Joe's exceptional talents could not be limited to one team or even one sport. In 1994, Fox hired the then twenty-five-year-old Buck to announce NFL Football, making him the youngest man to ever announce for the NFL on network TV. In 2022, ESPN lured him away to join its Monday Night Football broadcast booth for a reported salary of nearly $15 million a year.

Clearly there is a lot about Joe Buck that makes him a multitalented standout. But like anyone performing in the public eye at the top of his game, Joe has his fair share of critics. Yet when one considers some of the criticisms lodged against Buck, such as that he is not impartial and only got his start because of his father, they are simply comical. As a television broadcaster competing in the field of communication, Joe Buck is not biased. He is quite brilliantly serving the fashion of our times, generating competitive content that draws healthy debate. In other words, he is engaging his audience in a format capable of transitioning across multiple platforms—including social media, which is particularly geared toward opinions and debate and the unmoderated voices of fans.

In the art world, there is a French term that describes the situation when an artist or his work reflects the times accurately. The concept also applies to Joe as he continues to create new commentary. Put simply, Joe Buck is *au courant*. Artists who are *au courant*, who read the times accurately, are often somewhat ahead of their time. They are able to perceive societal shifts just before they happen. Consequently, they do not miss the change. Buck's regard for certain old-school broadcasting techniques, combined with an ability to take the pulse of his audience today, suggests he exhibits a distinctive maturity. I am convinced that one day he too will enter the Hall of Fame.

The bedtime stories of my childhood were told to me through the magic of radio by the legendary Mel Allen. I hope that tradition is continuing for young fans today. When the brilliance of the broadcaster prevents you from slipping into sleep, you have truly been transported to another world.

CHAPTER
TWENTY-FIVE

COMMISSIONERS, OWNERS, AND MONEY

"There are many people who know me

who can't understand...why I would go to work on

something as unserious as baseball. If they only knew."

– BART GIAMATTI

A Major League Baseball owner finds himself or herself in one of the world's most exclusive clubs. It is also a great privilege. The prestige of ownership, however, was never what attracted me. I always wanted to own a baseball team based purely on my love for the game. I found interacting with my twenty-nine other owner colleagues enjoyable, stimulating, and challenging. It was fascinating to have a front-row seat to this side of baseball. Although the game of baseball is often about one-on-one confrontations on the field, there was also an abundance of serious off-field discussions on important issues, where key decisions about the future of the game would be made.

There is no doubt that there were strong egos and individual agendas among the thirty people in the room at baseball's quarterly owners' meetings, always held in a different city to accommodate the travel needs of thirty teams from Seattle to Miami. Each team had a designated "control person" who acted as a liaison with the commissioner's office for matters that related to the team. Every-

OPPOSITE PAGE: *Major League Baseball Commissioner Rob Manfred.*

one's common goal was always to manage the game collectively, while preserving the interests and valuations of individual franchises. Outside of baseball, most owners were recognized leaders in their respective industries, including real estate, fast-food chains, retail stores, communications, and private equity, among others. I remember occasional healthy disagreements, often about competitive balance and the ever-present opposing interests of large-market versus small-market clubs. Discussions often focused on the periodically tense issue of league-wide revenue sharing. In general, everyone operated with the best of intentions for the good of the game. Consensus was important, and Commissioner Bud Selig was the master of consensus building. The owners frequently confronted historic issues during my tenure that resembled the same problems faced in other professional sports.

The pace of the game was an important topic. Baseball shared the universal need to reach a new and younger audience. These particular challenges persist in most sports but are especially acute in baseball. The average Major League Baseball game lasts almost three hours and ten minutes. With increased competition from faster-paced sports, baseball stands at a crossroads. It will never be basketball, nor should it be. But small tweaks introduced over time can help speed up the game and attract a younger generation of fans.

At many owners' meetings, committee recommendations focused on limiting the time between innings and also reducing delays, such as the number of mound visits, pitching changes, and on-deck warmup routines. For example, to speed up the game, relief pitchers now are required to face a minimum of three hitters, if they start an inning. More recently, in an effort to limit long extra-inning marathons, baseball has adopted a novel innovation: if a game is tied after nine innings, the top and bottom of the tenth inning (and any innings thereafter), start with a man on second base. That base runner is always the last hitter to have been struck, fouled, tagged, caught, or thrown out in the previous inning. These and other changes have become an effective way to use managerial strategies to speed up the game for a quick and fair resolution. The hope is that these changes will cut the overall playing time for a game by as much as 10 or 15 percent, while still keeping the game's purity intact. Ongoing reform and adjustments are always necessary, especially with the continued influx of new technologies to help fans capture the experience in ways that still make baseball fun and attractive.

———

Performance-enhancing drugs have long been the scourge of amateur and professional sports, making competitive play unfair. They repel fans who want to admire players as heroes. Baseball was disproportionately affected by this problem. In 1998, when I was already a part of the baseball fabric, Mark McGwire and Sammy Sosa, while shattering Babe Ruth's home run record of sixty home runs per year, exposed the impact of performance-enhancing drugs on the game. Commissioner Bud Selig was aggressive in combating the issue and, in combination with the Major League Baseball Players Association, eventually set in motion guidelines for testing, regulating, and limiting steroid use.

The players association was initially opposed to random drug testing, claiming it to be a violation of the players' privacy. However, there was unanimous agreement that the best path forward for everyone was to deal with the issue in conjunction with the commissioner's office. This was good for everyone, and clearly good for the game. In 2005, ownership and ultimately the union mutually agreed to a stricter policy that became one of the strongest in sports. It included a fifty-game, then hundred-game suspension, followed by a lifetime suspension for third-time offenders. By 2018, it had increased to a mandatory eighty-game suspension for a first-time offender. These types of honest and necessary concessions were what baseball sorely needed to preserve the game.

Now, we are witnessing a new golden era of player performance. Athletes like Aaron Judge, Mike Trout, and Bryce Harper among others have demonstrated that dedication, passion, and talent alone are all that is needed to run quickly or hit mammoth home runs. They also proved that when you do it fairly, the results are even more rewarding and exciting. Today the game is flourishing under the leadership of Commissioner Rob Manfred, who, to his credit, is steadfast in his conscientious dedication and resolve to maintaining the integrity of the game.

———

Without a doubt, the single most controversial word in all of sports is "money." The concept of money probably represents the greatest disconnect between ownership and the fans. From a fan's standpoint, the financial well-being of their favorite baseball team is wholly irrelevant. They care only about wins, losses, and championships. They believe that owners should care only about those things as well. This misconception is promulgated by the media. However, having been both a fan and an owner, I will not apologize for the following statement: I do care about wins, losses, and championships, but from the moment when I became an owner of a professional baseball team, I had to pay attention to the wins and losses on the financial statements as well.

While very few owners would discuss this publicly, I am not alone. There is not one owner of any team in baseball who enjoys writing checks at the end of the season to cover losses. I will never forget Bud Selig's words to all in attendance at my first owner's meeting in Phoenix, Arizona, in January of 2000. He said he could never understand why an owner would approve a budget that ended the year at a financial loss instead of a profit. Why would we, as owners, want to sit through 162 grueling games, live through the aggravation that certainly comes each and every day on and off the field, all for a twenty-nine-out-of-thirty chance to end the season miserably, not winning or even competing in the World Series, and on top of that, write a check from our own funds? Unfortunately, as much as I heard him that day, I didn't exactly follow his advice. The vast majority of my years as an owner in Miami ended with a monetary loss, and fourteen out of fifteen ended without a championship. Walking the tightrope between trying to win and the realization of the difficulty of achieving that goal is much harder than one would think.

In addition to the personnel challenges the Marlins faced, we also faced financial obstacles. The financial dimensions of baseball are complex, governed by multiple revenue streams, delayed income, long-term earnings, and shared income streams with the rest of the teams in the league. What was always crystal clear to me was that the larger, big-market teams had the most lucrative television arrangements. The basic formula is that the broadcast companies pay a substantial annual fee for the exclusive rights to air your games. These guarantees are usually in the form of long-term contracts, often in excess of ten years. Unfortunately, that was never our situation in Miami.

Our television contract was a major hindrance to our financial success. The terms we inherited required the broadcast companies to pay the Marlins a maximum of $18 million per year, and we were contractually obligated to that arrangement for many years. At the same time, team payrolls were rising throughout the industry, and fans as well as the media were demanding competitiveness. This situation created a painfully unsustainable situation in which I was forced to pour more money into the team. Most owners occasionally need to invest in their team, but they are fortified by massive outside revenue streams. We never had the luxury of these sources of income.

━━━

When Steve Ross became the majority owner of the Miami Dolphins in 2009, he approached me with an idea to launch a new regional television network in which the four major South Florida teams would participate in a year-round sports channel. I explained to him that baseball would provide key programming for at least six months; Ross proposed that he own 50 to 60 percent of the network, and the other three teams would split the remainder. I pointed out the disparity between baseball's 162 games and the

National Football League's 17. I further pointed out to him that this network could only rely on football summer practice camp, since the National Football League controlled the national television rights to all NFL games. I suggested that we explore a more equitable arrangement. In the end, we agreed to disagree.

In anticipation of the opening of our new Miami stadium, the organization took a gamble on making some major investments in free agent players. It became obvious shortly thereafter that these new players, who significantly added to our rapidly expanding payroll, weren't performing up to expectations. Even with the managerial problems we faced, the only option for us, given the unsuccessful product we were putting on the field, was to trade these players. I certainly understood the fans' frustration, since we all wanted continuity. As the owner, however, I had to make decisions for the long-term health of the franchise. The new players just didn't complement each other or gel together, nor did they perform adequately as individuals. We had one of the largest payrolls in the league, with unquestionably the worst television deal. It left us in an untenable situation.

Every year after our championship in 2003, I followed my heart and agreed to sign that extra player or take on additional payroll beyond our budget, all in the name of hope and the faith that we would achieve a second championship. That action would be followed by a conversation with my financial department. Such conversations always ended with a list of dates by which I needed to put money into the team. What didn't change over my nearly two decades of ownership was the maddening desire to win and the concomitant indifference that fans and media felt about our balance sheet. What did change were the team expenses required to attain that elusive next championship. The minimum salary for players almost tripled during my tenure. The cost of even average free agents continued to rise year after year, always disproportionately to the increase in revenue.

In retrospect, I smile knowing that normal business concepts don't always apply in sports, and not all of my personal business rules applied either. In the vast majority of businesses, maybe even all, when expenses go up, prices to consumers go up in lockstep. When the price of production for a car increases, so does the base price of that car. When the price of production of reading glasses increases, so does the price of reading glasses. When the price of coffee beans increases, your morning cup of coffee increases equally. I could go on and on, because the point stays the same. In baseball, it was inconceivable to increase the price of tickets as well as signage or TV rights to offset the increase in player payroll and other expenses. You may find this argument disingenuous because you believe that the sale price I was able to attain in 2017 more than made up for any losses incurred throughout the year, but that is not a metric that is used in any other business. It would be inexcusable for a business owner to simply rely on anticipated future asset appreciation to cover current annual operating losses.

There is no reason to finance annual losses in any business, simply hoping to recoup your investment when the business is sold. Even in an industry like professional baseball, where franchise values seem to increase with reckless indifference toward multiples found in other industries, I never wavered from the lessons of my business education. Simply put and permanently understood, there are no guarantees in business. While outside observers may think that it was a slam dunk to recoup all the annual losses I financed, I was the one who had to take the risk every year and the one who had to work tirelessly to protect my investment, while at the same time attempting to feed everyone's insatiable desire to win, including my own.

Sports teams are not charities; they are businesses. We are in the business of making money. Like any other business. I will always regret not winning more and not making more successful decisions regarding player acquisitions, in conjunction with our executive office. Team building is a unique challenge no matter who is in charge. By the time I sold the team, we had accumulated a very strong lineup, but the new ownership chose to trade many of our star performers to build the team their way. However, trading Christian Yelich for four players, for example, did not result in any major performance gains for the team. And those four players are now gone!

Looking back and thinking about my tenure, I refuse to apologize for treating my team like a business and not a 501(c)(3) charity. Every time I am approached by a fan who wonders why I didn't pour even more of my own money into the team, I always respond the same way. I turn the conversation around and ask that fan whether he or she would operate his or her business that way. Ultimately it is a question of risk versus reward, and I felt the level of risk that I took throughout my ownership tenure would hopefully be worth the reward. The new owners have faced similar challenges; they opted to trade Giancarlo Stanton, a player we had deemed to be significant for the team's success, to the Yankees to eliminate his salary and reduce yearly payroll expenses.

There is no doubt that during my almost two decades, I was well aware that Major League Baseball is a growing industry and that team ownership is an honor and an exclusive club that many people want to enter. As I saw industry revenue increasing, I always thought that the value of my team would increase, but thinking something to be true does not make it so. Knowing that I had created the value that I worked so hard to achieve was satisfying. Certainly, I have never met another owner who wasn't focused on the current and future value of his team. I, of course, was no different. The dollar amounts required to maintain baseball franchises have increased dramatically with time, from player salaries to player signing bonuses to general manager and manager salaries, and it remains to be seen whether franchise values can continue to rise to keep pace with the annual expenses. But that is for another day and now for another group of people.

———

There is one area where I believe we may have actually gone too far in the recent changes to baseball. I miss the verbal confrontations that occurred with some regularity in the past on the field. Other sports still have them, and undeniably fans crave them. I loved watching Lou Piniella, who was a crafty and smart manager, occasionally get extremely upset and angrily kick up infield dirt or pick up a base and throw it into the outfield. Managers and players can no longer dispute balls and strikes called by the home plate umpire for fear of automatic ejection. The excitement of a tirade from the Yankees' Billy Martin or the Orioles' Earl Weaver no longer enlivens the game. Perhaps the restrictions on behavior have become too regulated. Baseball never wants to lose some of its earlier spontaneity, color, and flavor.

During my tenure in the league, I was exceptionally fortunate to collaborate with two of the very best commissioners any professional sport has ever known. Bud Selig served as commissioner of Major League Baseball from 1992 to 2015. He was without a doubt the game's most influential leader. With a steadying hand, he brought the sport into the modern era with innovative ideas such as realigning teams and creating a playoff model for the concept of the Wild Card. The Wild Card enabled more teams to have the hope to make the playoffs well into September. By creating three divisions in each league, there is always a race to see who will make the Wild Card and compete as one of the four teams in the playoffs. Without question, there will be more modifications to league alignment and structure, all in the name of growing the game and building more excitement and hope for fans.

Bud also struck lucrative television deals, instituted necessary revenue-sharing formulas to help achieve competitive balance, and implemented the instant replay. He was also innovative in starting MLB Advanced Media, a limited partnership of all club owners. Most of all, he was passionate about the game, which is crucial for a leader. Aside from those critics who rarely like new ideas taking away from the "purity" of the past and those who failed to understand him, most baseball owners and executives admired his vision and tenacity. In time, Bud's innovations will be celebrated as part of his legacy with well-deserved appreciation. In addition to his great baseball intellect, he and his wife, Sue, are incredibly generous contributors to their community and tireless believers in working on behalf of many important charities.

I first met Bud Selig at the Regency Hotel in New York in the early 1990s. He spoke about his baseball experiences, both good and bad. He was very candid with me from the outset, explaining how important it was for him to have a team in Milwaukee, which was his hometown. When the Milwaukee Braves left for Atlanta in 1966, Bud worked tirelessly to attract the Seattle Pilots to move to Milwaukee. Renamed the Milwaukee Brewers, the franchise flourishes today under the leadership of one of its best owners, Mark Attanasio. Bud always maintained that nothing was perfect in sports, but baseball was still the greatest sport in the world.

It's not all fun and games, and there are certainly ups and downs. Only one team can win each year. Many owners have been in the game a long time and have never experienced the ultimate thrill and exhilaration of winning a World Series. If the team is not winning, an owner is definitely not popular with the fans. I didn't enter the game seeking adulation and, as Bud once told me, "There is no such thing as a beloved owner." He was right.

When he decided in September 2013 to retire after the end of the 2014 season, it appeared that Bud's shoes would be almost impossible to fill. Nonetheless, the competition to replace him was keen. For months there was intense speculation about which candidate had the inside track. David and I had an excellent long-term relationship with Bud's then chief operating officer, Rob Manfred. He was (and still is) fair, smart, focused, and firm, four qualities needed to take the game to its next level.

After Bud announced his retirement, many months of behind-the-scenes discussions, speculation, and lobbying ensued. The selection process for the next commissioner culminated in a contentious four-and-a-half-hour voting session in August 2014. Rob finally received the needed twenty-third vote on the sixth ballot, being selected over Boston Red Sox chairman Tom Werner in the first contested vote for a new commissioner in forty-six years. Tom remains an excellent executive and a great asset to the game. (The third candidate, former executive vice president of business Tim Brosnan, withdrew his nomination just before the start of final balloting.)

Rob has spoken publicly about David's and my strategic efforts in garnering the final votes necessary for his election. I'm happy to have been able to participate in this way. Without a doubt, baseball made the right decision for its future. With the inevitable impact of new technology and increased competition for fan loyalty, Rob is uniquely positioned to navigate the future evolution of the game. Baseball hasn't changed much in 150 years, but in order to keep moving forward, the sport needs to adjust to the circumstances and the rhythms of time. Change doesn't always make you popular, but leadership isn't a popularity contest. Rather, it's always about doing the right thing, and being both current and courageous.

Rob Manfred is a man of his word. In life and in business, one's word is all-encompassing. In 2016, I asked him to consider being the honoree at the annual dinner for the ALS Foundation's New York chapter, a charity that I support. He couldn't do it that year because of a scheduling conflict but said he would commit for 2017. Even though I had sold the Marlins in October of that year and was no longer an owner, he still kept his commitment. His presence made the event one of the most successful in the history of the New York chapter. Rob is the right man to be the commissioner of baseball, and ownership is fortunate to have him.

CHAPTER TWENTY-SIX

LOOKING AHEAD

WILLIE MAYS

> "Why does everyone talk about
>
> the past? All that counts is tomorrow's game."
>
> – ROBERTO CLEMENTE

Not long after José Fernández's tragic death, I began to consider life after baseball. After almost two decades in the game, I was filled with conflicting thoughts. I had already begun to receive numerous inquiries about selling, but I wasn't convinced that I was ready. As the offers kept coming, I began to consider them seriously, and I decided at least to discuss options for selling the team. Having previously executed many complex baseball transactions, the role of an outside investment banker seemed unnecessary. We reasoned that the process of selling the partnership could be more cost-effective by employing very few external consultants. I asked David to collaborate with the Marlins' New York attorney, Proskauer partner Wayne Katz, who is without a doubt one of the most capable and knowledgeable sports attorneys in America. Additionally, the team CFO Michel Bussiere drew on his reservoir of financial experience to advise us. He had long ago proven himself to be one of the best chief financial officers in the game.

To put the team in play for a possible sale, we established a multipronged strategy. We first let it be known by word of mouth to the many entities and people who had already inquired about a

OPPOSITE PAGE: *A prized bobblehead of the great Willie Mays.*

possible sale that we were now considering selling the team. With a spectacular stadium facility and a new media arrangement on the horizon for 2020, not to mention an exciting team with the best outfield in baseball and unmatched confidence, we felt that at most we were missing only one or two front-line starting pitchers for another run at a championship.

We then set the initial price at $1.6 billion to establish a market number and test the waters. We only wanted serious bidders. After all, in any negotiation it's possible to come down in price but not to raise an initial price. We also wanted to always have at least three groups at the negotiating table, which would create a rotating mix of possible preferred buyers—as each one indeed was at different times during the process. Each participant also happened to possess a very strong ego. Each felt he would be the savior of baseball in Miami, which, quite frankly, embodied the right quality for new ownership.

In some ways, the process was akin to a reality television show. Leading one effort was Jeb Bush, a former two-term governor of Florida, brother and son to United States presidents, and now a private equity executive. Jorge Mas—a favorite of the Cuban community, whose father was beloved in Miami and had led the Cuban American National Foundation, and was running MasTec, a $5 billion company—headed another group. Mas is one of the Miami community's true leaders. He was always honest and a straight shooter in all negotiations. And lastly, we had the interest of Derek Jeter, who is one of the most renowned retired baseball players alive. He had financial backing from serious investors such as Bruce Sherman.

When I was first contacted by Jeter, he asked if I would speak with one of his new backers. Bruce and I didn't know each other, but my initial introduction to him was a prearranged conference call. Bruce was on a boat in the middle of the Mediterranean at the time, and he sounded excited and seriously interested. When I eventually met him, I inquired about why he wanted to buy the Marlins. He responded by telling me that he had sold his business a few years earlier and wanted to try his hand at owning a professional sports team, specifically the Marlins. Clearly, we had built a sustainable and important franchise in South Florida.

The sale process, however, was not without problems. In the beginning, each party conveyed tremendous confidence in their ability to complete the deal, but all were susceptible to the chicken-or-the-egg dilemma. It was apparent that several of the potential investors would only commit publicly if they could ensure that they were committing to the winning bid. We required that bidders had to have firm financial commitments in place before a public announcement. This was a very high-stakes game with many potential outcomes. To succeed, I had to employ several lifelong strategies that have repeatedly served me well, namely the importance of thorough information gathering as we evaluated competing bids, seeking parallel paths between the bidders, and always finding alternatives with a plan B.

The process also proved to be a leaky faucet. All the groups were strategically leaking their positions and stories to news outlets. For example, at one point, another baseball star, Alex Rodriguez, was reported to be interested. It was common knowledge that Derek Jeter and Alex were former teammates but not close friends. The rumor got back to Derek that Alex was an interested bidder. Although we didn't fuel the rumor, we also did nothing to stop it, since the media was trying to write the story anyway with their own "facts." The process dragged on through the entire 2017 season, with rumor and innuendo running rampant. A new story would appear almost daily, revealing that one of the groups had won the bid, when nothing could have been further from the truth.

We communicated nearly every day with Major League Baseball commissioner Rob Manfred to garner his thoughts, as well as his guidance. It was fascinating to watch the emotions, intellects, maneuvers, and passions of these men positioning themselves to acquire what I had cherished for so long. I honestly didn't have a favorite. It had to be someone ethical, the highest bidder, and acceptable to baseball (which all the bidders were). I remained committed to selling and was unwavering once I made this decision. I knew there was no going back, and I was ready.

The sale of the franchise in October in 2017 ultimately changed the economics of baseball forever. The transaction was approved by a unanimous vote of the owners and to the satisfaction of the commissioner. Every single team's value increased that day in October. It seems likely that, in the future, no team will sell below $1 billion. To prove this point, the Kansas City Royals were sold in 2019 for $1 billion. We received more value for the team than I thought possible. I still think Miami is a franchise that will continue to appreciate if handled properly.

After the lengthy and agonizing sale process, we were initially pleased to sell the team to Bruce Sherman and Derek Jeter. In addition to his successful career spanning two decades and five World Series rings, Derek had been an important presence in the game, and I enjoyed our conversations. In 2012, when the Yankees were playing the Marlins in a preseason game in Miami, he approached me about wanting to buy a team. "One day, after I retire," he said. I mentioned to him that if I ever decided to sell the team, I would gladly give him an opportunity. I always envisioned him being an owner with long-term vision, integrity, and solid instincts. But being a player in the eyes of the fans and being an owner in the world of big business are two entirely different worlds, with different challenges. Fans want a winning team, and they want it sooner rather than later. Not long after the deal was done, the new ownership immediately began a new chapter. They were entitled to do it their way.

They have, however, learned the hard way that it is far easier to earn accolades when you sit in the dugout as opposed to the owner's box. DEREK JETER HAS GONE FROM ON THE FIELD LEGEND TO OFF THE FIELD BUFFOON, headlined the sports fan website *The Comeback* in a column. "When Jeter faces criticism, like he did in the HBO Real Sports interview with Bryant Gumbel, he comes across as defensive, evasive, and dismissive," opined sportswriter Michael Grant. Even *Florida Trend*'s glossy "Florida 500" noted in its short entry that "Jeter has drawn criticism for not engaging more with fans as he's traded big-name players." The numbers have borne this out. In 2018 and 2019, the last pre-COVID-19 seasons, the Marlins ranked dead last for attendance of teams in the league. In 2020, Andre Fernandez, writing in *The Athletic*, noted that if Derek didn't deliver on some of his promises, "Jeter would seem destined to join other legendary players turned executives like Michael Jordan…who were never able to translate their success as players to their second lives as owners." (Interestingly, in addition to being part owner of an NBA team, Jordan has also long been rumored to be one of the secondary investors and minority owners of the Marlins.)

On February 28, 2022, Fernandez's words became prophetic when Jeter made a surprise announcement that he would be exiting the Marlins and quitting the management side of baseball with a full year still left on his contract. The Marlins' principal owner, Bruce Sherman, issued a statement saying, "The Miami Marlins and Derek Jeter announced today that they have agreed to officially end their relationship. The Marlins thank Derek for his many contributions and wish him luck in his future endeavors." After watching this rather ignominious end to Derek Jeter's front office career, I wonder how many other successful pro athletes will continue to be interested in or eager to explore the owner's side of professional sports.

On reflection, it was the right time for me to sell the club and move on to the next stage of my life. But, as can be expected, it has not always been easy to watch so much change in Miami from the sidelines. I have profound pride in what our team built together, and I feel sadness for those who are no longer part of the Marlins universe. Of course, change is the norm, as new ownership almost always wants to put its own stamp on the club. I know I did. I am hopeful, as one who has long loved the Marlins, that its future will be filled with success.

Our staff was, and in retrospect remains, among the best executive teams in the industry. It took considerable time to assemble these talented evaluators and superb baseball minds. However, they were all fired soon after the team was sold. Derek instructed David to fire all of them on the first day of the new ownership and then promptly fired David the next day. I have great affection and admiration for Jeff McAvoy, Mike Berger, Jim Benedict, and Marc DelPiano. Happily, they quickly found work with other clubs. The Chicago Cubs immediately hired Jim to evaluate and improve their pitching, as he had done so creatively for us. The Milwaukee Brewers pursued Mike because of his wisdom and knowledge of the game. Jeff now assists Andrew Friedman with the Los Angeles Dodgers. Marc, a superb talent developer, soon joined the Yankees. Three of these four teams reached the playoffs in 2018. The decision to fire these talented baseball evaluators, particularly with three years of guaranteed salary left on their contracts, still baffles my mind.

The firing of Marlins special assistants and Hall of Fame players Andre Dawson and Tony Pérez was handled in the same poorly thought-out way: Derek instructed David to fire them rather than have a conversation himself. Many in and out of the league commented that this smacked of disrespect, and nearly two years later, both players indicated they would boycott Derek's induction ceremony to the Hall of Fame (which occurred during COVID). Dawson bluntly told Scott Miller of Bleacher Report, "But I don't have a sense or feeling like I want to sit on that stage to hear what [Jeter] has to say."

Our former manager Jack McKeon is in a league of his own—a baseball treasure who has been highly respected in the game for more than sixty years. Jack retired in 2005, and he asked me if he could come back in twelve years to manage for just one game. He would be eighty-seven years old. That would have made him the oldest manager in the history of America's national pastime. Connie Mack held the record, and Jack wanted to surpass it. Having reached ninety, he is still as sharp as anyone at analyzing baseball talent and the flow of the game! Will he get the chance to fulfill that dream? Probably not. But he has continued to share his wisdom with another club. The Washington Nationals recognized that McKeon is still sharp, creative, and honest and hired him to assist their world champion general manager, Mike Rizzo, to evaluate players in their Minor League system and scout in the Dominican Republic as well. He also is close to their World Series-winning manager Dave Martinez, who was no doubt the beneficiary of Jack's wisdom.

The talent of our staff was matched only by the strength and spirit of our players. I will miss what was surely the best outfield in baseball—Christian Yelich, Marcell Ozuna, and Giancarlo Stanton, as well as men like Dee Gordon and J. T. Realmuto. They all had a special chemistry that added to their God-given talent.

In the case of Christian Yelich, I spoke with former commissioner Bud Selig shortly after the new owners had traded Yelich to Milwaukee, the team Selig formerly owned. I explained what an exceptional young man Christian is, with a solid presence and superb skills. These qualities were the reason I rewarded him with his first large contract early in his Major League career. Christian's genius is that he is gifted with tremendous vision that allows him to quickly recognize the spin of a ball out of the pitcher's hand. Because of that gift, and in conjunction with his elite offensive game clock, he is able to consistently deliver the barrel of the bat to the point of impact, from at-bat to at-bat. Clearly, players like Christian and others before him, such as Ted Williams and Barry Bonds, define sustained brilliance and excellence on the field. They are winners. Christian once told me that while he was a high school player, his contemporaries and classmates would tease him for constantly playing so much baseball. They claimed he was wasting his life. I guess he is having the last laugh, as he is today one of the most elite players in the game.

Opinions differ on the successful ways to best equip a franchise for success. In my opinion, trusting your instincts and recognizing superior talent is key to owning a successful sports franchise. When I acquired the Marlins in 2002, I made the decision to build upon existing talent on and off the field. We won the World Series the following year. Taking chances can be its own reward! That is what ownership in sports is about. You win some and you lose some. You have to be lucky and healthy. You have to have instincts, courage, and thick skin. And you have to remain focused. There are no guarantees. Winning a championship in any sport is no easy feat, but taking a chance is the first major step toward success.

CHAPTER
TWENTY-SEVEN

IN DEFENSE OF PUBLIC ART

"There are two distinct languages.

There is the verbal, which separates people...

and there is the visual that is understood by everybody."

– YAACOV AGAM

reating Marlins Park, an edifice of stunning originality, brought the worlds of art, architecture, and baseball together. Art and architecture have always had a natural relationship. Both are intended to exist in perpetuity. Our lives are finite. The individual footprint each of us leaves is rarely as obvious as the monuments and images that we create. Art serves as evidence of our existence, beliefs, and intent. We value it for its ability to communicate to the future the aspirations and ideas that our own individual lives may never reach. To many fans, baseball is an American religion. Major League Baseball is a seasonal activity, and as with the seasons, change is inevitable. I think it is fair to say that baseball changes daily. Art does not. It is meant to be forever.

People can have very different views of art. But I do think that public entities have a different responsibility. I was very disappointed by the decision made immediately after the team's sale to remove a sculpture by Red Grooms from the Marlins' baseball stadium. That one act risked devaluing the artist's reputation as well as Miami's reputation for being a community that promotes the arts. But it went beyond the fate of an individual artwork. It is a troublesome precedent when government officials fail to recognize the difference between public art and baseball. They are not equivalent and cannot be treated as such.

Public art, unlike baseball, is a community trust, which is why the parameters for the initial designs and plans for a stadium, including any art, are often created by committee. The intent is to consider from the outset a variety of opinions that best represent the community served by the art. The decision to include public art in the new Marlins ballpark was a mandated commitment made by the county of Miami. The Marlins organization never underestimated the cultural sophistication of the people of Miami, for either baseball or art. Obviously, people do not visit an art museum to watch a baseball game, nor do they attend a baseball game to empathize with the artistry of a painting or a sculpture. In choosing public art capable of appealing to the local community spirit, Miami-Dade County, through its Art in Public Places program, sent out an RFP (request for proposal) to all artists, seeking ideas to satisfy the mandated art requirements for the new Marlins ballpark.

A committee comprised of county officials, as well as members of the Miami art community, eventually selected Red Grooms's *Homer*, a unique seventy-foot-tall sculptural tour de force. The committee also chose two other proposals: an installation that is an illumination of the exterior columns on the stadium's west side, and the large block letters installed abstractly on the east side of the building, which are an homage to the original Miami Orange Bowl. The artist for those works, Daniel Arsham, is a leading contemporary artist and, like Grooms, envisioned something truly special.

Perhaps better than any living artist, Grooms understood how to create an interactive work of art that extends beyond a static statement and is wholly specific to its site. The committee had very high hopes. The artist gave a great deal of serious consideration to Latin culture, particularly the vibrant colors and whimsical flair that are so characteristic of Miami. Grooms clearly hit a "home run," exceeding all expectations. His masterpiece assimilated those aesthetic concerns to empathize with the audience's primary interests during a game. He created an interactive work of art that captured the spirit of the crowd. In reply to the singularly most exciting moment in the sport, Grooms made a sculpture that celebrated the act of hitting a home run and each home team victory.

Grooms appropriately bestowed the name *Homer* on his creation. Unyieldingly positioned on its perch directly in center field, the sculpture patiently waited for that perfect pitch and listened for the unique sound of the ball hitting the bat's sweet spot and flying over the players' heads. When the ball cleared the field into the stands in fair territory, *Homer* was activated and became one with the audience. Just like any fan celebrating a hit, the artwork, whose imagery was an amalgamation of Floridian iconography, became animated. Symbols of the team's namesake, marlins, leapt amid spraying water, while seagulls took flight toward an illuminated Florida sun. Pelicans danced as lights glowed above the simulated waves of water.

The echoing sound of the fans' cheers emanated excitedly from *Homer*. Each element was part of an integrated and harmonious whole. It was an animated moment of celebration. As Michael Kimmelman wrote in the *New York Times*, "The game aside, the main attraction is clearly the kinetic sculpture by the Pop maestro of kitsch, Red Grooms." Grooms's creation was dressed in Florida garb, performing on behalf of the entire city of Miami, a part of the atmosphere and architecture, a part of the game, a part of the crowd and its excitement. It also followed in a wonderful tradition at other stadiums. In Milwaukee, Bernie Brewer celebrates a home run. In Houston, a large moveable train activates when its team celebrates. At New York's Citi Field, a big Apple suddenly appears in center field, joining the team in their celebration. Red Grooms's *Homer* celebrated every Marlins home run and victory, and that response in turn cheered on the players and inspired their performance. Through art, athlete and audience interacted in a hymn to victory.

The seventy-foot sculpture has now been moved to an open area outside the stadium, a site that has *nothing* to do with its original intent. The area where it once stood has been painted a severe gray and turned into additional seating. From a distance, it appears like the façade of an aging battleship, floating behind the center field fence. Meanwhile, the sculpture, with all of its delicately painted, detailed surfaces and its fragile mechanical elements, has been thrust from the climate-controlled, enclosed ballpark into Florida's harsh outdoor elements, completely unprotected against wind, rain, humidity, and hurricanes. I have been part of the art world long enough to know what disasters will follow. This work of art was not designed to be dismantled, and it definitely was not designed to be moved into the elements beyond the enclosed protection of the stadium.

Removing a major work of art, particularly one with specific symbiotic connections to its original site, sets an unfortunate precedent. The county's actions regarding *Homer* will almost certainly deter artists from submitting work for public places in the future. By moving the sculpture, the county has also declared that it isn't bound by what it agreed to and that public art is no longer a public trust. Seen in this light, an artist's work is consequently of no lasting value. Art is intended to live in perpetuity and to create a dialogue with changing opinions. By being placed outside the stadium, *Homer* is inappropriately located to perpetuate the intended dialogue. Rather than be condemned to neglect and outdoor decay, perhaps it could eventually be returned to the artist so he may control its future.

But there is an unfortunate personal precedent as well. Throughout history, we have examples of how changes in leadership have brought about the desecration of works of art. As far back as ancient Egypt, new pharaohs who were determined to make a statement often did so by removing and even defacing the art and images produced under their predecessors. Unfortunately, this was *Homer's* fate. But while targeting art is an old impulse, it is one that ultimately harms our collective respect for images and the artists who produce them. It also rarely ceases. Instead, the behavior recurs with the next transition, to the point where the focus shifts to how to tear down the past rather than how to build upon it and create something universal that will last and thrive well into the future. I had thought that the new owners would take the second path when it came to Marlins Park and its distinctive international style, which so reflects the diversity of Miami, rather than attempt to re-create a version of the old Yankee Stadium among palm trees.

Despite these challenges, however, art lives on. *Homer* will persist as a memory of what it once was, in the heart of the artist who created it, in the commentary of sports announcers, in the fans who enjoyed it, and even in the critics who despised it. *Homer* will be the subject of a continuing dialogue of changing opinions. But it no longer joins the fans celebrating in the stands for a shared moment of success and at the end of a victorious game. This beloved part of the community no longer can speak from its intended platform. It has become a ghostly shadow of a soul displaced. I certainly hope the team and baseball in Miami fare better than *Homer* in the long run.

CHAPTER TWENTY-EIGHT

THE ART OF THE GAME

INSTINCT AND INTUITION

"Our goals can only be reached
through the vehicle of a plan, in which
we must fervently believe, and upon which we
must vigorously act. There is no other route to success."

– PABLO PICASSO

True wisdom is born mostly out of experience. Knowledge can be gained by reading and observing. However, to truly understand the lessons learned, so that we can generate a system of rules and parameters to help us make decisions with conviction, it's also important to cultivate experiential wisdom. I have tried to do that in my own life.

My years of experience in the art world were an important source of information when dealing with the complexities of people and their personalities in the world of baseball, as well as the business side of owning a team. Indeed, the tools required to effectively navigate both art and baseball are far more alike than they are different. I can assure you that the world of baseball has as many eccentric characters as the art world. I also had some very solid and genuine experiences with artists and collectors that afforded me a great deal of confidence to navigate the intricate business of baseball. Of course, I encountered a sufficient number of unknowns that required patience and a willingness to learn. A dear friend once told me, "The strength of an individual is the ability to move from problem to problem." Life is, hopefully, more than an unending series of problems, but much of our success is determined by the strength with which we face the problems placed before us. And without problems, there would also be no solutions.

The many lessons and wisdom I have acquired in sports came from myriad valuable sources: commissioners Bud Selig and Rob Manfred; fellow owners including George Steinbrenner, Bill Giles, Fred Wilpon, and Jerry Reinsdorf; and special people like Stan Kasten, John Schuerholz, Sandy Koufax, and many more. They all contributed in different ways to the game and to enriching my experiences. In addition, no single person impacted my ownership thinking more than Jack McKeon.

From what is now the better part of a lifetime in the worlds of baseball and art, I have formulated a coterie of principles that together constitute my philosophical guide to business practices. Paramount among these principles is the idea that it is imperative to *surround yourself with the best people*. A team is only as good as its personnel. There are many factors that contribute to success, but putting together an organization with the hardest working and most talented staff is ultimately the surest route to success. I always placed a strong emphasis on personnel who can teach, communicate, evaluate, and motivate players.

It's easy to say that you will surround yourself with the best people, but it's not as easy to know who "the best" are. Many can look good on paper, but those skills may not translate into practice. It is important to be able to delegate; have consistent leadership, policies, and procedures; and rely on objective evaluations rather than become caught up in personality conflicts. When making strategic decisions, I have also relied on a second maxim: *trust your gut*. "All stat and no gut" can lead to lifeless mediocrity. Pure data alone is not enough.

My next principle follows closely on the others: just as you never want to be over-reliant on any single data source, it is also vital to *be flexible and open to the idea of change*. In other words, to stay fresh and reinvent. Successful artists like Clyfford Still and Niki de Saint Phalle understood this. Baseball is a separate example of a game of evolution. If I were still an owner, I would be very open to putting a qualified woman in the dugout as a Major League manager. With women already serving as on-field base coaches and Minor League managers, I'm sure this change will happen sooner rather than later. Nontraditional thinking needs to have a major and pivotal place in the game. After all, I hired a seventy-three-year-old manager in the middle of the season, who ultimately helped us win a World Series. I brought up a third baseman (Miguel Cabrera) and moved him to the outfield. I encouraged bringing up a pitcher, José Fernández, from our Single-A team directly to the Major Leagues. He became Rookie of the Year.

Yet, while I am proud of my instincts and my successes, I have tried very hard to also *maintain a level of humility*. Pride is important, but not to the point where we neglect to recognize that success is dependent on many factors. No one person should receive or insist on all the credit. That is why I also live by the credo: *don't be greedy*. Although many of the artists I worked with have commanded high prices, I never tried to extract the last penny in any particular arrangement. Generosity of spirit in investments ultimately leads to success. When building an art business, my philosophy was that smaller profit margins led to more business. It is the same in baseball. One needs to invest when quality demands it, such as when the Marlins signed Giancarlo Stanton to what was then the single largest contract in the history of American sports. Talent commands its own price.

These maxims have served me well, but they are also not necessarily infallible. As such, I found it important to commit to *expect the unexpected*. Chance often plays a major role in business and in one's personal life, and outside forces often determine outcomes. The Marlins didn't always have great luck over the years: the devastating injury to Giancarlo Stanton, when a fastball shattered his cheekbone and jaw in Milwaukee in 2014; José Fernández's tragic death in 2016; and Ozzie Guillén's misguided remark that he "loved" Fidel Castro in 2012 are examples of how a team can unravel in an instant. The important thing is to adapt to the situation and to navigate a flexible course, looking to the future.

Long-term vision and a *long-term commitment* are very important. Most owners never feel the exhilaration of winning a World Series during their tenure. Understandably, they often become impatient. But success in any business, including baseball, takes persistence, time, and financial commitment. Long-term commitment underscores the need to keep a team, in any field, together for an extended period of time so they can form a working bond and hopefully create camaraderie. I always tried to do this, starting when I was in my twenties, with my visits to artists in their homes and studios.

In baseball, one way to create bonds and camaraderie among players is by focusing on developing a good Minor League system to cultivate homegrown talent. It's easy to do impulsive trading, but until you have the right mix of important core players in your organization, that sort of impulsiveness and immediate gratification makes no sense. After you are close to being at the top and are competing well in your division, adding and trading for top-tier players can be explored. Ultimately, a championship organization cannot rely exclusively on a farm system nor on highly publicized trades. It requires a combination of each approach to put a complementary and winning group together. Leadership also means creating programs that keep things fresh in order to motivate both players and managers and to give them autonomy to be innovative.

All these principles require another key ingredient to succeed: *respect*. You need to maintain respect for the things you aspire to achieve. I developed my deep respect for art at Yale and honored it throughout my career as I pursued art and artists. My respect for baseball was fomented in my youth and only grew deeper with time and experience as my love and appreciation for the game increased.

Finally, a personal maxim that has guided me well in work and in life is *pain is inevitable, but suffering is optional.* I have helped bury deeply loved family, friends, and a terrific young baseball pitcher, José Fernandez, all while they were still in the prime of life or only just beginning. And I've had other difficult losses as well. No one lives a life free from hurt. Where there is true love, grief leaves a hole that never truly closes. The question is can you find ways to channel that pain into a deeper appreciation for life and for your family and friends, and can you ultimately make something beautiful out of pain, which, not coincidentally, is also what often produces some of our most meaningful and greatest art?

———

Baseball and art may seem like two separate worlds. From my perspective, they are as connected to each other as the desire to communicate is connected to language. Baseball and art are creative endeavors that celebrate the exceptional. They simply come to the field wearing different uniforms, but on any given day either discipline can provide a metaphor for the other.

My thoughts on operating a championship baseball team were in part born out of business rules and practices that I adapted over the years as an art dealer. First, *information gathering* was always of central importance to achieving my goals. Information is knowledge, and learning all the intricacies firsthand about both art and baseball was a logical progression in my professional life. Sharing information with colleagues is also vital. It often leads to discovery, and it is essential when making wise decisions. Indeed, learning how to decipher and evaluate the importance of the information that I gathered was in itself a lesson.

I've been fortunate to have the opportunity to observe both blue-chip artists and superior players as they addressed situations that on the surface seemed to be impeding their efforts. And I've witnessed how both found ways of *articulating* what was seemingly on the surface to reveal deeper issues. Too often, we offer solutions for problems before fully understanding their depth. It's a very natural tendency to want to fix something that appears to be wrong as quickly as possible, but when we do that, we may not be fully addressing the deeper issue that lurks below the surface. It is vital to understand any root causes so that we can effectively offer a comprehensive solution and ultimately resolve the problem. I've found articulating that which appears on the surface to be immensely helpful for gaining clarity regarding problems that lie below.

Surface appearances can be misleading in other ways. For instance, on the surface, it might appear that athletes and artists have little in common. We see the athlete as a physical being and the artist as a cerebral or emotional creature. But if you've ever had the opportunity to observe the focused eyes of artists when they're working, it becomes very apparent that their intensity is unshakable. A great artist can harness a mental focus equal to a marathon runner's physical endurance. Similarly, the successful artist needs the energy level of an endurance runner to carry out the demanding process of creation. For the athlete, physical endurance of course is vital, but that same unshakeable acuity that I've witnessed in the eyes of an artist at work is equally vital for an athlete.

Another important business principle I have acquired and adhered to is my belief that *hesitation can be a detriment.* As is apparent from observing both athletes and artists, it's vital to remain focused on one's vision and to move forward at an uninterrupted pace. The times that I have hesitated have often resulted in missed opportunities. I still kick myself for those possibilities I forfeited to hesitancy, such as delaying my visit to Alberto Giacometti's studio. Postponing a meeting from a Thursday to a Monday caused me to miss acquiring a major painting by the Spanish artist Joan Miró. By contrast, soon after I bought the Marlins, I insisted on signing the Hall of Fame catcher Pudge Rodríguez against others' counsel. He was a major reason why the team won the World Series in 2003; hesitation would likely have derailed a championship dream.

I began my professional life as an art dealer by imagining success. I worked to do the same in professional baseball. The concept of aiming for important goals illuminated how I approached my two careers. The best athletes and artists are always thinking ahead. Moreover, that sense of anticipation applies not only to the mechanics of one's craft. It is often about anticipating the value of people as well. I embraced disparate professional cultures because I believed that these various worlds could coexist successfully. Baseball is a magnificent balance of the familiar and the unexpected. It can keep us on the edge of our seats and addresses the idea of living in the moment. We are naturally drawn to the inclusivity of team sport. An emotional bond is created when we witness the efforts of individual players to advance the common interest of a team. We become part of something bigger than ourselves. One can watch a thousand baseball games and still see something different each time. To paraphrase what the great American artist and illustrator Saul Steinberg once told me in a discussion about baseball, "Things happen that you have never seen before. Every day is a new adventure in a ballpark. It's a kind of an intellectual game. There are so many possibilities as a result of a single pitch."

Steinberg's view of baseball is the same view I have of art. Every work of art is a new adventure. Like baseball, art has rules, but few are codified. The first rule in art might be that there are no rules. Of course, there are rules: rules of geometry, rules of color, rules of perspective, rhythm, and pacing, to mention a few, but in art perhaps the second most highly regarded rule among artists might be that the rules are meant to be broken.

So, when an artist approaches a canvas, which is his or her playing field, the rules may not be obvious. This allows for a wide range of opinions about what we see. A work of art can sometimes be ignored at its creation, only to be rediscovered years later as pioneering or even revolutionary. The public expression of an emotional response to a work of art can sometimes involve risk. Art allows us to experience new adventures over longer periods of time; our initial thoughts may change as we discover fresh aspects of an object. As such, a painting may appear to address one issue at the moment of its creation, but perhaps fifty years later it might relate differently to new cultural and/or societal issues, potentially making a different but no less important and timely statement, and yet nothing about the work itself will have changed. This is one of the most fascinating things about art; it has the ability to exist and to speak effectively across centuries without ever changing a single brushstroke, color, pencil line, or shape.

In our lifetime, we may not be able to tell which works of art will have the ability to live such vital extended lives, but we do have the ability to set aside any preconceived notions and look very carefully at the art. When we do this, there is a good chance we may find clues to a work's potential power and stamina.

Among my various principles, there are three that I group together but that serve as independent rules to apply to different situations. They are: *don't be afraid to take risks, fear of failure is not an option*, and *always use your eyes*. These three principles help one to be open, to art and to more.

———

In business and in life, one must be willing to take risks. Without risks there also is no possibility of a reward. Second, fear of failure should never be an option. There is nothing wrong with weighing one's fears against one's goals, but when fear has no purpose other than to serve as an obstacle to one's goal, it's best to move past it. Of course, when striving for excellence, top players and artists will experience some disappointments. But the idea of failure will not dissuade them from seeking their objectives.

There is also always something to be learned when we set fear aside and simply use our eyes. Looking is an undervalued concept. I always tried to look before speaking, whether I was in the studio of a famous artist or in a meeting of baseball executives. Deciphering responses, reactions, and context can only happen when we use our eyes.

It was my father who instilled an unswayable determination in me. He gave me the confidence to reach beyond any inhibitions or hesitations and realize my dreams. He understood the likelihood that in life we will hear the word "no" more often than we care to. He did not want that message to be a deterrent for me. My father would repeatedly say, "No is just a temporary impediment on the way to yes." What a gift it was. Later, when many people told me that professional baseball was a difficult business, the warnings only served to drive me to join its ranks. When I tried for the first time to meet a prominent artist, it never occurred to me that "no" could be the final word in our exchange. I think it was the sense of confidence I projected in my initial letter to the world-renowned sculptor Henry Moore that produced a positive reply.

As I continued to reach out to the artists who interested me, I rarely met with resistance. The practice of meeting artists helped humanize their art. I gained a deeper appreciation for the lives behind the images. They exhibited the same kind of determined effort in their work that an athlete does in his or hers, and it is one of the many similarities between athlete and artist. Their mutual commitment to a *work ethic* can bring both to the pinnacle of success in their drive for excellence.

Even the most prosperous artists practically live in their studios. They are constantly working on their craft. It is the same in sport. For the best players, baseball is not a seasonal activity. The most successful athletes train all year, continually challenging themselves and improving their skills. During the winter, Giancarlo Stanton was often in a batting cage in Los Angeles. He once told me that in the off-season, he preferred working after midnight when there was nobody around and there were no distractions. That enabled him to remain focused longer, without interruption. He was determined to improve every aspect of his already outstanding skills.

Henry Moore often worked long hours in his studio next to his house, sometime late into the night and early morning. He labored quietly by himself, trying to arrive at the precise angle or definition of a form, usually on a sculpture that already looked perfect to anyone else. His was a constant drive, not simply to achieve, but to exceed his own expectations. While I didn't think it was a conscious decision for him, his determination and disciplined practice to be in his studio on a regular basis emphasized a highly evolved, dedicated work ethic that I learned early and never forgot.

The extracurricular interests of a successful artist may seem like distractions, but in fact most often, he or she is dedicated to the studio. Larry Rivers had a reputation for wildness that often overshadowed the art he created. But regardless of his newsworthy activities outside the studio, somehow, he managed to spend eight or ten hours a day in his studios, which adjoined his residences, and to devote a single-minded focus to his art. Indeed, despite his sensational extracurricular life, he lived for his art.

For the artists and athletes who achieve great success, there is very often considerable uninvited distraction. Criticism seems to follow anyone who achieves a certain amount of recognition—with public success comes public scrutiny. I tried to *never let scrutiny become a distraction*. In baseball, there is often no opportunity to counter inaccurate reporting. The best players, like the best artists, often find themselves as the subjects of criticism. Of course, it affects them, but top-performing athletes and artists learn to manage the negativity so that it doesn't compromise their primary focus and become a distraction.

Larry Rivers was a favorite target of the critics. Certainly controversial, he often received harsh attacks. While the criticism may have bothered him, he refused to let it alter his focus. Similarly, elite baseball players are not easily spooked by distasteful or demeaning remarks. As a rule, they work diligently to perform at their best, regardless of their temporary feelings. Naturally, they carry a certain personal fragility. Many successful artists and baseball players can be thin-skinned. The great ones learn to *develop a thick skin*. By concentrating on their goals, both the player and artist can conquer their sensitivities. For my part, I let these important rules guide me as well. Years of public scrutiny and criticism did not distract me from my desire to build a Major League ballpark and save professional baseball in Miami.

———

Premier artists and athletes live on a grand stage in the public spotlight. Top performers perceive the precarious nature of their image. Consequently, they work hard at their craft to ensure a permanent legacy. Many will find new ways to *reinvent themselves.* When pitchers age and their skills deteriorate, changing how they pitch can keep them fresh and relevant. In the same way, artists alter their focus, styles, and approaches, Picasso made many changes throughout his career. Artists and athletes also have their "blue periods." But the genius converts that depression into a brilliantly hued canvas of insight and wonder—a home run for the ages! Reinvention keeps a performer moving forward.

The foremost players and artists constantly drive themselves to excellence in new ways. Their skills have monetary value. In reality, their efforts are commodities for trade in open and defined markets. Through their enormous dedication, players and artists become a desirable commodity. And when talent assumes a marketable value, the demand for a high level of performance creates a responsibility for fulfilling those expectations. Ironically, it is at this point that both artists and athletes have to relinquish some of their control. A player, for example, can be traded to another team. Artists are obliged to watch their work enter secondary markets once it leaves the artist's studio, with little or no say over valuations or sales.

Many successful artists and players actively push themselves to achieve great financial gain. Those rewards, in turn, need to be managed carefully. Everyone needs support, and nobody achieves great success without help. That help might come in many forms, but as a rule we are not nearly as independent as we want to believe. Some of the greatest talents we've ever known have died in anonymity for lack of a better source of support. As far back as 1623, while struggling to recover from an unknown illness, the writer John Donne wrote the famous line, "No man is an island," which certainly applies today. Artists have their patrons and baseball players have their professional and business supporters, as well as the sports media and fans. When they work in concert, these valued relationships can produce successes together.

It is also important to have a vision of one's goal. Sticking to a plan is important. But being able to navigate around the inevitable obstacles is also absolutely critical. Someone or some event can derail the focus. I once heard it said that the reason roads curve is because it was more practical to go around a boulder then to try to move it or blast through it. When the inevitable obstacle appears on the road to success, it's important to have another path, namely, *Plan B*.

In line with having multiple plans, *sometimes the best deals are the ones you don't make*. I was once presented with an opportunity to acquire an important American artist's watercolor. Instinctively, I felt the situation wasn't right. The sale needed to happen too quickly; the ownership also seemed unusual. Ultimately, I worked with the Federal Bureau of Investigation to help return a stolen watercolor to its rightful museum owner.

Quality over quantity is another maxim that has served me well. Everything from the design of a plan to the talent displayed by an artist or player needs to be considered carefully. Time and again, investing in quality over quantity has proven to be beneficial. One brilliantly skilled player on a team may be worth five players of average talent. One masterpiece can be worth a dozen works of lesser quality by the same artist. Adhering to quality over quantity as a business practice applies equally to investing in the best players, in the finest works of art, in an astute colleague or manager, in strong supporting staff, or in first-rate facilities. For me, quality over quantity has yielded dividends. In the end, it's all about high standards.

There is always subjectivity when determining quality. This is why it was very important to me, whether in baseball or in art, to adhere to one of my basic principles: *Buy what you want to buy, not what someone else is trying to sell you.* I always tried to do thorough research, to seek input and advice, to have a solid understanding of what I wished to acquire, and to know what my goal was for what I was acquiring.

One of my principles in baseball was that every athlete in the organization had to be very well conditioned. I rarely settled for athletes who were not, and those who were not often did not remain in the organization for long. Similarly, I never settled for work from an artist that I thought wasn't among their best. An exemplary artwork sells itself. Name recognition alone, while helpful in establishing price, is not enough. The work must hold up on its own.

Salvador Dalí created numerous great paintings and drawings in the 1930s and 1940s. In the late 1970s, he created mass-produced prints that were often meant for cruise ship auctions. Many of Dalí's early works are wonderful, but later prints were often sold for their signature value rather than for their innate quality. Only now, years after Dalí's death, has the market for his best paintings and drawings increased. The rarity of his early works and renewed appreciation for his art means that these works almost always sell for at or above the highest pre-sale auction estimates—a special tribute from the marketplace for one of the world's iconic modern artists.

In any pursuit, one should start out knowing what one wants. Salespeople know how to focus on what they want. The sale is their priority. But is it what *you* want? A gifted salesperson, be it an opposing baseball executive or an art dealer, has the advantage of knowing their products, probably better than you do. A salesperson can convince you that what he or she has fits your priorities. Perhaps it does, but you must ultimately make the decision, not the seller.

I always felt a responsibility for my decisions. I researched all options and consulted those whom I trusted. I weighed everything carefully in the interest of the organization. I wasn't easily swayed by rumors, opinions, hurt feelings, or accusations that would compromise executing the final decision. The uninformed emotions of others can distract from longer-term goals. Often people rationalize problems with the cliché, "Things happen for a reason." In other

411

words, for every problem there is a cosmic cause that may be revealed in the future. This notion offers comfort, but no logical explanation. In business, it is important to determine causes. Properly evaluating successful decisions is important for future momentum. Reviewing poor decisions is equally critical for future progress.

In all my efforts in both baseball and art, it was absolutely vital to subscribe to the principle *do it right or don't do it at all*. The future is largely unpredictable. But if we strive to the best of our ability, a successful result is probably more likely. Half-hearted efforts are vulnerable to failure. The best artists and the best players frequently rework with painstaking care the most minor features of their respective crafts. This discipline often ensures a better outcome. Top artists and players bring the best of themselves to everything they do.

The Japanese baseball superstar Ichiro Suzuki is a great example. He never cut corners. He adhered to the highest possible personal standards for excellence and did the work of training daily to achieve his goals. This future Hall of Famer was always professional. It was a pleasure to be in his company, to observe his professional approach to his craft, and to have him on my team. Indeed, having him as a player remains one of the thrills of my baseball life.

A truly competitive game in baseball is always exciting. The pitcher brings his best efforts to the mound, and the batter offers his best. In the flash of a second, one or the other will prevail. Even the player who loses in that moment, as long as he gives his best effort, can withstand his loss of dignity. He will be ready for the next encounter. Surely the motto for any career should be "do it right or don't do it at all." A credo I have tried to adhere to at all times.

CHAPTER
TWENTY-NINE

EXTRA INNINGS

> "When you are dealing with talent,
>
> you are not in business, you are in life."
>
> – SCOTT BORAS

I have always taken great pride in looking forward and not harboring too many thoughts of the past. Baseball has been an extraordinary gift to my life. It has been in my blood since childhood. Simply put, I accomplished what I had set out to do, and after almost twenty years, it was time to move on and let someone else try his hand at it. I'm deeply proud to have won a Triple-A Championship in 1992 and a World Series Championship in 2003; to have played host to an All-Star Game in 2017; to have hosted two World Baseball Classics; to have built an architecturally renowned, award-winning, and environmentally sensitive stadium; and to have mentored some of the best young talent the game has ever seen.

My life has certainly changed since selling the team. My least favorite part of being an owner was the almost daily telephone call from an executive or someone else that began, "Let me give you a heads-up." For two decades, scarcely a day went by without such a call, and the news was almost always negative. I definitely do not miss that.

In my art pursuits, I'm less interested in dealing in art and more fascinated with looking, studying, and appreciating the treasures that surround us. My guiding principle is pursuing what I call "iconic images." I want to see more works of art that define the geniuses who created them, in much the same way I enjoyed the superbly gifted athletes who played for me. Examples of such masterpieces would be a Salvador Dalí drawing of a reclining figure from 1936, a Pablo Picasso depiction of one of the many great loves of his life from the 1940s, or the superb Max Ernst painting that I pursued for more than fifty years. The chase never gets old, just as in baseball you discover new possibilities, talent, and adventures every day.

I recognize that this philosophy puts me a bit out of sync with the direction of the current art market, where the latest trend is for products like digital art and NFTs, terms which sound more suited to a complex, Wall Street financial instrument or an evolving form of credit swaps. Even traditional art is increasingly about commodities. Consider what is thus far the most expensive work of art ever sold: *Salvator Mundi*, otherwise known as the "Last Leonardo," a painting purported, but not entirely proven, to have been done by Leonardo da Vinci. Rediscovered at an auction house in New Orleans in 2005 and heavily restored, it was ultimately sold privately to a Swiss dealer, who promptly resold it in 2013 to a Russian oligarch for a reported $127.5 million. In November 2017, the painting was sold publicly at auction at Christie's in New York, with much fanfare, to a mystery bidder, later revealed to be a Saudi prince, for the very princely sum of $450 million. Thus far locked away from public view, the current trajectory of the Last Leonardo is far closer to a sixteenth century piece of bitcoin than a picture whose central purpose is to touch, move, and captivate us—as the *Mona Lisa* did for me as a young art history student.

In my personal approach to art, I am happy to go against the current grain.

Baseball and art have been wonderful pursuits. But there are two other passions in my life that have been deeply rewarding and which have given me tremendous satisfaction and joy. The first is Paris. I have traveled to Paris hundreds of times. My passion for France began when I graduated from Yale and took a trip to Europe with a classmate in 1962. I arrived in Paris on a train from London, and I still smile at the sign outside that station whenever I pass by. Looking for a place to stay on my initial trip, I found a small hotel and, with my college French, began a lifelong love affair with France. I vividly remember a small bistro opposite the hotel on the rue de Bourgogne, where I ate. At the time, I thought I had died and gone to heaven. Little did I know how much more I would discover during the ensuing years about France's artistic, cultural, and culinary heritage. Even today, whenever I visit, I walk everywhere in Paris; there is something to see on every street. Business effortlessly mixes with pleasure in the place known as the city of lights or the city of love.

A second passion of mine is philanthropy. Giving back and giving to others has always been an integral part of who I am and what I value. It started with art. Three years after I graduated from Yale, I donated a Cubist painting by an important French artist to the university's art museum. I knew the collection had a gap, and this addition would help complete the visual history of that pivotal era. Ever since, I have frequently donated works to museums and other public institutions, sometimes at the personal request of the artist or the artist's family, often to help complete collections or create a richer experience of an artist or an era. I have lent many more works for shows and collections. I have always considered myself only the caretaker of these works, not their owner in perpetuity. It is my deep belief that art is a living thing to be shared.

My business success has also allowed me to be generous in other ways, particularly to medical and educational institutions, a variety of religious institutions, and other important causes. I have been able to honor my mother by donating a hospital wing in her name, and I felt no small tug of emotion when recently I heard the hospital PA system paging a doctor, an orthopedist who happened to also be my mother's grandson, to the "Ruth Loria Wing." Finding treatments and a cure for the devastating disease ALS is also a cause dear to my heart. And I have been fortunate to be able to give to a variety of educational institutions.

More than a decade ago, Rick Levin, the incredible, long-serving president of Yale, asked me if I would support and fund an effort to build an art history building adjacent to the School of Art and Architecture. When I was a student, my art history classes were held in various spaces around the campus. I saw his inquiry as a welcome opportunity for me to "give back" to Yale, which I credit for so much of what my life became. Every time I am on the Yale campus, I visit the Loria Center, and it gives me great joy and great satisfaction to see the activity and positive effects that the center has on students seeking to open their eyes to the visual world around them. Every artist has their *oeuvre*, mine, I hope, ultimately resides in the people and places that I have been able to help.

———

Perhaps it is a natural instinct to want to lift your child on your shoulders as you try to give him or her a front-row view when parades go by. You navigate the crowd in which each individual is jockeying for that same pole position. Somehow, as if it is universally understood, the crowd slowly obliges and makes room for the smallest among us to have a front-row spot. You sneak a peek at your child's face, full of wonder as the grandeur and the pageantry unfolds. Privately you recall those formative moments from your own youth. Maybe part of you hopes the experience will help give your child the incentive not simply to reach for the best seat in the house but to believe confidently that with genuine effort they will earn it. I hope this is what I've given to my children. I know that it is what my parents did for me.

Those early impressions are vitally connected to learning a first language. You can learn many languages in life, but the first one connects them to thought. That language forever becomes a part of the way one processes information. I still feel as if baseball was part of my first language. In the same way that I think in English, the language and imagery of baseball became part of my deepest being. So, I was naturally inclined to want to know that world more intimately. As with any language, the broader one's vocabulary, the more one is able to comprehend.

If baseball is part of my first language, then art is my second language. It is the language that I chose. When one selects a second language, it may come from a felt need to communicate, or it may derive from a passion in one's soul. For me, it was the latter. It started with my courses at Yale, with the imagery projected on a screen or viewed in a museum. I was profoundly affected almost immediately by my art history classes. It was fitting that the very first work of art that opened up my mind and heart to a broader way of seeing was a painting by Pablo Picasso in the Yale University Art Gallery collection. Its title, in an appropriate irony, is *First Steps*. It represents a mother bent over her infant, holding each hand while the child takes its very first steps. The sharp edges of the painting dramatize the risks involved: stepping forward, maturing, and visiting places you have never been. Apart from the assuring image of the protective mother, there is clearly the suggestion of the confidence gained from taking those initial steps and discovering one's independence.

I began taking my "first steps" into the art world with that painting imprinted in my mind. The image gave me the confidence to reach out for the first time to a celebrated artist, when I connected with Henry Moore. At the time, I did not consider the fact that one of Moore's most important themes was also that of the mother and child. It should have been no surprise, consciously and subconsciously, that the messages from works of art greatly influenced my future. Art helped me to reach out to artists, whose works, in turn, reached out to me. I have had the rare opportunity to be front and center in some of the most important places where art is born, as well as in the most hallowed halls of professional baseball. Among other ties that bind, these two lifelong passions were driven by my burning desire to constantly reinvent myself.

Culturally, the languages of baseball and art might seem completely alien. We often build invisible walls around our interests. But the language of one culture is not really any different from that of another. They share the same purpose of bringing clarity and connection to thoughts and actions that touch our hearts and souls.

As we age, we seek distance to perceive more clearly what we have witnessed from the front row. We retreat in order to see the grand collage. In my own small way, I have stepped back to recount what I have witnessed and to offer my thoughts on the meaning of it all. I hope that these shared experiences may connect with you and become part of your experience. In the end, maybe that is why we all reach for the front row, not out of selfish needs, but because of the desire to make a connection and share what we have seen and come to know.

Ah but a man's reach should exceed his grasp,

Or what's a heaven for?

– ROBERT BROWNING

ACKNOWLEDGMENTS

In my careers, I've had help from many people. No one, however, has made more consistent and meaningful contributions to organizing my businesses than my intelligent, talented, and loyal friend Keli Zaloudek. She has worked with me for many years, helping me navigate multiple undertakings, which she always handles deftly. She is an exceptional problem solver and embodies my consistent principle to surround oneself with the best people.

I would like to thank my dear friend, Matthew Kamens, whose wisdom and counsel have been invaluable to me and my family. And for the many years that Murray Friedland was by my side, a heartfelt thank you. So too to Alan Frankel for his consummate professionalism.

I am grateful for my friendship with Maxwell Davidson III, with whom I've been talking about art for more than fifty years. My friend Danny Berger, always a delight, has gifted me with great advice over many decades. And also to David Joel with whom I've had many lively and enlightening conversations about art since we first met in Larry Rivers's studio. I want to thank Cameron and Jackie Wilson, whom I have known most of my professional life, for their amazing conservation talents, as well as Robert and Larry Berman for their constant help. The architectural team of Peter Stamberg and Paul Aferiat has shared their innovative vision, ideas, and imagination in all of our projects.

I have never known anyone more enthusiastic than Jack McKeon. He has always said something interesting and thought-provoking.

In retrospect, if I had to do it over again, I would have made Trader Jack my general manager in 2006 before Joe Girardi's departure. Then perhaps Joe, whom I admire very much, would have enjoyed a longer and happier tenure with us.

Thanks to Jennifer Weiss Monsky for her sage publishing advice. Robert Grant Irving, Mike Valdes-Fauli, and Roger Labrie offered valuable guidance when I began this project.

And I appreciate my friend Lyric Winik's very helpful suggestions for getting this book over the finish line, as well as our witty conversations about art, baseball, and everything in between.

Thanks to the terrific team at Post Hill Press, led by Adam Bellow, and including Aleigha Kely, Allison Griffith, and Jon Ford. Thanks also to Justin Striebel for his brilliant cover design, Carly Loman for her excellent graphic talents, and Keith Handley for his magical photographic skills.

Mary Cobin has been a special and invaluable part of my home for decades. So too Gladys Senior, Marzena Ruszkowski and David Corporan. For years, I have benefitted from John Tavarez's loyal assistance and dedicated professionalism. I am also grateful to have been able to work with the exceptional Beth McConville during my many years in Miami with the Marlins. And also thanks to Bobby Diaz, Matty Nagel, Tim Blenk, Scott Armusewicz, Perry Guillot, and Karen Foley for their many contributions.

I have been deeply fortunate to have had many wonderful friends, artists, and clients in my life, too numerous to name, but thank you all for all the ways that you have elevated my world.

My family will always have the highest place of honor in my heart. I have been blessed to have three beautiful children: My extraordinarily loving daughter, Samantha, who has been a special light in my life since her birth. My incredibly caring and compassionate daughter, Nancy, of Blessed Memory, and my truly amazing son David, whose mother Sivia graced me with their presence starting at six and four years old. They have enriched my years and my world.

I am deeply grateful for Nancy's husband, Josh, for the loving care he gave her during her battle with cancer and for being such a wonderful father to their children. And to Samantha's brilliant husband Jeffrey; their family has been a joy to watch.

I have also been privileged to be a close part of the lives of my wonderful and accomplished nephews, Glenn, Allen, and Richard, my late sister's sons, and their equally special wives, Randy, Emily, and Rosie. I have an abundance of splendid grandchildren, Ryan, Parker, Harris, Ross, Julia, Dana, Hannah, Kyra, and Caleb, and remarkable grand-nieces and nephews, Matthew, Haley, Jonathan, Noah, Max, Mason, Emma, and Alex. My hope is that this book will inspire them to seek happiness, friendship, and passion in their lives, while always remembering their roots (and perhaps they will indulge me and pay a bit of extra attention to Chapter 28). The joys of my own life have been amplified by the lively and loving spirit of my family.

I want to thank my incredible wife, Julie, whose devotion to baseball, like mine, was learned by going to games with her sweet father. Without her encouragement, this book would not have been written.

Lastly, I have greatly enjoyed the baseball fans who, in spite of negative media coverage, were always kind. I know those fans appreciated Miami's beautiful new ballpark, the World Series, the All-Star Game, and other events we were proud to bring to the community. In short, their gratitude has made me feel enormously fortunate. Just like art, baseball will always be part of my life. Once baseball and art are in your blood, they never leave.

PHOTO CREDITS

INTRODUCTION

PAGE XII: Photographer Unknown; Louvre Museum, Paris, France.

CHAPTER ONE

PAGE 2: Photo courtesy of the Loria Family Archive.

PAGE 7: Photo by Dr. Jon LaPook.

PAGE 9: Photo by Robert Vigon.

PAGE 11: Image © Daily News, L.P. (New York). Used with permission.

CHAPTER TWO

PAGE 14: Photo by Denis Bancroft.

CHAPTER THREE

PAGE 24: Photo by John Tavarez; Artwork ©2021 Estate of Larry Rivers/Licensed by VAGA at Artists Rights Society (ARS) NY.

PAGE 30: Image © Copyright 1963 Sears Roebuck and Co.

PAGE 33: Photo courtesy of the Loria Family Archive; Artwork © 2021 Salvador Dali, Fundació Gala-Salvador Dali, Artists Rights Society.

CHAPTER FOUR

PAGE 42: Photo by Jeffrey H. Loria / Loria Family Archive.

PAGE 47: Photo by Jeffrey H. Loria / Loria Family Archive.

PAGE 51: Photo courtesy of the Loria Family Archive.

CHAPTER FIVE

PAGE 56: Photo courtesy of the Marina Marini archive; Artwork ©2021 Artists Rights Society (ARS), New York / SIAE, Rome.

PAGE 59: Photographer unknown; courtesy of the Henry Moore Archive; Artwork ©2021 Artists Rights Society (ARS), New York / SIAE, Rome.

PAGE 62: Photo courtesy of ©Tate; Artwork ©2021 Artists Rights Society (ARS), New York / SIAE, Rome.

CHAPTER SIX

PAGE 70: Photo courtesy of the Loria Family Archive; Artwork ©2021Artists Rights Society (ARS), New York / SIAE, Rome.

PAGE 72: Photo courtesy of the Archives of the Giacomo Manzù Foundation.

PAGE 75: Photo by Jeffrey H. Loria / Loria Family Archive.

PAGE 76: Photo courtesy of the Archives of the Giacomo Manzù Foundation.

PAGE 83: Photo courtesy of the Loria Family Archive.

CHAPTER SEVEN

PAGE 86: Unknown photographer / Courtesy of The Roy Lichtenstein Foundation Archives.

PAGE 92: Photo by Alister Alexander / Camerarts; Artwork © Estate of Roy Lichtenstein.

CHAPTER EIGHT

PAGE 100: Photo by G. Proust.

PAGE 113: Photo courtesy of ©Estate of Larry Rivers / Licensed by VAGA at Artists Rights Society (ARS), New York.

PAGE 117: Photo courtesy of the Loria Family Archive.

CHAPTER NINE

PAGE 120: Photograph by Patricia Still. Courtesy of the Clyfford Still Archives, Denver Colorado; © 2021 City & County of Denver, Courtesy Clyfford Still Museum / Artists Rights Society (ARS), New York; CPSA.F001.S003.SB001.B006.627.

CHAPTER TEN

CHAPTER ELEVEN

CHAPTER TWELVE

CHAPTER THIRTEEN

Chapter Fourteen

PAGE 182: Photo by Jeffrey H. Loria / Loria Family Archive.

PAGE 185: Photo by George Platt Lynes, World History Archive, Alamy Stock Photo.

Chapter Fifteen

PAGE 194: Photo by Jill Krementz, 1965.

PAGE 200: Photographer Unknown; Larry Rivers Papers, Fales Library and Special Collections, New York University, Courtesy of the Larry Rivers Foundation.

PAGE 203: Photo Courtesy of the Larry Rivers Foundation; Artwork © 2021 Estate of Larry Rivers/Licensed by VAGA at Artists Rights Society (ARS), New York, © 2021 Niki Charitable Art Foundation. All rights reserved / ARS, NY / ADAGP, Paris.

PAGE 205: Photo by Jeffrey H. Loria / Loria Family Archive; Artwork © 2021 Niki Charitable Art Foundation. All rights reserved / ARS, NY. / ADAGP, Paris.

PAGE 208: Photo by Julie Lavin Loria / Loria Family Archive; Artwork © 2021 Niki Charitable Art Foundation. All rights reserved / © 2021 Artist Rights Society ARS, NY / ADAGP, Paris.

PAGE 211: Photo courtesy of the Loria Family Archive; Artwork © 2021 Niki Charitable Art Foundation. All rights reserved / © 2021 Artist Rights Society ARS, NY / ADAGP, Paris.

PAGE 214: Photo by Philippe Turpin / Photononstop Alamy Stock Photo; Artwork © 2021 Niki Charitable Art Foundation. All rights reserved / © 2021 Artist Rights Society ARS, NY / ADAGP, Paris.

Chapter Sixteen

PAGE 220: Photo by Norton Simon Art Foundation; Artwork ©The Henry Moore Foundation. All rights reserved.

Chapter Seventeen

PAGE 242: Photo courtesy of the Loria Family Archive.

Chapter Eighteen

PAGE 258: Photo by Michael Bush UPI, Alamy Stock Photo.

Chapter Nineteen

Page 272: Photo courtesy of the Loria Family Archive.

Page 279: Photo by Reuters photographer Jason Reed, Reuters, Alamy Stock Photo.

Chapter Twenty

Page 284: Photo from the Fernandez Family Archive. Courtesy: Maritza Fernandez.

Page 287: Photo from the Fernandez Family Archive. Courtesy: Maritza Fernandez.

Page 290: Photo by Denis Bancroft.

Page 293: Photo by Peter Rentschler.

Page 297: Photo by Robert Vigon.

Page 301: Photo courtesy of the Loria Family Archive.

Chapter Twenty-one

Page 304: Photo by George Kalinsky.

Chapter Twenty-two

Page 314: Photographer unknown, Photo courtesy of the Loria Family Archive.

Page 317: Image courtesy of Loria Family Archive.

Chapter Twenty-three

Page 336: Image from Miami, Fla.: Gulfstream Card Co., Inc. (top) and Photo by felixtm/Depositphotos.com (bottom).

Page 342: Photo courtesy of the Loria Family Archive.

Chapter Twenty-four

Page 350: Archive PL/Alamy Stock Photo.

Chapter Twenty-five

Page 364: Photo by Ron Antonelli / MLB Photos.

Chapter Twenty-six

Page 378: Photo by Alister Alexander / Camerarts.

Chapter Twenty-seven

PAGE 390: Photo by Robert Vigon; Artwork © Red Grooms, Member of Artists Rights Society (ARS).

Chapter Twenty-eight

PAGE 398: Photo courtesy of the Loria Family Archive.

Chapter Twenty-nine

PAGE 416: Photo by Kokyat Choong, Alamy Stock Photos; Artwork © Estate of Roy Lichtenstein.